Your Personal
HOROSCOPE
—1994—

Your Personal
HOROSCOPE
—1994—

*Month-by-month Forecasts
for Every Sign*

Joseph Polansky

Aquarian/Thorsons
An Imprint of HarperCollinsPublishers

The Aquarian Press
An Imprint of HarperCollins*Publishers*
77–85 Fulham Palace Road,
Hammersmith, London W6 8JB
1160 Battery Street,
San Francisco, California 94111-1213

Published by The Aquarian Press 1993
1   3   5   7   9   10   8   6   4   2

Star ★ Data, Inc. 1993

Joseph Polansky asserts the moral right to
be identified as the author of this work

A catalogue record for this book
is available from the British Library

ISBN 1 85538 281 4

Typeset by Harper Phototypesetters Limited
Northampton, England
Printed in Great Britain by
HarperCollinsManufacturing Glasgow

Contents

ACKNOWLEDGEMENTS

The author wishes to give special
thanks to STAR ★ DATA, who originally
commissioned this work. Without their
help – both financial and technical –
this book could not have been written.

Introduction

Welcome to the fascinating and intricate world of astrology!

For thousands of years the movements of the planets and other heavenly bodies have intrigued the best minds of every generation. Life holds no greater challenge or joy than this: knowledge of ourselves and the universe we live in. Astrology is one of the keys to this knowledge.

Your Personal Horoscope 1994 gives you the fruits of astrological wisdom. In addition to general guidance on your character and the basic trends of your life, it shows you how to take advantage of planetary influence so you can make the most of the year ahead.

The section on each sign includes a Personality Profile, a look at general trends for 1994 and in-depth month-by-month forecasts. The glossary on page 11 explains some of the astrological terms with which you may not be familiar.

One of the many helpful features of this book is the 'best and worst days' section at the beginning of each monthly forecast. Read these sections to learn which days in each month will be good overall, good for money and good for love. Mark them on your calendar – they are your best days. Similarly, make a note of the days that will be stressful for you. It is best to avoid important meetings or taking major decisions on these days, as on those days when important planets in your horoscope are *retrograde* (moving backwards through the zodiac).

The Major Trends section for your sign lists those days when your vitality is strong or weak, or when relationships with your co-workers or loved ones may need a bit more effort on your part. If you are going through a difficult time, take a look at the colour, metal, gem and scent listed in the

At a Glance section of your Personality Profile. Wearing a piece of jewellery that contains your metal and/or gem will strengthen your vitality; just as wearing clothes or decorating your room or office in the colour ruled by your sign, drinking teas made from the herbs ruled by your sign or wearing the scents ruled by your sign will sustain you.

Another important virtue of this book is that it will help you know not only yourself but those around you: your friends, co-workers, partners and/or children. Reading the Personality Profile and forecasts for their signs will provide you with an insight to their behaviour that you won't get anywhere else. You will know when to be more tolerant of them and when they are liable to be difficult or irritable.

I consider you – the reader – to be my personal client. By studying your Solar horoscope I gain an awareness of what is going on in your life – what you are feeling and striving for – and the challenges you face. I then do my best to address these concerns. Consider this book the next best thing to having your own personal astrologer!

It is my sincere hope that *Your Personal Horoscope 1994* will enhance the quality of your life, make things easier, illuminate the way forward, banish the obscurities and make you more aware of your personal connection to the universe. Astrology – understood properly and used wisely – is a great guide to understanding yourself, the people around you and the events in your life – but remember that what you do with these insights – the final result – is up to you.

Astrological Terms

Ascendant

We experience day and night because the Earth rotates on its axis once every 24 hours. It is because of this rotation that the Sun, Moon and planets seem to rise and set. The zodiac is a fixed belt (imaginary, but very real in spiritual terms) around the Earth. As the Earth rotates the different signs of the zodiac seem to rise at the horizon of the observer. During a 24-hour period every sign of the zodiac will pass this horizon point at some time or another. The sign that is at the horizon point at any given time is called the Ascendant, or Rising sign. The Ascendant is the sign denoting a person's self-image, body and self-concept – the personal ego, as opposed to the spiritual ego indicated by a person's Sun sign.

Aspects

Aspects are the angular relationships between planets, the way in which one planet stimulates or influences another. If a planet makes a harmonious aspect (connection) to another, it tends to stimulate that planet in a positive and helpful way. If it makes a stressful aspect to another planet, the stimulation is stressful and uneasy, causing disruptions in the planet's normal influence.

Astrological Qualities

There are three astrological qualities into which all the 12 signs are divided: *cardinal*, *fixed* and *mutable*.

The cardinal quality is the active, initiating principle. Cardinal signs (Aries, Cancer, Libra and Capricorn) are good at starting new projects.

Fixed qualities are stability, persistence, endurance and perfectionism. Fixed signs (Taurus, Leo, Scorpio and Aquarius) are good at seeing things through.

Mutable qualities are adaptability, changeability and balance. Mutable signs (Gemini, Virgo, Sagittarius and Pisces) are creative if not always practical.

Direct Motion

When the planets move forward – as they normally do – through the zodiac they are said to be going 'direct'.

Houses

There are twelve signs of the zodiac and twelve houses of experience. The twelve signs are personality types and ways in which a given planet expresses itself. The houses show 'where' in your life this expression takes place. Each house has a different area of interest (see the list, opposite). A house can become potent and important – a house of power – in different ways: if it contains the Sun, the Moon or the ruler of your chart, if it contains more than one planet, or if the ruler of the house is receiving unusual stimulation from other planets.

ASTROLOGICAL TERMS

1st House of Body and Personal Image

2nd House of Money and Possessions

3rd House of Communication

4th House of Home and Family, Domestic Life

5th House of Fun, Entertainment, Creativity, Speculations and Love Affairs

6th House of Health and Work

7th House of Love, Romance, Marriage and Partnership

8th House of Elimination, Transformation, Other People's Money

9th House of Travel, Education, Religion and Philosophy

10th House of Career

11th House of Friends, Group Activities and Fondest Wishes

12th House of Spiritual Wisdom and Charity

Karma

Karma is the law of cause and effect which governs all phenomena. We are all in the situation we are in because of Karma – of actions we have done in the past. The universe is such a balanced instrument that any unbalanced act immediately sets corrective forces into motion – Karma.

Long-term Planets

The planets that take a long time to move through a sign are considered long-term planets – these planets are Jupiter (which stays in a sign for about a year), Saturn (which stays in a sign for two and a half years), Uranus (seven years), Neptune (fourteen years) and Pluto (fifteen to thirty years). These planets show the long-term trends in a given area of life and thus they are important when astrologers forecast the prolonged view of things. Because these planets stay in one sign for so long, there are periods in the year when the faster-moving (short-term) planets will join them, further activating and enhancing the importance of a given house.

Lunar

Relating to the Moon.

Natal

Literally means 'birth'. In Astrology this term is used to distinguish between planetary positions that occurred at birth (natal) and transiting (current) ones. For example, Natal Sun refers to where the Sun was when you were born; the transiting Sun refers to where the Sun's position is currently at any given moment – which usually doesn't coincide with your birth or Natal Sun.

Out of Bounds

The planets move through our zodiac at various angles relative to the celestial equator (if you draw an imaginary extension of the Earth's equator out into the universe you will have the celestial equator). The Sun – being the most dominant and powerful influence in the Solar system – is the measure astrologers use as a standard. The Sun never goes more than approximately 23 degrees north or south of this celestial equator. At the Winter solstice the Sun reaches its maximum southern angle of orbit (declination) and at the Summer solstice it reaches its maximum northern angle. Any time a planet exceeds this Solar boundary – and occasionally they do – it is said to be 'out of bounds'. This means that the planet exceeds or trespasses into strange territory – beyond the limits allowed by the Sun, the ruler of the Solar system. The planet in this condition becomes more emphasized and exceeds its authority, becoming an important influence in a forecast.

Phases of the Moon

After the full Moon, the Moon seems to shrink in size (as perceived from the Earth), gradually growing smaller until it is virtually invisible to the naked eye – at the time of the next new Moon. This is called the *waning* Moon phase – or the waning Moon.

After the new Moon, the Moon gradually gets bigger in size (as perceived from the Earth), until it reaches its maximum size at the time of the full Moon. This period is called the *waxing* Moon phase – or waxing Moon.

Retrogrades

The planets move around the Sun at different speeds. Mercury and Venus move much faster than the Earth, while Mars, Jupiter, Saturn, Uranus, Neptune and Pluto move more slowly. Thus there are times when, relative to the

Earth, the planets appear to be going backwards. In reality they are always going forward, but relative to our vantage point on Earth they seem to go backwards through the zodiac for a period of time. This is called 'retrograde' motion and it tends to weaken the normal influence of a given planet.

Short-term Planets

These are the fast-moving planets: the Moon (which stays in a sign for only two and a half days), Mercury (20 to 30 days), the Sun (30 days), Venus (approximately a month) and Mars (approximately two months). Since these planets move so quickly through a sign their effects are generally of a short-term nature. They show the immediate, day-to-day trends in a horoscope.

Transits

This refers to the movements or motions of the planets at any given time. Astrologers use the word 'transit' to make the distinction between a birth or Natal planet and its current movement in the heavens. For example, if at your birth Saturn was in the sign of Cancer in your 8th House, but is now moving through your 3rd House, it is said to be 'transiting' your 3rd House. Transits are one of the main tools with which astrologers forecast trends.

Aries

)(

THE RAM
Birthdays from
21st March
to 20th April

Personality Profile

ARIES AT A GLANCE

Element – Fire

Ruling planet – Mars
  Career planet – Saturn
  Love planet – Venus
  Money planet – Venus
  Planet of home and family life – Moon
  Planet of wealth and good fortune – Jupiter

Colours – carmine, red, scarlet

Colours that promote love, romance and social harmony – green, jade green

Colour that promotes earning power – green

Gem – amethyst

17

Metals – iron, steel

Scent – honeysuckle

Quality – cardinal (= activity)

Quality most needed for balance – caution

Strongest virtues – abundant physical energy, courage, honesty, independence, self-reliance

Deepest need – action

Characteristics to avoid – haste, impetuosity, over-aggressiveness, rashness

Signs of greatest overall compatibility – Leo, Sagittarius

Signs of greatest overall incompatibility – Cancer, Libra, Capricorn

Sign most helpful to career – Capricorn

Sign most helpful for emotional support – Cancer

Sign most helpful financially – Taurus

Sign best for marriage and/or partnerships – Libra

Sign most helpful for creative projects – Leo

Best sign to have fun with – Leo

Signs most helpful in spiritual matters – Sagittarius, Pisces

Best day of the week – Tuesday

Understanding the Aries Personality

Aries is the activist *par excellence* of the zodiac. The Arien need for action is almost an addiction and those who do not really understand the Arien personality would probably use this hard word to describe it. In reality 'action' is the essence of the Arien psychology – the more direct, blunt and to-the-point the action, the better. When you think about it, this is the ideal psychological makeup for the warrior, the pioneer, the athlete or the manager.

Ariens like to get things done and in their passion and zeal often lose sight of the consequences for themselves and others. Yes, they often *try* to be diplomatic and tactful, but it is hard for them. When they do so they feel that they are being dishonest and phony. It is hard for them even to understand the mind-set of the diplomat, the consensus builder, the front office executive. These people are involved in endless meetings, discussions, talks and negotiations – all of which seem a great waste of time when there's so much work to be done – so many real achievements to be gained. An Aries can understand, once it is explained to him to her, that talks and negotiations – the social graces – lead ultimately to better, more effective actions. The interesting thing is that an Aries is rarely malicious or spiteful – even when waging war. Aries people fight without hate for their opponents. To them it is all good-natured fun; a grand adventure; a game.

When confronted with a problem many people will say 'Well, let's think about it, let's analyse the situation.' But not an Aries. An Aries will think 'Something must be done. Let's get on with it.' Of course neither response is the total answer. Sometimes action is called for, sometimes cool thought. But an Aries tends to err on the side of action.

Action and thought are radically different principles. Physical activity is the use of brute force. Thinking and deliberating require one not to use force – to be still. It is not good for the athlete to be deliberating his or her next move;

this will only slow down reaction time. The athlete must act instinctively and instantly. This is how Aries people tend to behave in life. They are quick, instinctive decision-makers and their decisions tend to be translated into actions almost immediately. When their intuition is sharp and well tuned, their actions are powerful and successful. When their intuition is off, their actions can be disastrous.

Don't think this will scare an Aries. Just as a good warrior knows that in the course of combat he or she might acquire a few wounds, so too does an Aries realize – somewhere deep down – that in the course of being true to oneself, one might incur a disaster or two. It's all part of the game. An Aries feels strong enough to weather any storm.

There are many Aries people who are intellectual: Ariens make powerful and creative thinkers. But even in this realm they tend to be pioneers – outspoken and blunt. These types of Ariens tend to elevate (or sublimate) their desire for physical combat with intellectual, mental combat. And they are indeed powerful.

In general, Aries people have a faith in themselves that others could learn from. This basic, rock-bottom faith carries them through the most tumultuous situations of life. Their courage and self-confidence make them natural leaders. Their leadership is more by way of example than by actually controlling others.

Finance

Aries people often excel as builders or estate agents. Money in and of itself is not as important as are other things – action, adventure, sports, etc. They are motivated by the need to support their partners and to be well thought of by partners. Money as a way of attaining pleasure is another important motivation. Aries people function best in their own businesses or as managers of their own departments within a large business or corporation. The less orders they have to take from higher up the better. They also function better out in the field rather than behind a desk.

Aries people are hard workers with a lot of endurance; they can earn large sums of money due to the strength of their sheer physical energy.

Venus is their money planet, which means that Ariens need to develop more of the social graces in order to realize their full earning potential. Just getting the job done – which is what an Aries excels at – is not enough to create financial success. The co-operation of others needs to be attained. Customers, clients and co-workers need to be made to feel comfortable. Many people need to be treated properly in order for success to happen. When Aries people develop these abilities – or hire someone to do this for them – their financial potential is unlimited.

Career and Public Image

One would think that a pioneering type would want to break with the social and political conventions of society. But this is not so with the Aries-born. They are pioneers within conventional limits, in the sense that they like to start their own businesses within an established industry rather than to work for someone else.

Capricorn is on the 10th House (of Career) cusp of Aries' solar horoscope. Saturn is the planet that rules their life's work and professional aspirations. This tells us some interesting things about the Arien character. First off, it shows that in order for Aries people to reach their full career potential they need to develop some qualities that are a bit alien to their basic nature. They need to become better administrators and organizers. They need to be able to handle details better and to take a long-range view of their projects and their careers in general. No one can beat an Aries when it comes to a short-range objective, but a career is long term, built over time. You can't take a 'quickie' approach to it.

Some Aries people find it difficult to stick with a project

until the end. Since they get bored quickly and are in constant pursuit of new adventures, they prefer to pass the old project or task to somebody else in order to start something new. Those Ariens who learn how to put off the search for something new until the old gets done will achieve great success in their careers and professional lives.

In general, Aries people like society to judge them on their own merits, on their real and actual achievements. A reputation acquired by 'hype' feels false to them.

Love and Relationships

In marriage and partnerships an Aries likes people who are more passive, gentle, tactful and diplomatic – people who have the social grace and skills they sometimes lack. Our partners always represent a hidden part of ourselves – a self that we cannot express personally.

An Aries tends to go after what he or she likes aggressively. The tendency is to jump into relationships and marriages. This is especially true if Venus is in Aries as well as the Sun. If an Aries likes you, he or she will have a hard time taking no for an answer; many attempts will be made to sweep you off your feet.

Though Ariens can be exasperating in relationships – especially if they are not understood by their partner – they are never consciously or wilfully cruel or malicious. It is just that they are so independent and sure of themselves that they find it almost impossible to see somebody else's viewpoint or position. This is why an Aries needs someone with lots of social grace to be his or her partner.

On the plus side, an Aries is honest, someone you can lean on, someone with whom you'll always know where you stand. What he or she lacks in diplomacy is made up for in integrity.

Home and Domestic Life

An Aries is of course the ruler of the home – the Boss. The male will tend to delegate domestic matters to the female. The female

22

Aries will want to rule the roost. Both tend to be handy around the house. Both like large families and both believe in the sanctity and importance of the family. An Aries is a good family person, although he or she doesn't especially like being home a lot, preferring instead to be roaming about.

For natures that are so combative and wilful, Aries people can be surprisingly soft, gentle and even vulnerable with their children and partner. The sign of Cancer, ruled by the Moon, is on the cusp of their solar 4th House of Home and Family. When the Moon is well aspected – under favourable influences – in the birth chart an Aries will be tender towards the family and want a family life that is nurturing and supportive. Ariens like to come home after a hard day on the battlefield of life to the understanding arms of their partner and the unconditional love and support of a family. An Aries feels that there is enough 'war' out in the world – and he or she enjoys participating in that. But when Aries comes home, comfort and nurturing are key.

Horoscope for 1994

Major Trends

1993 was a year of tremendous social expansion. Many Aries people will have got married or been involved in a relationship that was 'marriage-like'. All Ariens expanded their social sphere, making new friends of the heart. Many of these friends will be with you for a long time. You strengthened your social graces in 1993.

Now, in 1994, the cosmos is asking you to develop different faculties. The emphasis will be on eliminating the unnecessary from your life. This applies to friendships, social activities and romantic affairs. Those of you who 'overexpanded' socially last year will now be forced to cut back a little. You will be more concerned with purifying and improving the relationships you have rather than starting new ones.

1994, in general, is going to be easier than 1993 was. It won't be totally easy, of course, because Uranus and Neptune (that volatile, dynamic celestial duo) are still in your 10th House of Career, shaking up your professional activities. Ultimately this shake-up will release you – free you – upon your true and pre-destined life's work. Uranus and Neptune are also forcing you to deal with issues of ego and self-esteem. Not that you lack these things, Aries – on the contrary, you generally have too much of them. But when Uranus and Neptune are through you will have neither too much nor too little self-esteem. Your ego will be healthy and you will understand its niche in the scheme of things.

Saturn makes a major move into your 12th solar House of Spiritual Wisdom this year and stays there for the next two to three years. This is going to force you to reorder and restructure your spiritual and philanthropic life. Those Ariens who belong to spiritual organizations will find that more demands are made on you while your share of the glory diminishes: your charitable deeds spring from a sense of duty rather than love. You do good deeds but the glow and the good feelings are not there. This dissatisfaction is the first key to healing as you are forced to reshape this area of your life. This Saturn transit is also important for your career, but more on this later.

Health

1993 was a stressful health year. Seldom in this life have you faced such planetary stress. The mere fact that you are now walking around sane and healthy represents a major victory. You have demonstrated how strong you really are. You should feel proud, heroic and good about yourself – even if vitality is not what you have been accustomed to.

1994 will be a lot easier healthwise. You don't seem overly concerned about it. The emphasis is more on psychological health than physical health. The psychological barriers to good health will come tumbling down this year almost by themselves. This is because the universal tendency of the cosmos is always slanted towards health, wholeness, beauty and balance. Your involvement with depth psychology – the exploration of *why* you feel the way you do – will happen because of your need to advance careerwise. But it will produce side-effects that improve your physical health.

Your best health periods overall this year will be 20th March to 20th April, 23rd July to 23rd August and 22nd November to 21st December.

Your most stressful health periods overall will be 21st June to 22nd July, 23rd September to 23rd October and 22nd December to 20th January (1995). Try to rest and relax more at these times.

Home and Domestic Life

Whatever needed to be done in the home – whether it involved moving, rebuilding or making major repairs – was done in 1993. You don't seem too focused on domestic issues this year. Career, finance and spiritual issues will be greater priorities in your life during 1994. If you do move, it will be because of a job or career change. This is most likely to happen from 21st June to 22nd July and from 17th August to 4th October. These two periods, by the way, will be your most active domestic times this year.

Dealings with your family seem much smoother this year than they were last year. Changes in your psychological attitude and personal philosophy of life seem to ease tensions. However, over-asserting your personal will – particularly from 17th August to 4th October – could lead to a short-term conflict. Neither you nor your family seems willing to compromise – so a clearing of the air is likely to happen.

Keep in mind that because the Moon is the planet that governs your domestic life there will always be short-term fluctuations in family relations. This is because the Moon moves around your entire horoscope every month. If you have domestic projects to accomplish the phases of the Moon become important to you. The waxing phase (see the month-by-month forecasts) will give you more zest and personal enthusiasm for domestic affairs than will the waning phase. If you want to do some DIY, for instance, do it when the Moon is waxing. If you want to eliminate things from your house – getting rid of old furniture and the like – use the Moon's waning phase. Dealings with family, too, will generally be better on the waxing Moon than on the waning.

Love and Social Life

Your love and social life and your career are by far the most interesting aspects of your 1994 horoscope, Aries. As mentioned earlier, 1993 was a year of social expansion and 1994 is going to be a year of social compression. You are going to winnow down your social list and agenda. You are going to focus more on quality than quantity. You have a need to purify your existing love relationship – to purge it of things that make you unhappy. This is good and basically healthy – only don't go overboard and start 'throwing out the baby with the bath water'. By all means get rid of the impure elements in your marriage or relationship but cling fast to the good things. You must approach it as a surgeon would: leave what is healthy and cut away what is not.

As we all know, there are two aspects to romance. The first and probably the more important is the love that you feel for another as a human being, the general affection that exists between you and your love on all levels. The second aspect is the sexual relationship between you. It is this relationship that distinguishes romance from mere friendship. If two people love each platonically, this is usually not considered romance, nor is it when there is only a sexual relationship. It is only when you have both aspects in harmony that you have what's called romance.

1994 is a year when you explore – on much deeper levels – the sexual relationship you share with your partner. This exploration, by the way, is very happy, fulfilling and expansive. Important life lessons come to you this way, life lessons about gender differences in general and about the true nature of physical intimacy. You will expand your capacity for bliss by breaking the barriers that obstruct it. Your emphasis here will cement the bonds of love between you and your partner and will help you gain deeper knowledge of yourself and him or her.

Human sexuality has many dimensions. Most of us are familiar with its pleasurable nature. Not so many are familiar with it as a primary creative power in the universe. Taboos about physical intimacy arose because those who saw into the deepest nature of things were trying to caution others against misusing or abusing this sacred force.

This is not a prediction of promiscuity. Quite the contrary. You will focus on one person exclusively and you will get to know your partner more deeply and intimately than you ever dreamed possible. If you truly understand one person you understand, in essence, all people. If you understand the femaleness or maleness of your partner you have insight into the divine principle that he or she expresses here on Earth. Since this principle is universal you will understand – by means of your partner – all the members of that sex. Thus you will find that you have little need to 'experiment' with other partners. This may sound strange and shocking to many of you. But further meditation – plus the events that will take place in the coming year – will verify the truth of what is being written. Every person is – in essence – infinite.

This one-pointed, almost 'scorpionic' focus on your partner could make you more possessive and thus more prone to jealousy this year. Be aware of these feelings – they come from an incredibly ancient collective past – but don't let them control you. Jealousy is the 'green monster' that destroys true love.

Enjoy, Aries, for there is much personal pleasure for you

27

in 1994 and your capacity for pleasure is being deepened and expanded.

Career and Finance

This is a most interesting area this year. The emphasis on career has been going on for many years now – since 1988 – and will continue this year. You are gradually being liberated – through a lot of trial and error – into your true life's work. This is what distinguishes a career from a mere job. Buddhists would call it the *Dharma* – your duty to life and to others, your mission for this lifetime.

With Saturn (the lord of your career) moving into your 12th House of Spiritual Wisdom for the next few years, your idealism about career and your search for your spiritual mission in life are intensified. Those of you who have found it need not worry about the changes and upheavals going on in career matters. For you these changes will be pleasant and bring you closer to your goals. For those of you who are still searching, these upheavals can seem frightening. Rest assured that each experiment that goes awry brings you closer to what you should do. Carry on experimenting; don't be afraid to try different fields, skills and companies. Launch out into your own business. As long as your intentions are in harmony with the cosmos you will be safe, even in apparent failure. You are gaining much needed experience for later on.

In order to be cosmically in tune when selecting a career, you must think in terms other than mere money or status. You must think about your gifts, your skills and talents. You must consider where these came from and why they were given to you. This is not a time to be overly modest. You must also reflect on where you can be of greatest service to society and the world at large. Ask yourself these questions when in a quiet, prayerful state – you will be amazed at the answers you receive. You are being led to your highest career ideals.

Money comes to you from others this year. Of course you will probably be working and earning your living, but the major amount of money comes from others. Marrieds can expect to see their partner's income greatly increased this year. Lump sum payments come through insurance settlements, royalties and profitable stock transactions. This is a year where your debts will be paid off – and rather easily at that. But be careful not to incur new ones. Someone remembers you in his or her will.

20th April to 4th July and 7th September to 9th December will be especially powerful and favourable financial periods this year.

Self-improvement

With Jupiter and Pluto moving through your 8th House of Transformation and with Saturn moving through your 12th House of Spiritual Wisdom there is no question that you should be focused on psychological and spiritual conversion. Psychotherapeutic or spiritual counselling is very rewarding this year and has beneficial side-effects that are surprising. It will improve your career and professional status, your love life and your religious and philosophical faculties. You should pay particular attention to a few primary areas for maximum benefit. First, learn how to take a negative and transform it into a positive (this was the true, hidden meaning behind the ancient alchemists' quest to transmute lead into gold). Second, learn that your present condition has its roots in events that occurred long before you entered this world. Third, learn how to contact the source of all wisdom and knowledge within yourself – directly and without intermediaries.

Month-by-month Forecasts

January

>Best Days Overall: 1st, 8th, 9th, 17th,
18th, 19th, 27th, 28th

>Most Stressful Days Overall: 4th, 5th, 10th,
11th, 25th, 26th

>Best Days for Love: 2nd, 3rd, 4th, 5th,
10th, 22nd, 23rd, 31st

>Best Days for Money: 2nd, 3rd, 6th, 7th,
10th, 15th, 16th, 20th, 21st, 22nd, 23rd,
25th, 26th, 31st

The unusual line-up of 60 to 70 per cent of the planetary power in the sign of Capricorn for most of this month has both a universal and a very personal meaning for you, Aries. Not only does it make your career the number one priority and activity for the month but it shows the psychological mood of the general populace – the people around you.

So much power in Capricorn is not very comfortable for you. It is a practical Earth energy that makes people more cautious, calculating and prudent. To your highly active mentality it seems to make others over-prudent and over-cautious. In their minds, on the other hand, you can be viewed as hot-headed, rash and brazen – if you're not careful. All career and financial proposals that you make to superiors must be clearly thought out. Take it as given that people will be more critical, pessimistic and 'nit-picking'. Take this into account when making your proposals and try to answer every objection, no matter how far-fetched. You must show clear advantages if your propositions are to be accepted.

This power in Capricorn is not only stressful

psychologically but physically as well. Definitely rest and relax more this month – especially until the 20th. You are going to be working hard promoting your career, but try to focus on priorities. Let lesser issues go for the time being. After the 20th you feel much better physically and psychologically as power in the Air signs (Gemini, Libra, Aquarius) increases. When this cool mental energy takes hold your fiery activism and optimism will be more appreciated. You will be seen as the true leader and motivator that you are.

With 100 per cent of the planetary power in direct motion (very unusual) you are in a period of achievement. Your plans go forward – the problem is your tendency to overwork.

Your whole life – love and social relationships, finances, even domestic issues – are subordinate to your career this month. Major – and happy – career breakthroughs are likely.

February

> Best Days Overall: 4th, 5th, 14th, 15th, 23rd, 24th
>
> Most Stressful Days Overall: 1st, 7th, 8th, 21st, 22nd, 27th, 28th
>
> Best Days for Love: 1st, 9th, 10th, 11th, 12th, 21st, 22nd, 27th, 28th
>
> Best Days for Money: 1st, 2nd, 3rd, 9th, 10th, 11th, 16th, 17th, 21st, 22nd

Your health and vitality are very much improved over last month as the short-term planets have shifted from 'hostile' Capricorn to 'kinder' Aquarius. The general energy of the people around you is more mental, communicative and receptive to the new. Aquarian energy is good for you, Aries, because it cools you down without smothering your fire. It opens you up to higher levels of thought, making you less likely to jump into action rashly and impulsively. When you do act, your actions are likely to be more powerful because they have been thought through. But communication projects – sales, marketing, mailings and the like – which normally would blossom under this benign Aquarian influence are disturbed because of Mercury's retrograde on the 11th of the month. Try to get major communication projects done before then. When ordering goods or dealing with bureaucracy, make sure all the details are nailed down precisely. Don't give others an excuse to make mistakes.

This power in Aquarius for the better part of the month – Mars, your ruling planet, will be there all of February – energizes your 11th House of Friends. Thus you will be preoccupied with group activities most of this month. You find something comforting about relating to people on an equal basis. Ego games can be dispensed with and you can get right down to appreciating the mind and unique gifts of the other.

Venus (your love and money planet) is also in Aquarius for the early part of the month. Thus you enjoy the platonic, mental side of relationships. You might even treat your lover more platonically this month. Those of you involved with Ariens need not fear that there is anything wrong with the relationship – your Arien partner merely sees you as a friend right now. More passion and ardour are aroused after the 12th when Venus moves into emotional Pisces.

Finances will be better after the 12th of the month than before. This is not because earnings are less but because you are probably overspending before the 12th. Until the 12th your friends and acquaintances are a source of income and earning opportunity. Your activities with groups and organizations provide you with important financial contacts. Singles find romantic opportunities at these group activities as well.

March

Best Days Overall: 4th, 5th, 13th, 14th, 23rd, 24th, 31st

Most Stressful Days Overall: 6th, 7th, 20th, 21st, 22nd, 27th, 28th

Best Days for Love: 1st, 2nd, 13th, 14th, 23rd, 24th, 27th, 28th, 31st

Best Days for Money: 1st, 2nd, 10th, 11th, 12th, 13th, 14th, 15th, 16th, 20th, 21st, 22nd, 23rd, 31st

The unusual power of the Water Element (Cancer, Scorpio, Pisces) in this month's solar horoscope doesn't sit too well with you, Aries. Not that your health or vitality are affected in any way – they are excellent all month – but because this Water influence creates a mood of sensitivity and introversion. The people around you seem overly sensitive – often with a tendency to depression. They may even feel that everything is hopeless and that they are helpless. This is not your attitude, yet even though your fiery nature does much to dispel the temporary gloom around you, you find it hard getting people to move or act. Moreover, your blunt manner tends to affect them over much – even to make them feel hurt. Tread softly this month. Little things – little slights – are apt to be magnified out of all proportion.

With all this power in the sign of Pisces – your 12th solar House of Spiritual Wisdom – you should express your activism in ways that help the unfortunate and needy. Get more involved in voluntary, altruistic activities and you will be more in tune with the cosmos. More introspection, more prayer, meditation and a review of your life over the last year are also in order. This will clear the decks for your new solar cycle to begin after the 20th and you will be in a better position (psychologically) to spring ahead during the coming year.

Venus, your planet of love and money, is in Pisces until the 8th of the month. Venus is exalted in this sign and thus exerts her influence with greatest strength. Thus, in spite of the heavy emotions all around you your earnings increase and your love life blooms. Venus in Pisces makes you very charitable with your money. You definitely give more to worthy causes and to those in need. This position enhances your financial judgement and intuition: financial guidance often comes to you in dreams or through psychics and astrologers.

Venus in Pisces also makes you altruistic and self-sacrificing in love – generally not your nature. It improves your love life in that you have a greater appreciation and insight into how others feel and this makes you more popular. Your ability to attract the opposite sex is very much enhanced this month.

April

> Best Days Overall: 1st, 9th, 10th, 19th, 20th, 27th, 28th
>
> Most Stressful Days Overall: 2nd, 3rd, 17th, 18th, 23rd, 24th
>
> Best Days for Love: 2nd, 3rd, 12th, 13th, 21st, 22nd, 23rd, 24th
>
> Best Days for Money: 2nd, 3rd, 7th, 8th, 12th, 13th, 17th, 18th, 21st, 22nd, 25th, 26th

After a month of introspection, self-examination and emotional mush you are reborn again into your true self. Gone are the doubts, worries and insecurities. You live, you act, perform and achieve. Spring has come and with it your energy and vitality. This is both a month of happiness and challenge. Happiness comes because you are functioning according to your true nature. You assert yourself boldly. You are sure of yourself and your actions are powerful. Any opposition is simply overwhelmed by your zeal and ardour.

The challenge comes because of this: with the Sun and Mars in your own sign – and with 70 to 80 per cent of the planets in the eastern hemisphere of your solar chart – *you* are shaping events now. You have greater freedom and greater control over your life – but what kind of conditions are you creating? If you have used last month's introspective period properly you need have no fear, for you will create according to a well-thought-out plan. If you have not thought things through, this greater freedom and creative power could cause problems in future.

Your health, energy, vitality and self-esteem are all strong. You have all the energy you need to achieve any goal or desire. Your earnings are thus naturally increased. Mercury's speedy forward motion shows that work goals are accomplished swiftly and with confidence.

Both your romantic and financial situations are stable for most of the month. Venus (your love and money planet) is very happy and powerful in the sign of Taurus. Money is earned pleasurably and you spend it wisely. Partners and social contacts are supportive financially. Your partner prefers that you earn your own money this period rather than rely on his or her generosity and you seem very amenable to this.

Singles find love in the normal pursuit of financial goals. Banks, farms, estate agencies and shopping precincts are likely meeting places. Romantic partners show their love by creating earning opportunities and through material gifts. You seem overly possessive in love this month, but no one is about to fight you now.

May

Best Days Overall: 6th, 7th, 8th, 16th, 17th, 25th, 26th

Most Stressful Days Overall: 14th, 15th,
21st, 22nd, 27th, 28th

Best Days for Love: 1st, 2nd, 3rd, 11th,
12th, 13th, 21st, 22nd, 23rd, 24th, 31st

Best Days for Money: 1st, 2nd, 3rd, 4th,
5th, 9th, 10th, 11th, 12th, 13th, 14th,
15th, 23rd, 24th, 31st

With Mars (the lord of your horoscope) moving through your
own sign your usual passion and aggressiveness are very
much amplified this month. Nothing scares you, nothing
shakes you and there is no problem you can't solve. Haste
and impulsiveness are the main dangers to watch out for.
Over-asserting your personal will – which you almost can't
help doing right now – could put you in conflict with
superiors and hurt your career. While superiors admire your
courage and militancy and are in awe of your ability to work,
they feel that you are only seeing your side of the story. There
is something in what they say – try to understand their
needs and position as well as your own. Career matters are
going to work out and no amount of rushing on your part
is going to hasten them along. In the early part of the month
you go beyond the call of duty – and get involved in spheres
not usually yours. But you will see that superiors need time
to think and evaluate: they are not yet in a position to make
a judgement.

There are two important eclipses this month. The solar
eclipse of the 10th occurs in your 2nd House of Money –
suggesting long-term and major changes in the way you earn
a living and in the earnings of your partner. Any short-term
financial upheavals later in the month are overcome by hard
work and lead to long-term boons. Your earnings increase
because of clever marketing and advertising. Neighbours and
siblings bring you profitable ideas and opportunities. In
short, money matters are important all month.

The lunar eclipse of the 25th occurs in your 9th House of

Travel, Education, Religion and Philosophy, showing long-term changes in your religious and philosophical views. Your personal philosophy will probably be attacked or undermined and only what is real and true will remain. A spiritual or religious guide will leave your life and another will come in.

Your health is excellent all month.

Love is friendly – almost platonic – until the 21st. After that it becomes more emotional, tender and nurturing but also much more unstable and fickle.

June

> Best Days Overall: 3rd, 4th, 13th, 14th, 21st, 22nd, 30th
>
> Most Stressful Days Overall: 10th, 11th, 17th, 18th, 23rd, 24th
>
> Best Days for Love: 1st, 10th, 11th, 17th, 18th, 21st, 22nd, 30th
>
> Best Days for Money: 1st, 5th, 6th, 7th, 10th, 11th, 19th, 20th, 21st, 22nd, 28th, 29th, 30th

Your efforts to achieve balance seem to be rewarded this month. The planets are equally dispersed between all the different sectors of your chart. You recognize – and give time to – the various important aspects of your life. Your need for success is balanced by the need for personal happiness, emotional harmony and a stable home. The ability to create events is balanced by the need to adapt to already existing ones. The need to assert yourself is balanced with an appreciation of the needs of others. Seldom have you seen things in such clear perspective.

With 60 per cent of the planetary power in retrograde (backward) motion this month you and most other people feel frustrated and puzzled. Pet projects, schemes and relationships all seem delayed. These retrograde periods are particularly tough on you because the psychology of the retrograde is alien to your active, forward-moving, blunt nature. You generally want to get on with things, the faster the better. You are in a cycle now where you need to learn some patience. Action is not the cure for everything. Right now, time is the cure. Rail as you might at the inactivity around you there is little you can do – apparently – to speed things up.

Take the opportunity to rest and relax more – especially after the 21st. Enjoy the pleasures of home and hearth; get on with those DIY projects you've been putting off for so long. Make your home more comfortable. Patch up disputes with the family. If a relationship is good make it better by calling on family members, who have probably felt neglected of late. Your home and family are centres of profit and love this month.

Your career seems on hold for now, so focus on other things. Review your career goals and see if you can make them more perfect. Then let go and let time do its work. Your earnings are strong, though family expenses could put a dent in your wallet.

Your love life is emotional and volatile. Until the 15th you want nurturing, afterwards just plain old fun. Your romantic situation is further confused by an overabundance of lovers – or potential lovers – after the 15th.

July

Best Days Overall: 1st, 10th, 11th, 19th, 20th, 27th, 28th, 29th

Most Stressful Days Overall: 7th, 8th, 9th, 14th, 15th, 21st, 22nd

Best Days for Love: 1st, 10th, 11th, 12th, 14th, 15th, 21st, 22nd, 30th, 31st

ARIES

Best Days for Money: 1st, 7th, 8th, 9th,
10th, 11th, 12th, 16th, 17th, 21st, 22nd,
25th, 26th, 30th, 31st

With 50 to 60 per cent of the planetary power in the Water
Element (Water signs), the general psychological atmosphere
is one of hypersensitivity, emotionalism, moodiness and
introversion. Combine this with the fact that 40 per cent of
the planets are still retrograde and you find this feeling of
introversion is further emphasized. Many signs enjoy this
kind of mood, but not you. It doesn't sit well with you either
physically or psychologically. You itch to move – to go out –
to get some action going and have some fun. But not much
is going on and no amount of prodding gets your friends and
acquaintances on the move. People enjoy being dormant just
now.

This introverted, subjective energy goes on for some
months to come – though in the next few months your
health won't be as affected by it as it is now. Rather than rail
at these feelings of sluggishness and lethargy, use them to
your advantage. Develop some of the virtues of the introvert,
like learning to listen more and to feel what others are
feeling. Be more receptive to your environment and the
people around you. Have no fear, Aries, you will never
become a real introvert. But this is a good period to develop
this introvert's psychological awareness.

The feeling of going backwards is easing just a bit this
month. Mercury and Jupiter start going direct. Your
intellectual abilities are being enhanced and your
educational interests are strong, happy and fulfilling. A
delayed trip now becomes possible. Physical intimacy
within a current relationship becomes much more fulfilling.

Rest and relax more until the 23rd. Be patient with career
delays. Good things are going on beneath the surface. The
feeling of sluggishness – and the general feeling of
depression around you – lightens up a bit after the 23rd of
the month.

Finances are good this month – though be careful about overspending.

August

Best Days Overall: 6th, 7th, 15th, 16th, 24th, 25th

Most Stressful Days Overall: 4th, 5th, 11th, 12th, 17th, 18th, 31st

Best Days for Love: 11th, 12th, 19th, 20th, 29th, 30th

Best Days for Money: 4th, 5th, 11th, 12th, 13th, 14th, 19th, 20th, 21st, 22nd, 23rd, 26th, 27th, 29th, 30th, 31st

The universal standstill – the general feeling of frustration – has eased up considerably since June. From 60 per cent of the planets going retrograde now there are only 30 per cent. People are on the move again. You feel a lot better personally and psychologically.

All sorts of personal pleasures offer themselves to you and you take them. You enjoy the companionship of children and display an uncanny knack for getting on with them. There's a lot you can learn from them about life – and of course there's a lot they can learn from you. Children derive pleasure from simple things. We adults would do well to emulate this.

You are tempted to speculate recklessly this period – and though speculations are favourable it's the recklessness, the overdoing that can be dangerous. Don't bet more than you can afford to lose and don't bet with money that you need for operating expenses.

Your health is excellent all month and your self-esteem and self-worth are much improved as well. Your solar horoscope shows that creativity – true self-expression – is an important if you are to maintain good health right now. Fun and entertainment, a light-hearted attitude to life tend to reduce stress and promote good health. After the 18th purity in your diet enhances your general constitution.

Your finances are stable until the 7th. Your financial judgement is sound. You are a careful shopper and have a knack for getting the most for your pound. After the 7th, however, finances are less secure. There is nothing wrong with what you're earning, but extra expenses at home and in your love life make you feel strapped. This is just temporary.

Singles find love at the workplace or in doctors' surgeries until the 7th. Your attitude to love is one of service and purity. Anything not matching this high – almost divine – ideal tends to get criticized. After the 7th you are much more romantic. You seek a true partnership in love.

September

>Best Days Overall: 3rd, 4th, 11th, 12th, 20th, 21st, 30th

>Most Stressful Days Overall: 1st, 7th, 8th, 13th, 14th, 28th, 29th

>Best Days for Love: 7th, 8th, 9th, 18th, 19th, 28th, 29th

>Best Days for Money: 1st, 8th, 9th, 10th, 18th, 19th, 22nd, 23rd, 24th, 28th, 29th

This is a month of learning experiences, Aries. It is a good month though not necessarily a pleasant one. You need to stretch yourself, to take attitudes and positions that are alien to you. First off, 70 to 80 per cent of the planetary power is now in the western hemisphere of your personal solar horoscope chart. Secondly, 50 to 60 per cent of the planets are in the Water Element – an element that you are not too comfortable with. Thirdly, 80 to 90 per cent of the planets are in negative, receptive, introverted signs.

41

So what does this all mean and how can you handle it advantageously?

Generally, you are an activist, a person who creates conditions and circumstances. Usually there are few in life who excel at this as much as you. You are the creator, the initiator *par excellence* and you are very comfortable in that role. But now you find less freedom to create your own circumstances. You are forced to adapt to situations created by others. Everything you want to do or be or have seems dependent on others. You have trouble going it alone – as is your usual custom – this month. Moreover – and this is really difficult for you – you are forced to see, understand and acknowledge that other people's needs and positions can be as valid as your own.

To succeed this month you must develop your social graces. You must be able to gain the co-operation of others in your projects and plans. Going it alone is going to be difficult. You must develop more emotional sensitivity, more tact, diplomacy and social skills (the cosmos will help you). Learn how to build a consensus in order to attain a specific goal. Learn to listen, without judging, to what others are actually saying. Be more receptive. Look for the points of common interest – the things that bind people rather than the things that separate them. When you depend on others, patience becomes primary – and patience is not one of your fortes, Aries. But you must understand that not every one leaps into action as quickly as you do. Not everyone has the psychology of a warrior.

October

Best Days Overall: 1st, 8th, 9th, 17th, 18th, 19th, 27th, 28th

Most Stressful Days Overall: 4th, 5th, 10th, 11th, 25th ,26th

Best Days for Love: 4th, 5th, 6th, 7th, 15th, 16th, 25th, 26th

ARIES

You are learning valuable lessons in character this month,
Aries. While this is somewhat uncomfortable it is worth it.
70 to 80 per cent of the planets are still concentrated in the
western half of your chart, forcing you to adapt to situations
that you never created. You need to see and to put the
interests of others above your own. With 50 to 60 per cent
of the planets in sensitive and subjective Water signs, you are
forced – against your natural inclination – to be less blunt,
less outspoken and more aware of other people's feelings.
With this many Water influences, people are so over-
sensitive that you need to bend over backwards not to hurt
them. Things that in other times endear you to others are not
considered endearing right now – in fact they're seen as
actually cruel. Of course you are not a cruel person by nature,
but your fiery tone and outspokenness can be perceived that
way.

The new Moon of the 5th is going to teach you everything
you need to know about the social graces and how to gain
the co-operation of others. Watch how this information
comes to you as the month progresses. A new tact,
diplomacy and sensitivity open up new financial and social
vistas for you. Love blooms – but with Venus going
retrograde proceed cautiously. It's better to avoid scheduling
a marriage this month – though you will be sorely tempted
to do so.

Though your personal earning power is strong this month,
the real financial banner headline is the incredible power in
your 8th House of Other People's Money. Between 40 and 50
per cent of the planetary power is there – and the planets are
beneficent ones as well. Thus, large lump sums of money
come to you in the form of royalties, dividend income, stock
transactions and the largesse of a partner. Someone
remembers you in his or her will – and substantial sums are
involved. You have a knack for earning money for others and

it is appreciated. You have the ability to take a dead – almost worthless – business and resurrect it and make it profitable again. You seem willing to forgo short-term profits for the sake of long-term growth. Investors are interested in your proposals. Outside capital is obtained rather easily – though avoid signing contracts between the 9th and 30th October, when Mercury retrogrades.

November

> Best Days Overall: 5th, 6th, 14th, 15th, 24th, 25th
>
> Most Stressful Days Overall: 1st, 7th, 8th, 21st, 22nd, 28th, 29th
>
> Best Days for Love: 1st, 2nd, 3rd, 4th, 11th, 12th, 21st, 22nd, 28th, 29th, 30th
>
> Best Days for Money: 3rd, 4th, 11th, 12th, 16th, 17th, 21st, 22nd, 30th

Though this is a highly tumultuous month – not so much for you but for those around you and the world in general – it is also a month of achievement and progress. By the end of the month *all* the planets will be moving forward. Anything that blocks progress gets eliminated. Two eclipses this month see to this. The celestial powers are saying, in effect, 'either lead, follow or get out of the way'.

People are overly intense and suspicious this month, so tread softly on their feelings. Hurt feelings – even if caused unintentionally – are likely to bring drastic retribution. The upheavals that you see around you – though not often pleasant – make sense when viewed from this perspective. The universe wants to go forward and those that lag will be shoved out of the way. Of course, Aries, this suits you down to the ground.

With 50 per cent of the planets in Scorpio (your 8th House

44

of Other People's Money), for the better part of the month the activity in this house is dominant. This is a time when you should eliminate any undesirable conditions, character traits or possessions from your life. It is especially important to do some 'housecleaning' in your social life. Focus on your true friends and those who truly love you; let the others go. Physical intimacy and passion are more important to you than romance right now. You are learning important lessons about love.

Any debts are paid off this month – and rather easily at that. Investors are interested in your ideas. Outside capital comes to you effortlessly. Your partner's income is increased – though only after some upheavals. You make profits for others and they appreciated it. In fact, you seem better able to make profits for others than for yourself right now.

The solar eclipse of the 3rd is a particularly powerful one – especially for those Ariens who live in southern latitudes. It will cause important changes in your self-image, love life and social life. It can lead to marriage – if a relationship is good – or a break-up.

Your health is good all month, but take a reduced schedule on the 3rd and 18th – the two eclipse periods.

December

> Best Days Overall: 2nd, 3rd, 11th, 12th, 21st, 22nd, 30th
>
> Most Stressful Days Overall: 8th, 9th, 10th, 16th, 17th, 23rd, 24th
>
> Best Days for Love: 1st, 8th, 9th, 10th, 19th, 20th 25th, 26th, 28th, 29th
>
> Best Days for Money: 1st, 11th, 12th, 13th, 14th, 15th, 21st, 22nd, 30th

This is a happy and very lucky month for you, Aries. Enjoy. Jupiter, your planet of wealth and good fortune, makes a major move out of Scorpio into Sagittarius. This does wonders for your self-esteem, health and career. It's a long-term signal for increased wealth, happiness and success.

In addition, most of the planets are concentrated at the top half of your solar horoscope chart. This means you are really focused on your career, professional status and success. Family, emotional and domestic issues take a back seat to your career right now.

For the better part of the month there is great – and benevolent – planetary power in your 9th House of Travel, Education, Religion and Philosophy. All these activities are favourable. This is the time to take that trip or to do that course. This is the time to prepare yourself educationally for your new career status. Bible, scriptural and mythology classes inspire you now. Your ability to understand the philosophical rationale for things is greatly enhanced. With this understanding come the resolution of conflicts and an inner peace. Your faith in yourself and in the universe is strengthened – and this will affect your happiness and your finances.

You are making great career progress. Shifts at the top of your corporate hierarchy are benefiting you. Stalled projects start going forward. All the planets are moving forward this month – highly unusual – and you are being swept forward to your goals by the progressing universe.

50 to 60 per cent of the planets will be in Earth signs (Taurus, Virgo, Capricorn) by the middle of the month. People are more utilitarian, prudent and practical. When proposing new things to superiors and others, be sure to emphasize the practical aspects of your ideas. Show how the nitty gritty details work. You must demonstrate that your idea or method is not only workable but also most cost-efficient.

Rest and relax more after the 22nd.

Taurus

THE BULL
Birthdays from
21st April
to 20th May

Personality Profile

TAURUS AT A GLANCE

Element – Earth

Ruling planet – Venus
  Career planet – Uranus
  Money planet – Mercury
  Planet of wealth and good fortune – Jupiter

Colours – earth tones, green, orange, yellow

Colours that promote love, romance and social harmony – red-violet, violet

Colours that promote earning power – yellow, yellow-orange

Gems – coral, emerald

Metal – copper

Scents – bitter almond, rose, vanilla, violet

Quality – fixed (= stability)

Quality most needed for balance – flexibility

Strongest virtues – endurance, loyalty, patience, stability, a harmonious disposition

Deepest needs – comfort, material ease, wealth

Characteristics to avoid – rigidity, stubbornness, tendency to be overly possessive and materialistic

Signs of greatest overall compatibility – Virgo, Capricorn

Signs of greatest overall incompatibility – Leo, Scorpio, Aquarius

Sign most helpful to career – Aquarius

Sign most helpful for emotional support – Leo

Sign most helpful financially – Gemini

Sign best for marriage and/or partnerships – Scorpio

Sign most helpful for creative projects – Virgo

Best sign to have fun with – Virgo

Signs most helpful in spiritual matters – Aries, Capricorn

Best day of the week – Friday

Understanding the Taurus Personality

Taurus is the most earthy of all the Earth signs. If you understand that Earth is more than just a physical element, that it is a psychological attitude as well, you will get a better understanding of the Taurus personality.

A Taurus has all the power of action that an Aries has. But Taureans are not satisfied with action for its own sake. Their actions must be productive, practical and wealth-producing. If Taureans cannot see a practical value in an action they will not bother taking that action.

Taureans' forte is the power to make real their own or other people's ideas. They are generally not very inventive but they can take another's invention and perfect it, make it more practical and useful. The same is true for all projects. Taureans are not especially keen on starting new projects, but once they get involved in new projects they will bring them to perfection. A Taurus carries everything through. He or she is a finisher and will go the distance as long as no act of God intervenes.

Many people find Taureans too stubborn, conservative, fixed and immovable. This is understandable, because Taureans dislike change. They dislike change in their environment or change in their routine. Taureans even dislike changing their minds! On the other hand, this is their virtue. It is not good for a wheel's axle to waver. The axle must be fixed, stable and unmovable. Taureans are the axle of the wheel of society and the heavens. Without their stability and so-called stubbornness, the wheels of the world (and especially the wheels of commerce) wouldn't turn.

Taureans love routine. A routine, if it is good, has many virtues. It is a fixed – and ideally perfect – way of taking care of things. When one allows for spontaneity mistakes can happen and mistakes cause discomfort and uneasiness – something almost unacceptable to a Taurus. Meddling with Taureans' comfort and security is a sure way to irritate and anger them.

While an Aries loves speed, a Taurus likes things slow. They are slow thinkers – but don't make the mistake of assuming they lack intelligence. On the contrary, Taureans are very intelligent. It's just that they like to chew on ideas, to deliberate and weigh them up. Only after due deliberation is an idea accepted or a decision taken. Taureans are slow to anger, but once aroused you'd better take care!

Finance

Taureans are very money-conscious. Wealth is more important to them than it is to many other signs. Wealth to a Taurus means comfort and security. Wealth means stability. Where some zodiac signs feel that they are spiritually rich if they have ideas, talents or skills, Taureans only feel their wealth when they can see and touch it. Taurus's way of thinking is 'What good is a talent if it has not been translated into a home, furniture, car and swimming pool?'

These are all reasons why Taureans excel in estate agency and agricultural industries. Usually a Taurus will wind up owning land. They love to feel their connection to the Earth. Material wealth began with agriculture, the tilling of the earth. Owning a piece of land was humanity's earliest form of wealth: Taureans still feel that primeval connection.

It is in the pursuit of wealth that Taureans develop their intellectual and communication abilities. Also, in this pursuit of wealth and need to trade with others Taureans are forced to develop some flexibility. It is in the quest for wealth that they learn the practical value of the intellect and come to admire it. If it weren't for the search for wealth and material things Taureans might not try to reach a higher intellect.

Some Taureans are 'born-lucky' people who usually win in any gamble or speculation they make. This luck is due to other factors in their horoscope and is not part of their essential nature. By nature they are not gamblers. They are hard workers and like to earn what they get. Taureans' innate conservatism makes them abhor unnecessary risks both in finance and in other areas of their lives.

Career and Public Image

Being essentially down-to-earth people, simple and uncomplicated, Taureans tend to look up to those who are original, unconventional and inventive. Taureans like their bosses to be creative and original – since they themselves are content to perfect their superiors' brain-waves. They admire people who have a wider social or political consciousness and they feel that someday (when they have all the comfort and security they need) they too would like to be involved in these big issues.

In business affairs Taureans can be very shrewd – and that makes them valuable to their employers. They are never lazy; they enjoy working and getting good results. Taureans don't like taking unnecessary risks and do well in positions of authority, which makes them good managers and supervisors. Their managerial skills are reinforced by their natural talents for organization and handling details, their patience and thoroughness. As mentioned, through their connection with the earth Taureans also do well in farming and agriculture.

In general a Taurus will choose money and earning power over public esteem and prestige. A position that pays more – though it has less prestige – is preferred to a position with high prestige but less earnings. Many astrological types do not feel this way, but a Taurus does, especially if there is nothing in his or her personal birth chart that modifies this. Taureans will pursue glory and prestige only if it can be shown to them that these things have a direct and immediate impact on their wallet.

Love and Relationships

In love, the Taurus-born likes to have and to hold. They are the marrying kind. They like commitment and they like the terms of a relationship to be clearly defined. More importantly, Taureans like to be faithful to one lover and they expect that lover to reciprocate their loyalty. When this doesn't happen the whole world comes crashing down. When they are in love Taureans are loyal but they are also very possessive. They are capable of great fits of jealousy if they are hurt in love.

Taureans are satisfied with the simple things in a relationship. If you are involved romantically with a Taurus there is no need for lavish entertainments and constant courtship. Give them enough love, food and comfortable shelter and they will be quite content to stay home and enjoy your company. They will be loyal to you for life. Make a Taurus feel comfortable and – above all – secure in the relationship and you will rarely have a problem with him or her.

In love, Taureans can sometimes make the mistake of trying to take over their partners, which can cause great pain on both sides. The reasoning behind their actions is basically simple. Taureans feel a sense of ownership over their partners and will want to make changes that will increase their general comfort and security. This attitude is OK when it comes to inanimate, material things but it can be dangerous when applied to people, so Taureans should be careful and attentive.

Home and Domestic Life

Home and family are vitally important to Taureans. They like children. They also like a comfortable and perhaps glamorous home – something they can show off. They tend to buy heavy, ponderous furniture – usually of the best quality. This is because Taureans like a feeling of substance in their environment. Their house is not only their home but their place of creativity and entertainment as well. The Taureans' home tends to be truly their castle. If they could choose, Taureans would prefer living in the countryside to being city-dwellers. If they can't do so during their working lives, many Taureans like to holiday in or even retire to the country, away from the city and closer to the land.

At home a Taurus is like a country squire – the lord of the manor. They love to entertain lavishly, to make others feel secure in their home and make them derive the same sense of satisfaction from it as they do. If you are invited for dinner at the home of a Taurus you can expect the best food and best entertainment. Expect a tour of the house – which the Taurus treats as a castle – and expect to see your Taurus friend exhibit a lot of pride and satisfaction in his or her possessions.

Taureans like children but they are usually strict with them. The reason is that they tend to treat their children – as they do most things in life – as their possessions. The positive side to this is that their children will be well cared for and well supervised. They will get every material thing they need to grow up properly. On the down-side, Taureans can get too repressive with their children. If a child dares to upset the daily routine – which Taureans love to follow – he or she will have a problem with a Taurus parent.

Horoscope for 1994

Major Trends

Saturn's transit through the sign of Aquarius – your primary challenge for the past three years – is just about over, Taurus. Rejoice. Starting on January 29th it moves from a stressful position to a harmonious one for you. This is going to lift many burdens and secret sorrows off your shoulders. It is going to improve vastly your health, vitality and sense of self-esteem. This will in turn increase your earning power. The stresses on your romantic relationships are leaving you as well. You've got a lot of good to look forward to.

1993 was basically a work and career year. You learned how to become more valuable by increasing your ability to serve. You became a better, more efficient worker. Many Taureans achieved great career success because of this. 1993 was a year where you *earned* your career status – it wasn't just given to you. 1994, on the other hand, is a romantic year. 'What good is it to own the whole world and yet lack love?' These are your sentiments as you enter this year of passionate romance and deep, committed love. What you lose in the form of superficial friendships and acquaintances you gain in greater intimacy with your 'significant other'. More on this later.

Your interest in religion, philosophy, foreign travel and foreign cultures continues this year. This has been a long-term trend and will continue beyond 1994. Uranus and Neptune (that potent celestial 'wrecking crew') are destroying all your false religious notions and personal philosophies. This destruction is liberating, however: you are free to explore something finer, truer and more workable. When the process is complete you will have a philosophy of life that is truly uplifting and fulfilling. You will have a deeper understanding of what religion is all about and you will be able to reap its considerable benefits.

Health

As mentioned earlier, your health is vastly improved this year. In fact, it is a very minor concern in your chart this year. For the past two to three years you have been like the athlete who practices with weights around the ankles. This builds strength so that when the real match or race comes up the athlete can jump that much higher and run that much faster. This year the 'weights around your ankles' are taken off and you are amazed at your strength.

There are other factors at play in your improving vitality. Elders and authority figures – bosses, people above you in social or professional status – who, for two to three years now, seemed to have denied you recognition and honour are now friendlier to you. They seem less intent on repressing you; they now allow you to shine. Increased self-esteem, greater inner and outer freedom are allowing life forces to flow through you with greater power.

It is almost universally acknowledged these days that stress and tension are the major causes of disease. Stress tends to weaken the immune system so that there is less resistance to opportunistic invaders. With Saturn moving away from you there is less stress in your life. You feel more in harmony with yourself and your universe.

Though your health is wonderful it is natural for your vitality to fluctuate. The healthiest and most robust people experience energy highs and lows – this is in the nature of things. Your periods of greatest overall vitality will be from 1st to 20th January, 20th April to 20th May, 23rd August to 22nd September and 21st December to 1st January (1995).

Your periods of lower overall vitality will tend to be 21st January to 18th February, 23rd July to 22nd August and 23rd October to 22nd November.

Home and Domestic Life

Though you don't seem too concerned with domestic and family issues this year – these take a back seat to romance, higher education and friendships – family matters and domestic harmony seem improved over 1993. Perhaps, as mentioned earlier, because things are basically good you don't need to pay too much attention to this area of your life. One reason for the improvement is that career issues are more or less settled; you are bringing home less tension. Another reason is that you are more concerned with your overall love relationship than with the nitty gritty details of everyday life. You seem content to live on love, letting lesser matters go.

There will be periods this year when domestic issues become a bit more important, however: 15th June to 11th

July, 23rd July to 23rd August and 4th October to 12th December. This last period seems particularly stressful. A major domestic project such as a repair or renovation causes some friction between you and your partner. Unresolved emotional issues from childhood – from the distant past – arise and must be settled. Your partner gets embroiled in your family's internal politics. An acquaintance from the distant past comes between you and your partner. But all of this is short term. The air gets cleared and family harmony resumes.

Love and Social Life

This is one of the major highlights of this year's solar horoscope.

For some years now you have been focused on your primary relationship, but in a rather sombre way. You have experienced some turmoil in love. You've seen the negative side of your partner and of relationships in general, close up. Revelation after revelation has come up in your love relationship. It is quite understandable that you felt compelled to make over your partner or vice versa. Many Taureans will have got divorced or separated – and when this happens things can get ugly. Some of your pet romantic illusions may have been shattered. Yet all of this was part of the great celestial plan which was doing a 'cosmic housecleaning' of your love life. You were being prepared for this year, when real and true romance comes into your life. Where, for the past few years you saw into the depths of hell, this year you see the heights of heaven.

You meet that special someone – your real and true soulmate – whom you can love on many different levels. This is not mere 'hand-holding-in-the-park' kind of romance – but something fiery, passionate, deep. You meet someone strong and loyal who can stand by your side and help you fight the battles of life. This person is very rich – much wealthier, more successful and prominent than you. This is a person you can look up to and respect. He or she also understands the dark aspects of human relationships and knows how to deal with them. This is a person you can share your deepest, darkest feelings with and who knows how to use power constructively and wisely. This person will make you feel safe in the midst of the gloomiest scenarios. The fires of hell cannot daunt his or her ardour or your happiness.

This new love will help you to heal your wounded feelings about relationships. Together you are able to transform yourselves into the people that you want to be.

Your social life – your circle of close friends (friends of the heart) – also expands this year, but in a curious way. By dropping those who are not really your friends – and your new insight into motivation will tell you who they are – you will almost automatically make room for the new and the better. These people were always there, but there was no room in your heart for them.

Curiously, while your circle of heart-friends is increasing your circle of casual acquaintances (or head-friends) is diminishing. Though we all need both types of friendship you seem enamoured of the deep things and have no patience with anything superficial this year.

Your most active and happiest social and romantic periods this year will be from 18th February to 20th March, 21st June to 22nd July and 23rd October to 22nd November. This last period promises to be the most rapturous. Marriage/serious commitment is most likely to happen then.

Career and Finance

Saturn moves out of your 10th House of Career, making professional issues much clearer for you. Bosses and superiors are going easier on you. They are much less inclined to repress or criticize you. In all probability a very repressive and over-controlling authority figure will move out of your life.

Neptune's influence on Uranus (the lord of your career)

makes you more idealistic about career issues and frees your vision as to what could and should be. Sometimes you can close your eyes and see yourself at the pinnacles of success. The gap between this vision and where you are now can cause you dissatisfaction. Use this dissatisfaction positively to spur yourself on to work towards your dreams. Uranus and Neptune have been in your 9th House of Religion and Philosophy for so many years now that you are beginning to see that the limits to career success were all mental and philosophical. You can only go as far as your philosophy of life allows you. Widen your philosophy and your career potential will widen almost automatically.

Many new career opportunities are coming out of your new social contacts. Your new lover and friends cannot take you to new career heights but they can and will create opportunities for you to reach them on your own – if you're ready. You are probably better prepared than you think – Saturn the Cosmic Tester and Taskmaster has seen to that. You can by now handle anything thrown at you. Be bold.

Money is always important to you, Taurus, but this year – as for the past few – it is less so. Your need for prestige and public recognition far outweighs your urge for wealth and comfort. This is definitely unusual and out of character for you.

Your earnings will reflect Mercury's adventures through the zodiac (see the month-by-month forecasts). When Mercury is well aspected and moving forward your earnings are strong and you achieve your financial goals easily. When Mercury receives stressful aspects or goes retrograde (backwards) your earnings may be delayed or come after much struggle. All these are short-term trends only.

Nevertheless, you are financially secure this year. As mentioned, your new relationship is with someone wealthy and supportive. You are mixing – on a social level – with wealthier people as well. The dissolution of a previous relationship or partnership seems to have left you well off. You are also likely to inherit a sizeable sum of money at some future time. A wealth of friendships is also wealth – but remember it is their quality, not quantity, that counts. Towards the end of the year you will have opportunities to pay off all debts. You will also have the chance to attract investors – or loan capital – for a new venture.

Self-improvement

You are going to have a wonderful love this year whether or not you do any work on improving yourself. Your love life can be even more wonderful, however, if you pay attention to the psychological aspects of relationships.

Much of your success this year depends on your ability to discern people's motives and to distinguish a 'head' friend from a 'heart' friend. There is also a need to learn how to look into your own darker motivations and come to terms with them. The more insightful you become about yourself the more tolerant you will become of yourself and of others. The problem is not in having unworthy motivations *per se* but in not understanding your own motivations and not recognizing them. Once they are understood you will realize they are not so dark – and that they can be used to good advantage.

The thrust of this delving into psychology should *not* be to understand others in order to get your way with them. You've gone this route for the past few years and you need to move on. This delving should make you more aware of what 'the other' is and what he or she needs. Thus you will be in a better position to deal justly with that soul – to fill those needs that you can fill and avoid getting entangled in impossibilities. Work as much as possible on developing the social graces. Entertain more. Recognize the differences between people but focus on the things that bind us together. Learn to love the differences as well as the similarities. This year, fulfilling the needs of others will bring you more happiness and satisfaction than merely fulfilling your own.

Month-by-month Forecasts

January

Best Days Overall: 2nd, 3rd, 10th, 11th, 20th, 21st, 29th, 30th

Most Stressful Days Overall: 1st, 6th, 7th, 12th, 13th, 14th, 27th, 28th

Best Days for Love: 2nd, 3rd, 6th, 7th, 10th, 15th, 16th, 22nd, 23rd, 25th, 26th, 31st

Best Days for Money: 2nd, 3rd, 6th, 7th, 10th, 11th, 15th, 16th, 22nd, 23rd, 25th, 26th, 31st

The unusual planetary line-up in the sign of Capricorn, though stressful for many of the other zodiac signs, works very well for you, Taurus. You are quite comfortable in the practical, utilitarian, prudent climate that surrounds you. Your own earthly virtues are very much appreciated and prized. Your health and vitality are superabundant and you feel that you can attain any goal no matter how seemingly impossible. Yes, life-force is the strongest type of magic there is. It is the elixir of eternal youth and the nectar of immortality. When we have it, our boundaries and limits naturally fall away and we are capable of things that we usually think impossible.

You are very much – perhaps overly – involved in foreign affairs, religion, philosophy and higher education right now. Mars, Uranus and Neptune are breaking all barriers to your goals, while the Sun and the new Moon of the 11th are giving you the enlightenment and ideas you need to deal with these issues. Philosophical and religious disputes work out in your favour. You are in a win-win situation: if you win the dispute, you've won; if you lose, you've gained new knowledge and are in a position to enhance your personal philosophy.

Opportunities for education and foreign travel are unusually abundant and bring great happiness – as well as profit.

Everything seems subordinate to your religious, educational and travel interests for most of this month. The pursuit of these interests brings love and financial opportunities. Developments in foreign countries – and your connections with foreigners – bring you profits. Bankers, though unusually prudent, see you as a good investment. Your refinement makes you more attractive to others and strengthens an already existing relationship. Romantic opportunities come from foreign travel and through your religious interests.

Church and university socials promise happy romantic opportunities for singles. Most importantly you attract more and earn more because your self-esteem is unusually high.

February

> Best Days Overall: 7th, 8th, 16th, 17th, 25th, 26th
>
> Most Stressful Days Overall: 2nd, 3rd, 9th, 10th, 23rd, 24th
>
> Best Days for Love: 1st, 2nd, 3rd, 9th, 10th, 11th, 12th, 21st, 22nd
>
> Best Days for Money: 2nd, 3rd, 10th, 11th, 12th, 19th, 20th, 21st, 22nd, 27th, 28th

Physically and emotionally you feel less at home this month than last month. The power in harmonious Capricorn has shifted to erratic, rebellious Aquarius (the signs of Capricorn and Aquarius display different characteristics according to which other sign of the zodiac they are relating to. This is why, for example, Capricorn is hostile for Aries and harmonious for Taurus). You find yourself in a situation where change is exalted and tradition bashed. Being such a conservative creature, it is natural for you to feel some discomfort. Basically you distrust the modern.

In career issues this month new techniques and technology are needed that can enhance your professional status. That new fancy machine or computer programme – which seems so complicated and unnecessary – is probably the vehicle that will make you more effective at your job and help you promote your professional position. Modern things have got their redeeming features, Taurus.

Definitely rest and relax more until the 19th. Wear your colours, scents, gems and metal. The increased use of technology can free up a lot of your time and physical energy – reducing the wear and tear on your vitality. A visit to a masseur, reflexologist or chiropractor might be in order this part of the month.

After the 19th your vitality improves considerably.

If you've read your yearly report you know that this is a super love year for you. But this month there is some short-term stress with your partner or lover. Basically this involves your career. The demands of your career conflict – in a dramatic way – with the demands of your relationship or social life. A delicate balance is needed. Don't let either your partner or your boss think that you have priorities above them.

These issues smooth out after the 19th, which promises to be an unusually favourable love period. Romance blossoms in a big and happy way. Singles meet wonderful romantic prospects. Current relationships become closer, more passionate and more romantic. Love becomes very altruistic.

With Mercury, your money planet retrograde (moving backwards) in the sign of Pisces from the 11th onwards, exercise caution in all financial dealings, investments and major purchases. Avoid signing leases or contracts after the 11th. Review and revise your financial goals. Be more careful about how you communicate about financial matters, as well as with those people involved in your financial life – bankers, investment advisers, brokers and the like.

March

>Best Days Overall: 6th, 7th, 15th, 16th, 17th, 25th, 26th

>Most Stressful Days Overall: 1st, 2nd, 8th, 9th, 23rd, 24th, 29th, 30th

>Best Days for Love: 1st, 2nd, 10th, 11th, 12th, 13th, 14th, 20th, 21st, 22nd, 23rd, 24th, 29th, 30th, 31st

>Best Days for Money: 1st, 2nd, 8th, 9th, 10th, 11th, 12th, 18th, 19th, 20th, 21st, 22nd, 29th, 30th

With so much planetary power in Pisces and the Water Element this month, even your hard-headed, down-to-earth psychology is softened. You are more aware of invisible, spiritual realities. You are more altruistic – especially towards your friends. You are much more open to getting involved in movements and causes that promise help for the needy and a better world. Your ESP powers and dream life will be active all month, for when the Sun leaves mystical Pisces it will enter your 12th House of Mysticism and Spiritual Wisdom. Don't be alarmed – you're not about to run off to the Himalayas and become an ascetic. This is a temporary, short-term phenomenon that has much to teach you.

The general introversion that all this Water Energy produces sits very well with you, Taurus. This is a period where your depth and receptivity (and you have ample amounts of both) are greatly valued. Your self-esteem and self-worth are high, your health and general vitality are excellent.

Two major long-term planets are going retrograde through your 7th House of Love all month. This shows that a current serious love relationship is being reviewed and re-evaluated. Both you and your partner are not sure where your relationship is headed – so some respite from each other is called for. Have no fear, your social charisma is still unusually strong. You might find greater happiness right now associating with friends of the mind. Platonic friends can help you fulfil your social urges and also help you straighten out a current affair. Moreover, these friends are a resource for future romantic opportunities.

There is another strong motivation for pursuing group activities and platonic friends this month: they seem to be a source of financial opportunity and growth. Your general financial condition is very much improved this month as Mercury starts to go forward on the 5th. Stalled projects and payments can now go forward. Financial misunderstandings are cleared up and fiscal confidence is restored.

April

> Best Days Overall: 2nd, 3rd, 12th, 13th, 21st, 22nd, 30th

> Most Stressful Days Overall: 4th, 5th, 19th, 20th, 25th, 26th

> Best Days for Love: 2nd, 3rd, 7th, 8th, 12th, 13th, 17th, 18th, 21st, 22nd, 25th, 26th

> Best Days for Money: 7th, 8th, 9th, 10th, 14th, 15th, 17th, 18th, 19th, 20th, 25th, 26th, 30th

Your charitable nature takes a more active form this month, Taurus. You are not just content with giving money and material to charitable causes but you give of yourself as well.

You give time, physical energy – yes, even free labour – to those less fortunate than yourself. You get a good feeling about this. This is a month to clear karmic debts and prepare for the new solar cycle that begins late in the month.

The power in Aries, though not stressful to your health, is a bit uncomfortable for you as it emphasizes action. You prefer the status quo and only act when forced to. When in doubt, people around you will tend to jump into action – as if everything can be solved by activity. But with Venus, your ruling planet in your own sign almost all month, your self-esteem is not bothered by this. Your personal magnetism and charisma are strong. You dress better, accessorize yourself better and in general project more glamour. You have no trouble attracting others, but social problems could crop up over conflicts of interest. However, these are minor side issues. Your ability to balance your own interest with that of your lover is the key to romantic happiness this month.

Finances are strong all month. Mercury's speedy forward motion shows that you are earning money quickly and easily. You make financial judgements rapidly. However, bear in mind that haste can bring some expensive surprises. Your financial judgement stabilizes after the 25th. Until the 25th you are apt to be an impulsive shopper – afterwards you tend to be more prudent and careful. Overall, the latter part of the month seems better financially than the early part. An increase in your self-esteem is the reason.

Psychologically you feel better after the 20th. Until the 20th you seem rushed, harassed, overly busy. After the 20th you are still achieving but with less haste and impatience. There is a greater calm – an inner peace – when the Sun moves into your own sign on the 20th.

May

> Best Days Overall: 9th, 10th, 19th, 20th,
> 27th, 28th

Most Stressful Days Overall: 1st, 2nd, 3rd, 16th, 17th, 23rd, 24th, 29th, 30th

Best Days for Love: 1st, 2nd, 3rd, 4th, 5th, 11th, 12th, 13th, 14th, 15th, 23rd, 24th, 31st

Best Days for Money: 4th, 5th, 11th, 12th, 13th, 14th, 15th, 21st, 22nd, 23rd, 24th, 31st

You are very much focused on your personal concerns and interests this month, Taurus, as there is a lot of power in your own sign. You assert your will with greater force because you have some difficulty seeing other people's positions. There is nothing – in itself – wrong with asserting yourself. It shows that you are a person with depth, with interests and needs and that you are not afraid to go after those needs. But the challenge this period is to balance your own needs with those of your lover. Over-asserting your position could cause problems.

Your personal appearance and physical energy are strong right now. Your charisma is powerful and, aside from partnerships, you generally get your way. You are more athletic and aggressive all month.

The solar eclipse of the 10th occurs in your own sign, suggesting long-term and dramatic changes in your personal appearance and self-perception. Those of you born on the 9th, 10th or 11th of the month will feel this eclipse more intensely than will others. You should definitely rest and relax more and try to take a reduced schedule around this time. Definitely avoid undertakings that are dangerous, taxing or require you to be at 100 per cent efficiency. This is not a period to try to break athletic or speed records!

The lunar eclipse of the 25th occurs in your 8th House of Elimination and Transformation. This suggests that you are going to get rid of – in a dramatic and perhaps forceful way – some unnecessary things, people and character traits. Your partner's income is going to change over the long term. These short-term upheavals in earnings, however, will lead to greater stability down the road.

Finances are always important to you, Taurus, but this month they are even more so – probably your primary interest. You are going out of your normal orbit to pursue greater earnings and to acquire high-ticket (expensive, long-lasting) possessions. You seem to be stretching your financial limits – trying to break earnings records. With Mercury moving quickly and direct you are likely to succeed (especially after the solar eclipse).

June

> Best Days Overall: 5th, 6th, 7th, 15th, 16th, 23rd, 24th
>
> Most Stressful Days Overall: 13th, 14th, 19th, 20th, 25th, 26th
>
> Best Days for Love: 1st, 10th, 11th, 19th, 20th, 21st, 22nd, 28th, 29th, 30th
>
> Best Days for Money: 1st, 8th, 9th, 10th, 11th, 19th, 20th, 28th, 29th

As for Aries, the planets are quite evenly dispersed between the different sectors of your solar horoscope this month, Taurus. You have a clear and balanced perspective on life. You pay attention to the major spheres of life without overlooking other important areas. Your health and self-esteem continue to be good this month. Your energy and personal charisma is strong. You give off a martial, militant appearance – others annoy you at their own risk! Generally slow to anger, this month you are quicker. If your energy is kept in constructive channels you will excel in athletics and exercise programmes. Your capacity for hard work is also increased.

Your self-assertion could provoke arguments with your lover right now. You are seen as too forceful and pushy. Probably you are not aware that you are acting this way – it seems unconscious, the work of some repressed force coming through.

Your earnings are excellent until the 12th. But then Mercury, your financial genius goes retrograde. Things slow down. Payments due you are delayed. Miscommunication – failures of communication equipment – could delay financial projects and payments as well. In general you need to be more cautious in money matters. Don't sign contracts or make major investments or purchases during the retrograde period. Do it before the 12th or wait till next month.

Of course you are not going to stop all business dealings completely at this time; you are not expected to. But take more time to make sure that those involved in your financial life – bankers, partners, insurance agents, employers and/or employees – are clear in what you are saying and that you understand them completely. This will save you a lot of heartache later on. Purchases made during the retrograde of Mercury usually have to be brought back or exchanged. Why ask for trouble? – Wait till after the retrograde period to buy important things.

Love is stormy and tempestuous right now. This is only temporary, but you really need to work hard to see another's point of view. This is the main problem. Your forcefulness makes your partner back off and you seem to win, but he or she is re-evaluating the relationship and his or her own opinions. Cool down.

July

> Best Days Overall: 2nd, 3rd, 4th, 12th, 13th, 21st, 22nd, 30th, 31st

> Most Stressful Days Overall: 10th, 11th, 16th, 17th, 23rd, 24th

TAURUS

Best Days for Love: 1st, 7th, 8th, 9th, 10th, 11th, 12th, 16th, 17th, 21st, 22nd, 25th, 26th, 30th, 31st

Best Days for Money: 5th, 6th, 7th, 8th, 9th, 16th, 17th, 25th, 26th

Unlike Aries you can really enjoy all the unusual power in Water Signs this month. All this water 'lubricates' you.

You can even enjoy the fact that 40 per cent of the planets are in retrograde (backward) motion. A part of you can relish this slow-down, not doing anything unless you absolutely have to. So, though not many things are taking place this month you enjoy it nevertheless.

Your health is excellent until the 23rd. After that rest and relax more. This is a psychologically-orientated period for all people, but especially for you. People are examining their feelings and why they feel as they do. Psychological issues are going to be covered more by the media and deep insights will come from pieces on the television and radio and in print media. Emotional harmony is the key to good health this month.

Your finances are vastly improved over last month. Mercury, your money planet starts going forward on the 3rd and Mars enters your 2nd House of Money on that day. Thus you are financially fearless and aggressive. You go after what you want – and get it. Your financial confidence is strong and your judgement is good. Trust your intuitions this month. You earn more and you give more this month. No charity is turned down.

Your love life is beginning to pick up as Pluto is unusually stimulated. Nevertheless, continue to exercise caution about committing yourself to a relationship or breaking up one. Neighbours, brothers, sisters and/or in-laws conspire on your behalf to promote true love.

Romantic opportunities come from members of your household and those involved in your finances. The bank, the shopping mall and parties – especially in your own neighbourhood – are likely meeting places for singles. Remember that most people are interested in being nurtured this month. Show feeling, tenderness and concern and love will follow more easily.

August

Best Days Overall: 8th, 9th, 17th, 18th, 26th, 27th

Most Stressful Days Overall: 6th, 7th, 13th, 14th, 19th, 20th

Best Days for Love: 4th, 5th, 11th, 12th, 13th, 14th, 19th, 20th, 21st, 22nd, 23rd, 29th, 30th, 31st

Best Days for Money: 1st, 2nd, 3rd, 4th, 5th, 6th, 7th, 13th, 14th, 15th, 16th, 18th, 21st, 22nd, 23rd, 26th, 27th, 31st

Rest and relax more until the 23rd. Creative self-expression, a light-hearted, childlike attitude to life and a healthy diet are important keys to maintaining good health this period. After the 7th harmony with others at the workplace and fulfilling romance influence your health as well. Your well-being, vitality and self-esteem improve considerably after the 23rd.

Emotional issues were important for you last month and they continue to be important now. You need to take time to understand your childhood and early experiences at home if you are to understand your present behaviour. Your ability to read your own moods and feelings helps you to read these same things in others. Greater tolerance is the result. You have great – even unusual – power in dealing with these issues now and your progress will be rapid. There are greater demands made on you at home. These demands are related to your need to explore your psychological roots. Progress made psychologically – in therapy, for example – will help you deal with family responsibilities; dealing with these responsibilities will in turn aid your psychological progress.

Your earnings are good all month and with Mercury going speedily forward you have great financial confidence. Until the 18th unusual domestic expenses put a temporary dent in your wallet. But this is only in the short term. By the 18th, whatever money was spent is replaced. Speculations become very favourable. Creative projects earn you extra income and you seem to enjoy the way that you earn your money.

Your love life – a current relationship – is greatly improved this month but still not perfect. You experience some tension with your beloved over your devotion to your family. Your family, on the other hand, resents your devotion to your lover. This is the sort of impossible situation that helps us grow. Tread the middle way. Give to each what you are able. Tensions will ease up after the 23rd.

September

Best Days Overall: 5th, 6th, 13th, 14th, 22nd, 23rd, 24th

Most Stressful Days Overall: 3rd, 4th, 9th, 10th, 15th, 16th, 30th

Best Days for Love: 8th, 9th, 10th, 18th, 19th, 28th, 29th

Best Days for Money: 1st, 7th, 8th, 9th, 10th, 15th, 16th, 18th, 19th, 25th, 26th, 27th, 28th, 29th

This month you must deal with the highly unusual phenomenon of having 70 to 80 per cent of the planetary power in the western hemisphere of your solar horoscope chart. But you can handle this. Venus, your ruling planet, is the mistress of tact, diplomacy and reaching consensus. The unusual power in Water and introverted signs during this period is also very helpful, as you are an introvert by nature. Your natural psychology is very well suited to the general temperament of this month.

Fun, work and love are the dominant themes this month. All of these are important, but the major headline is love. You are, unquestionably, in the strongest period of a generally strong love year. This time might even be one of the high points of your life. Love is simply rapturous, romantic, passionate and tender. Seldom have you been this happy in a relationship. Your personal interests and the interests of your lover are merged. What you want is what your lover wants. What your lover wants is what you want. Singles are likely to form serious commitments/marry this month, though such mundane thoughts are probably far from your consciousness: when love is so blissful talk of commitment seems not to matter.

You love the entire world and the entire world loves you. You are glimpsing what paradise on Earth can be. Make no mistake, this is serious committed love here, not something you manipulated to get, but something freely given by the celestial powers. When they decide to give pleasure to someone, that person finds rapture – to the degree that he or she is able to accept it.

Aside from romance, your general social circle expands vastly now. Rich, glamorous, powerful friends of the heart – jet-set types – come into your life. You are catapulted into a world of beauty and glamour. The reality is beyond your fantasy.

All the challenges you face this month – and there are a few – get overwhelmed in a tide of love. You hardly feel them.

October

Best Days Overall: 2nd, 3rd, 10th, 11th, 20th, 21st, 30th, 31st

Most Stressful Days Overall: 1st, 6th, 7th,
13th, 14th, 27th, 28th

Best Days for Love: 6th, 7th, 15th, 16th,
25th, 26th

Best Days for Money: 6th, 7th, 13th, 14th,
15th, 16th, 22nd, 23rd, 24th, 25th, 26th

There are even more planets focused in the western
hemisphere of your solar chart this month – between 80 and
90 per cent. This means that your whole life is wrapped up
in other people, their needs, wants and situation. And while
this has its down-side – the lack of independence, the need
to curry favour and co-operation – the up-side is much
stronger. For the conditions you are brought into are far more
pleasant and opulent than anything you would have created
for yourself – though you are getting ideas from this on how
to create your own future.

Your public life really glitters. Your previous social scene
dies and is reborn into something much more wonderful.
The rich, the beautiful and the powerful are now in your
sphere. With Venus, your ruling planet going retrograde on
the 13th you are not in a position to assert yourself too
strongly with them. Your social life is expanding so fast –
and so high – that you need to retrench, rethink and review
how far and how high you want to go. This Venus retrograde
period is a good time to do it. You are in one of the social high
points of your life. Love blooms but don't schedule a
marriage just yet – not with Venus going retrograde. Enjoy
the love – enjoy the relationship – but don't commit yourself
too soon.

You are in a potent position to attract outside capital into
your business or pet project. You have the ear and the favour
of the rich. You know how to make them even richer and
they like that. But with Mercury going retrograde from the
9th to the 30th you must sign all contracts and make major
financial commitments either before the 9th or next month.

This Mercury retrograde (the backward motion of your money planet) happens in your 7th House of Love and Partnerships – so be especially careful about how you communicate to your love and to friends – and to those involved in your financial life. You won't get away with slipshod communications now.

With the social agenda so active it's going to be tough to weed out the important from the unimportant during this period. But you need to spend more time resting and relaxing – especially after the 23rd.

November

Best Days Overall: 7th, 8th, 16th, 17th, 26th, 27th

Most Stressful Days Overall: 3rd, 4th, 9th, 10th, 24th, 25th, 30th

Best Days for Love: 3rd, 4th, 11th, 12th, 21st, 22nd, 30th

Best Days for Money: 1st, 2nd, 3rd, 4th, 9th, 10th, 11th, 12th, 19th, 20th, 21st, 22nd, 30th

You will be affected by one of the two eclipses that occur this period. Those with April birthdays will be more affected by the solar eclipse of the 3rd, while those with birthdays in May will be more affected by the lunar eclipse of the 18th. Take a reduced schedule on those days and avoid strenuous or taxing activities.

The solar eclipse of the 3rd occurs in your 7th House of Love and Marriage and influences both Venus and Mars. The lunar eclipse of the 18th occurs in your own sign of Taurus and affects Mars, Jupiter and Pluto. The love planets, both universal and personal, are very much affected. Thus, a marriage is likely to happen for those of you who are in a good relationship; a divorce is possible for those relationships that are not good. Some of you will experience both – a divorce and a remarriage. The effect of these eclipses tends to last about six months. The eclipse forces necessary actions to take place over that period of time.

Definitely rest and relax more this month. Social harmony, balanced sexual activities and the elimination of toxins from your system will do much to enhance your vitality this month. If you take life easier these eclipses will bring you blessings and their harmful effects will just pass you by.

Your social life continues to glitter but you must do some weeding out this month. Focus on the quality, not the quantity of your relationships.

With so many planets still in the western half of your chart you continue to be wrapped up in other people and their needs. But the social contacts this brings makes it all worthwhile. Moreover, your business life prospers because of this, as your social contacts bring you new business and earning opportunities. You will learn that wealth cannot be measured merely in pounds and pence; a wealth of friendships – though not on any financial statement – must also be considered.

December

Best Days Overall: 4th, 5th, 13th, 14th, 15th, 23rd, 24th

Most Stressful Days Overall: 1st, 6th, 7th, 21st, 22nd, 28th

Best Days for Love: 1st, 8th, 9th, 10th, 19th, 20th, 28th, 29th

Best Days for Money: 1st, 2nd, 3rd, 11th, 12th, 16th, 17th, 21st, 22nd, 23rd, 24th, 30th

Jupiter, the planet of wealth and good fortune, makes a major, long-term move from your 7th House of Love and Marriage into your 8th House of Passion, Transformation and Elimination. So, the trend of weeding out the impure from your social agenda continues. You have to continue to discern the motives of those in your social sphere and eliminate those people whose motives are not right.

With the Sun and Mercury, your money planet, also congregated in your 8th House for the better part of the month, you are going to be paying off your debts – and rather easily at that. You are becoming attractive to investors. Loans and other forms of financing are easy to get. You will probably explore the stock-market as a means of investment.

Your partner's income increases, not only this month but over the long term as well. The income of family members increases as well. Your partner is more generous towards you. A parent's financial speculations work out very well. The sale of a house is happy and profitable. Focus your attention on making profits for others and your own prosperity will follow naturally.

Love is tender but also passionate. Physical intimacy is more alluring right now than romance. There is still a need for you and your mate to know each other better and on deeper levels. Both of you feel the urge for greater unity between you.

Your health is excellent all month. With all the planets moving forward this month you are making great progress in all your goals. The enormous power in Earth signs towards the middle of the month increases your self-esteem and self-worth. You appreciate the general the mood of practicality and caution. You like to move ahead slowly. People admire your innate ability to materialize insubstantial ideas and make them workable.

Gemini

⚇

THE TWINS
*Birthdays from
21st May
to 20th June*

Personality Profile

GEMINI AT A GLANCE

Element – Air

Ruling planet – Mercury
  Career planet – Neptune
  Love planet – Jupiter
  Money planet – Moon

Colours – blue, yellow, yellow-orange

*Colour that promotes love, romance and social
harmony* – sky blue

Colours that promote earning power – grey,
silver

Gems – agate, aquamarine

Metal – quicksilver

Scents – lavender, lilac, lily of the valley,
storax

Quality – mutable (= flexibility)

Quality most needed for balance – deep rather
than superficial thought

Strongest virtues – great communication
skills, quickness and agility of thought,
ability to learn quickly

Deepest need – communication

Characteristics to avoid – gossiping, hurting
others with harsh speech, superficiality,
using words to mislead or misinform

Signs of greatest overall compatibility – Libra,
Aquarius

Signs of greatest overall incompatibility – Virgo,
Sagittarius, Pisces

Sign most helpful to career – Pisces

Sign most helpful for emotional support – Virgo

Sign most helpful financially – Cancer

Sign best for marriage and/or partnerships –
Sagittarius

Sign most helpful for creative projects – Libra

Best sign to have fun with – Libra

Signs most helpful in spiritual matters –
Taurus, Aquarius

Best day of the week – Wednesday

Understanding the Gemini Personality

The Gemini type is to society what the nervous system is to the body. It does not introduce any new information but is a vital transmitter of impulses from the senses to the brain and vice versa. The nervous system does not judge or weigh these impulses – this function is left to the brain or the instincts. The nervous system only conveys information. And does so perfectly.

This analogy should give you an indication of a Gemini's role in society. Geminis are the communicators and conveyors of information between people. To Geminis the truth or falseness of the information is irrelevant, they only transmit what they see, hear or read about. They teach what the textbooks say or what their managers tell them to say. Thus they are capable of spreading the most outrageous rumours as well as conveying truth and light. Geminis sometimes tend to be unscrupulous in their communications and they can do great good or great evil with their power. This is why the sign of Gemini is called the Sign of the Twins. They have a dual nature.

Their ability to convey a message – to communicate with such ease – makes Geminis ideal teachers, writers, media and marketing people. This is helped by the fact that Mercury, the ruling planet of Gemini, also rules these activities.

Geminis have the gift of the gab. And what a gift this is! They can make conversation about anything, anywhere, at anytime. There's almost nothing that is more fun to Geminis than a good conversation – especially if they can learn something new as well. They love to learn and they love to teach. To deprive a Gemini of conversation, or of books and magazines, is almost cruel and heartless punishment.

Geminis are almost always excellent students and take well to book learning. Their minds are generally stocked with all kinds of information, trivia, anecdotes, stories, news items, rarities, facts and statistics. Thus they can support any intellectual position that they care to take. They are awesome debaters and if they are politically involved make good orators.

Geminis are so verbally facile that even if they don't know what they are talking about they can make you think that they do. They will always dazzle you with their brilliance.

Finance

Geminis tend to be more concerned with wealth of learning and ideas than with actual material wealth. As mentioned they excel in professions that involve writing, teaching, sales and journalism – and not all of these professions pay very well. But to sacrifice intellectual needs merely for money is unthinkable to a Gemini. Geminis strive to combine the two.

Cancer is on Gemini's solar 2nd House (of Money) cusp, which indicates that Geminis can earn extra income (in a harmonious and natural way) from investments in residential property, restaurants and hotels. Given their verbal skills, Geminis love to bargain and negotiate in any situation, but especially when it has to do with money.

The Moon rules Gemini's 2nd solar House. The Moon is not only the fastest-moving planet in the zodiac but actually moves through every sign and house of the zodiac every 28 days. No other heavenly body matches the Moon for swiftness or ability for quick change. An analysis of the Moon – and lunar phenomena in general – describes Gemini's financial attitudes very well. Geminis are financially versatile and flexible. They can earn money in many different ways. Their financial attitudes and needs seem to change daily. Their moods about money change. Sometimes they are very enthusiastic about it; sometimes they couldn't care less.

For a Gemini, financial goals and money are often seen only as a means of supporting a family; it has little meaning otherwise.

The Moon, as Gemini's money planet, has another important message for Gemini financially: in order for Geminis to realize their financial potential fully they need to develop more of an understanding of the emotional side of life. They need to combine their awesome logical powers with an understanding of human psychology. Feelings have their own logic; Geminis need to learn this and apply it to financial matters.

Career and Public Image

Geminis know that they were given the gift of communication for a reason, that it is a power that can achieve great good or cause unthinkable distress. They long to put this power at the service of the highest and most transcendental truths. This is their primary goal, to communicate the eternal verities and prove them logically. They look up to people who can transcend the intellect – to poets, artists, musicians and mystics. They may be awed by stories of religious saints and martyrs. A Gemini's highest achievement is to teach the truth, whether it is scientific, inspirational or historical. Those who can transcend the intellect are a Gemini's natural superiors – and a Gemini realizes this.

The Sign of Pisces is Gemini's solar 10th House of Career. Neptune, the planet of spirituality and altruism, is Gemini's career planet. If Geminis are to realize their highest career potential they need to develop their own transcendental side – their spiritual and altruistic side. They need to understand the larger cosmic picture, the vast flow of human evolution – where it came from and where it is heading. Only then can a Gemini's intellectual powers take their true position and he or she can become the 'messenger of the Gods'. Geminis need to cultivate the ability of 'inspiration', which is something that does not originate *in* the intellect but which comes *through* the intellect. This will further enrich and empower a Gemini's mind.

Love and Relationships

Geminis bring their natural talkativeness and brilliance into their love and social life as well. A good talk or a verbal joust is an interesting prelude to romance. Their only problem in love is that their intellect is too cool and passionless to incite passion in another. Emotions sometimes disturb them and Geminis' partners tend to complain about this. If you are in love with a Gemini you must understand why this is so. Geminis avoid deep passions because these would interfere with their ability to think and communicate. If they are cool towards you, understand that this is their nature.

Nevertheless, Geminis must understand that it is one thing to talk about love and another to actually love – to feel it and radiate it. Talking about love glibly will get them nowhere. They need to feel it and act on it. Love is not of the intellect but of the heart. If you want to know how a Gemini feels about love you shouldn't listen to what he or she says but rather observe what he or she does. Geminis can be quite generous to those they love.

Geminis like their partners to be refined, well-educated and well-travelled. If their partner is more wealthy than them that is all the better. If you are in love with a Gemini you'd better be a good listener as well.

The ideal relationship for the Gemini is a relationship of the mind. They enjoy the physical and emotional aspects, of course, but if the intellectual communion is not there they will suffer.

Home and Domestic Life

At home the Gemini can be uncharacteristically neat and meticulous. They tend to want their children and partner to live up to their idealistic standards. When these standards are not met they moan and criticize. However, Geminis are good family people and like to serve their families in practical and useful ways.

The Gemini home is comfortable and pleasant. They like

to invite people over and they make great hosts. Geminis are also good at repairs and improvements around the house – all fuelled by their need to stay active and occupied with something they like to do. Geminis have many hobbies and interests that keep them busy when they are home alone.

Geminis understand and get along well with their children, mainly because they are very youthful people themselves. As great communicators Geminis know how to explain things to children; in this way they gain their children's love and respect. Geminis also encourage children to be creative and talkative just like they are.

Horoscope for 1994

Major Trends

1993 was a fun-filled, light-hearted year. You partied, were entertained and generally explored the pleasurable side of life.

In 1994 the party is over. It's time to get down to more serious issues – work, career and generally being of service to others. Understand that astrology doesn't elevate one aspect of life over others: each is valid at some time. What was right for you last year could be very much out of order this year. 'For everything there is a season,' say the Scriptures.

Perhaps more than any other sign you are most able to handle the sudden changes in life. Your versatile, mercurial nature makes you welcome the sudden adaptations that life forces on us. Your ability to shift gears suddenly and effortlessly is part and parcel of your genius. It makes you what you are. So don't anticipate any problems in making the necessary adjustments.

Saturn's move from Aquarius (a harmonious position for you) into Pisces (a more stressful position) is forcing you to develop new faculties – patience, endurance, the long-term view and the capacity for hard work. It makes you more serious, more inclined to think deeper about things and to keep your own counsel. Saturn's transits usually produce problems in your feelings of self-worth and self-esteem.

Your feelings about your self – your worthiness and your true position in life – are severely tested by events this year. When this testing time is over you will have a deeper, more realistic sense of who you are and where you belong. Welcome the test as it is in your best interest to have a more realistic sense of who you are. Wisdom begins with knowing your limits.

Health

Your health is a major concern in this year's solar horoscope, Gemini. First off, Saturn's transit makes you more aware of your physical limits. Your normal superabundant energy is not as plentiful this year. No matter how healthy you are – and most of you are basically healthy – you are beginning to see that you can't do everything, be everywhere and handle every project that arises. You need to focus, to set priorities, to determine where you will put your energies. Though the cosmic energy is basically Infinite, our capacity to absorb it at any given time is finite. If you ignore Saturn's warning you run a health risk. If you heed the warning and start conserving energy you will find that you have plenty of strength to do whatever really needs to be done.

You will be exploring health issues more deeply this year. Those of you who have had longstanding health problems now have a good chance of either improving your condition or actual healing it . You gain more knowledge of the role of diet, exercise and emotional well-being in maintaining physical health. You are delving deeper into the mind/body connection. Your innate healing power – both for yourself and for others – is very much strengthened.

This is a year when dietary, vitamin and exercise regimes

are very favourable. Those of you who want to lose weight will find the going much easier this year. Those of you who want to eliminate a bad habit for health reasons will also find doing so less arduous than before. The cosmos seems to impel you in these directions.

The solar horoscope shows other vital areas for maintaining good health: Jupiter, the lord of your love and social life, moves through your 6th House of Health practically all year, showing that love and social relationships are affecting your stamina and vitality. Lack of harmony in a relationship could be causing some physical uneasiness. Before you run looking for physical causes for this unease, therefore, try to repair your relationship. Even if you still need to see a health professional, this repair work will make recovery easier.

Jupiter's transit also shows that a harmonious, well-balanced, social life is unusually important for good health. In your zeal to work and be productive don't forget to play a little. Don't ignore your social life completely.

Though your vitality is not as robust as you are accustomed to, there will be periods when it is quite strong – as well as periods when it ebbs quite low. This is due to the natural fluctuations of planetary movements. Your best overall health periods this year will be from 20th January to 18th February, 20th May to 22nd July and 22nd September to 23rd October.

The most stressful health periods this year – the periods when your vitality is substantially less abundant – will tend to be from 19th February to 20th March, 23rd August to 21st September and 22nd November to 21st December. Be sure to rest and relax more at these times. Wear your colours and gems to strengthen yourself on the subtle realms. Avoid power struggles where possible. You might find it useful to see a chiropractor, reflexologist, masseur, aromatherapist or acupressure practitioner for natural, drugless preventive treatments.

Home and Domestic Life

Family and domestic issues were not that prominent in 1993 and they are not prominent this year, Gemini. Major domestic issues were resolved in 1992 when Jupiter activated this area of life. This was the most recent activation of this area of your life by a major planet. By now the moves and repairs that needed to be made have been made. The cosmos is giving you a free hand (more or less) in the home this year.

A potential challenge lies in relation to your parents. For men, your relationship with your father – or father figure – seems more stressful. For women, the stress is in the relationship with your mother – or mother figure. Perhaps this parent feels – this is what your chart shows – that you have been too light-hearted, irresponsible and neglectful of your real and serious duties, of late. He or she is concerned that you are just frittering your life away in the vain pursuit of pleasure. As with all stressful relationships you need to understand, compromise where possible and look truthfully at the points that are being made. Some will be valid, some not. Attend to the valid ones – it is in your interest to do so.

In spite of this hiccup, your domestic sphere – the details of everyday living – seem basically unaffected this year. Domestic issues will become important from 11th July to 7th August, 19th August to 23rd September and 2nd December to the end of the year. This last period shows an emotional clearing of the air with family members or parents.

Love and Social Life

Though your 7th House of Love and Marriage is not activated most of the year – it does become active very late in 1994 – Jupiter, your love planet, *is* unusually stimulated. So it is going to be an active and basically fulfilling social year.

You expand your social sphere by cutting away – not necessarily by adding. That is, you are better off compressing your social agenda than inflating it. Focus on those who are truly your friends and who sincerely love you and have your best interests at heart. If you do this you will find that the love you seek comes to you almost automatically. Furthermore, you will avoid one of the most common complaints in relationships: neglect. Your present circle of friends (or current love relationship) will not feel that your attention or loyalty is being divided. You will spend more time with the special people rather than in friendships that are going nowhere. Don't be afraid to trim your social agenda and focus on quality rather than quantity. One real friend is better than hosts of false ones. One true love is better than legions of faithless ones.

You have a need for purity in love. You want the real thing, purged of all the usual dross that comes with it. This urge is basically wonderful. Go with it. Only be careful that in your zeal you don't try to make your partner into your own image. Be careful too about over-controlling your partner.

The dirty linen of an old and established relationship is being hung out this year. Scandals – real and imagined – are arising. If your partner has some dark secrets, they will be revealed. If your relationship is basically sound – based on true love and proper motives – it will survive and be stronger than ever before. The relationship will be so transformed as to become – for all practical purposes – a new union. If the relationship is not fundamentally sound, these revelations will unravel its fragile underpinnings.

Some of you will dissolve your marriage or current relationship one way or another this year. But have no fear, a new relationship or marriage is very much in the offing – either this year or next. Do your best to keep the parting from being nasty and venomous. The temptation is unusually strong, but spite between you and your ex-lover only delays the healing process and keeps the new and better love from appearing.

Singles will find abundant romantic opportunities at their jobs and in hospital and doctors' surgeries. You are especially enchanted with people of the healing professions. You also have the need to be able to discuss your deepest, most secret feelings with your beloved this year. You want depth of feeling and depth of conversation in love. You admire people who are deep and perceptive. You admire those who ease the pain and suffering of others. This is very much out of character Gemini, but for this year it is the norm.

Your love and emotional support for someone ill could lead to a serious romance with that person.

Your ideal love is someone who serves your practical interests. You want someone who will serve and minister to you. True love, to you, means service. 'If someone does for me that person really loves me.' Those who have their eye on a Gemini native take note.

If you have done a good job at compressing your social list, expect a great social expansion – many new heart friends, more parties and socializing – after December 9th and well into 1995.

In 1994 your most active and favourable love periods will be from 18th February to 20th March, 21st June to 22nd July and 7th September to 9th December. Singles are most likely to marry or become involved in a serious commitment during this last period.

Career and Finance

Saturn's transit through your 10th House of Career on January 29th makes this area of life of major significance this year. So important is your urge for status and prestige that it dwarfs your interest in mere money-making.

However, career success is not going to be handed to you on a plate. Get used to the idea that you will have to earn it. You will be evaluated by your superiors and the general public, who will be looking for signs of real achievement.

Bosses and superiors are likely to be tougher on you than usual. They are more demanding, more repressive, more controlling and stricter in their judgements. They wear masks of great sternness, but if you pass the trials and ordeals they ordain, you will discern tremendous love and transcendent compassion.

Those of you who are worthy have no need to fear these tests. Stern though they are, these superiors are eminently fair. You will rise according to your current ability and no further. You will not be demoted below your ability. Political pull, nepotism or social connections could no doubt bring you career opportunities but they will not automatically bring you success or professional esteem.

Thus, many of you will actually experience career highs in 1994. You will be promoted, earn more, be given greater responsibility and more work. You will be called on to supervise the work of others. Your organizational ability is a great career asset this year.

With Saturn occupying the highest point in your solar horoscope, be very careful in your dealings with the corporate and governmental hierarchy. Obey rules to the letter. Avoid short-cuts. What may look to you like a mere 'technicality' is enforced with unusual severity. Your superiors are sticklers for detail; so when in doubt go by the book.

Your personal earning power is controlled by the Moon. Its movements, phases and general fluctuations determine the quality and quantity of your earnings. Since the Moon travels so rapidly around the zodiac – every 28 days or so – your earnings will fluctuate day to day and month to month. (Be sure to read your month-by-month forecasts for the short-term trends.)

The income of your partners will still be highly unstable this year, but less so than last year. A partner's earnings will be unusually high or unusually low. Big money is earned, but big money is also spent. Your partner is experimenting – and rightfully so – with different ways of earning money. Sometimes he or she succeeds and sometimes not. Your partner is being led, by means of this experimentation, to a predestined affluence. As long as the risks are calculated this is a healthy course. There is a need to break with or redefine conventional earning practices.

Self-improvement

The thrust of your self-improvement programme this year should be aimed at enhancing your career and public image. Think about what you need to be and to have in order to occupy the position you covet or dream about.

The first thing to focus on is your health and energy. Improve your diet and exercise regimes. Stay physically fit. Without this basic need taken care of you can forget about scaling the arduous and often perilous career heights. A healthy social life – neither too much nor too little (and better a little less this year than too much) – is also a factor here.

Perhaps most important is the quality and quantity of the work you do daily. Set out to become a more valuable person to your company or employer. Become more wisely productive. Your solar horoscope shows that the way for you to increase productivity is not necessarily to do more but to eliminate unnecessary and wasteful tasks. Cut away any activities that are useless, unprofitable and time-consuming; you will have more time and energy to do the things that really count. You need to sit down and consider what you do. What is real and what is unreal, where should you be focused and what can reasonably be dropped. One hour of *real* work – done with concentration and attention – is worth several days of lackadaisical, slipshod work. Work done improperly at the beginning only needs to be done over again later on – wasting further time and energy. Remember, you need all the energy you can muster this year.

GEMINI

Month-by-month Forecasts

January

> Best Days Overall: 4th, 5th, 12th, 13th, 14th, 22nd, 23rd, 31st

> Most Stressful Days Overall: 2nd, 3rd, 8th, 9th, 15th, 16th, 29th, 30th

> Best Days for Love: 2nd, 3rd, 6th, 7th, 8th, 9th, 10th, 15th, 16th, 22nd, 23rd, 25th, 26th, 31st

> Best Days for Money: 2nd, 3rd, 6th, 7th, 10th, 11th, 15th, 16th, 22nd, 23rd, 25th, 26th, 31st

You, along with most of the people around you, are feeling very prudent, practical and cautious this month. You are definitely getting things done – achieving your goals – but in a very careful, organized way. You are particularly sensitive right now to the call of duty and responsibility. You see duty – especially when unpleasant – as one of the highest forms of love. Be careful, though, that you don't take on too many responsibilities (ones that aren't really yours and that you will later regret having taken on).

Normally, this much power – 60 to 70 per cent of the planets – in the sign of Capricorn, making action paramount, doesn't sit too well with you. You prefer ideas and talk. For you, good communication is a form of action. But this month you seem to be in harmony with it all, for Mercury, your ruling planet, is also in Capricorn.

You have an uncanny ability to turn your ideas into reality this month. You also feel duty-bound to increase your partner's income and are very successful in so doing. Big and sudden lump sums of money come to you from your unusually prosperous partner, from stocks and/or insurance settlements. You are also an especially productive worker this month. You are productive because you've learned to enjoy your work.

Singles find a love interest at the workplace; marrieds enjoy the friendship of co-workers. All of this tends to generate extra earning opportunities.

Your health is good but will get even better after the 14th. Diets and weight-reduction regimes prosper.

On the love front, you seem more concerned with issues of physical intimacy and passion than with mere 'hand-holding' romance. Positive, constructive types of experimentation will enhance the joys of physical intimacy and make an existing relationship stronger. Your social agenda needs to be pruned this month. Focus on one good relationship rather than many lesser ones. More is not always better, as the events of January will prove to you.

Financially, your partner needs to experiment with various cost-cutting devices to further enhance his or her profitability. These financial experiments are successful this month.

February

Best Days Overall: 1st, 9th, 10th, 19th, 20th, 27th, 28th

Most Stressful Days Overall: 4th, 5th, 11th, 12th, 25th, 26th

Best Days for Love: 1st, 2nd, 3rd, 4th, 5th, 9th, 10th, 11th, 12th, 21st, 22nd

Best Days for Money: 1st, 2nd, 3rd, 9th, 10th, 11th, 12th, 21st, 22nd

Studies, travel and religious interests, though happy and fulfilling, seem to cause distress with partners, lovers and fellow employees this month. These individuals also interfere with your ability to achieve work goals. Try to maintain a delicate balance: give each person and aspect of your life its due. By the 2nd the situation is straightened out.

The unusual power in the sign of Aquarius is very harmonious to you. It emphasizes intellectual and communication interests and values. These are your strong points. Your virtues are recognized by others and your self-esteem is high.

Your health is also excellent for most of the month. After the 18th, though, try to rest and relax more. Your health is being affected by two causes – the power in the sign of Pisces and the retrograde of Mercury, your ruling planet.

Mercury's retrograde, which begins on the 11th, affects communications in general – often delaying things and increasing the possibility of miscommunication. For you personally, this makes you feel as though you were going backwards in life. Mercury's retrograde creates a cautiousness, a need to review and revise one's goals and self-image. It also affects your home and family life. Be especially careful about how you communicate to family members about sensitive emotional issues. Miscommunication will inflame rather than resolve issues. Avoid making any major purchases for the home until next month, when Mercury starts to go direct again.

Your relationship with your current love are strained right now but will smooth over by the 18th. Your love life in general is experiencing a temporary lull. After the 18th, though, you more than make up for it! The workplace and the pursuit of career objectives are the paths where love will find you. Elders and bosses are Cupids after the 18th. You socialize more with those above you in age and status.

Your finances seem stable and relatively unimportant this period. The cosmos gives you a free hand. Keep in mind that your earning power will increase as the Moon waxes – from the 10th to the 26th. Schedule yourself accordingly.

March

Best Days Overall: 8th, 9th, 18th, 19th, 27th, 28th

Most Stressful Days Overall: 4th, 5th, 10th, 11th, 12th, 25th, 26th

Best Days for Love: 1st, 2nd, 4th, 5th, 10th, 11th, 12th, 13th, 14th, 20th, 21st, 22nd, 23rd, 24th, 31st

Best Days for Money: 1st, 2nd, 10th, 11th, 12th, 20th, 21st, 22nd, 23rd, 24th, 29th, 30th, 31st

The unusual power in the sign of Pisces and the dominance of the Water Element for the better part of the month is definitely uncomfortable for you, Gemini. It is uncomfortable physically and psychologically. The general mood around you favours feeling rather than thinking. People would rather emote than communicate and any perceived lack of feeling is considered crude, barbaric, superficial and insensitive. Logic and intellect seem less respected now, so your self-esteem is not what it should be. Be sure to rest and relax more until the 20th. And remember that clear thinking – your strong point – doesn't necessarily equal insensitivity or lack of feeling – though you could be accused of this. Feeling and thought should work together, hand in hand.

The power in Pisces – though it impacts negatively on your self-esteem – does spur your career ambitions. You make a lot of career progress right now, but it takes hard work. The short-term, fast-moving planets are providing you with opportunities, but Saturn is going to make sure that you deserve them. Those of you who are deserving are going to receive promotions and wage increases during this period. But along with these come extra work and extra responsibility. Often you wonder whether it's all worth it.

Those of you in managerial positions must temper the rules with sensitivity and compassion right now. You must be firm but kind. Over-emphasizing force or authority will not go over well. The new Moon of the 12th is going to clarify power and administrative issues.

Your finances definitely take a back seat to career matters this month. The cosmos seems to give you a free hand in money matters.

Your social life is favourable but commitment or contractual types of partnership should be avoided. Jupiter, your love planet, is retrograde all month. Its favourable stimulation by the other planets brings all kinds of love opportunities, but you are not sure how serious these are. These things will become known as time goes on. Enjoy your relationship and these romantic opportunities for what they are, without looking to make them permanent right now.

April

Best Days Overall: 4th, 5th, 14th, 15th, 23rd, 24th

Most Stressful Days Overall: 1st, 7th, 8th, 21st, 22nd, 27th, 28th

Best Days for Love: 2nd, 3rd, 7th, 8th, 12th, 13th, 17th, 18th, 21st, 22nd, 25th, 26th, 27th, 28th

Best Days for Money: 1st, 7th, 8th, 9th, 10th, 11th, 17th, 18th, 20th, 21st, 25th, 26th, 30th

Your health and vitality in general are much improved over March. As April progresses your vitality will keep increasing. Spring is certainly welcome as you feel less depressed, less hemmed in and can see the answers to most of your problems. Things are not as hopeless as they seemed in March.

Where March was a career month, April is shaping up to be a social month. You mingle with new groups of people and make new platonic friends. Your gift of the gab is a special asset here. Seminars and courses you attend are educational and bring new friends into your life. Mercury's speedy forward motion shows increased personal confidence and an ability to get things done quickly. You know what you want and how to get it.

Overall you are in a period of finishing up old projects, Gemini. This is the time for winding down, for tying up loose ends and making plans for the future. When the Sun moves into your own sign next month, you will be in a better position to start new and important projects.

With most of the planets in the top half of your chart you are still very much career-minded now. You don't mind sacrificing personal happiness or emotional harmony for professional success. The time for getting your emotions in order will come later on. This is a time for manifesting some of your deepest, most cherished hopes and wishes. The new friends you are making now will help you do it.

In love you seem torn between altruism and selfishness. On the one hand you are well aware that the highest love is universal, free and unconditional, but your practical side wants something that suits your needs. This conflict will resolve itself towards the end of the month when you see that it's OK to get what you need from a relationship.

Your partner's income is unstable at the beginning of the month but is fine by month's end. This naturally will affect his or her generosity towards you. Your focus on your own fondest wishes conflicts with your ability – or desire – to enhance your partner's income. But this will straighten out by the 20th. As mentioned above, right now your personal earnings and acquisitions seem unimportant and take a back seat to friendship and career.

May

Best Days Overall: 1st, 2nd, 3rd, 11th, 12th, 13th, 21st, 22nd, 29th, 30th

Most Stressful Days Overall: 4th, 5th, 19th, 20th, 25th, 26th, 31st

Best Days for Love: 1st, 2nd, 3rd, 4th, 5th, 11th, 12th, 13th, 14th, 15th, 23rd, 24th, 25th, 26th, 31st

Best Days for Money: 4th, 5th, 9th, 10th, 14th, 15th, 19th, 20th, 21st, 23rd, 24th, 29th, 30th, 31st

This is basically a happy and harmonious month for you, Gemini, as almost all the planets are being kind right now. However, there are a few surprises thrown in just to keep you on your toes.

First, the good news. Your health, vitality and self-esteem are excellent all month. Your personal charisma and attractiveness are also strong, as you project both energy and glamour. You have a certain flair right now that makes you irresistible. Lovers or would-be lovers can't quite work out what makes you so alluring – is it your clothes? Your accessories? Let them wonder. You know it is merely the extra energy that comes when Mercury, Venus and the Sun move through your own sign.

Your love life will be much happier and more active after the 21st. The solar eclipse of the 10th seems to affect a current relationship. If there is something real between you and your partner the relationship will survive and become better as a result of the upheaval. If the relationship is not strong, it is doubtful whether it will survive. Not to worry, though: you're in a perfect position to meet a truer, more harmonious mate.

The solar eclipse is going to cause some upheavals in your dream life as well. It's going to bring to the surface deep, unconscious areas of yourself that you never knew existed or that you repressed long ago. While not comfortable, this is good, as once these issues are out in the open you can do something about them.

This solar eclipse is also going to bring dramatic and long-term changes in your charitable and religious life. You might decide not to contribute to certain charities any longer, or to start giving more to ones you have not supported before.

The more important eclipse for you this month is the lunar eclipse on the 25th. It will affect all Geminis to some degree but especially those of you born in May. Definitely rest and relax more during the eclipse period – from about a day before till a day after. Postpone strenuous and physically-taxing activities for another time. Avoid long trips – if possible. Allow yourself more time than usual to get things done. This eclipse seems to bring long-term change in your personal earning power and the earnings of partners. It produces changes in the way you dress and the kind of image you project. Your concept of yourself changes – ultimately for the good.

June

Best Days Overall: 8th, 9th, 17th, 18th, 25th, 26th

Most Stressful Days Overall: 1st, 15th, 16th, 21st, 22nd, 28th, 29th

Best Days for Love: 1st, 10th, 11th, 19th, 20th, 21st, 22nd, 29th, 30th

Best Days for Money: 1st, 8th, 9th, 10th, 11th, 17th, 18th, 19th, 20th, 28th, 29th

With 60 per cent of the planets going retrograde this month – including your ruling planet, Mercury – your edginess and frustration are understandable. However, don't feel that you are somehow being singled out by the celestial forces. Most people are feeling the same way. Also, things are not as gloomy as they look: Your health is excellent and, though you don't assert yourself as strongly as you'd like, with the Sun moving through your own sign you're not exactly a weed, either. This is not a good time to be self-assertive anyway. No amount of personal effort is going to speed things up.

You're in a period of review and re-evaluation: take a look at your thoughts and feelings. Keep a notebook for writing down anything that occurs to you. Ask yourself how you can improve your appearance and your image; how you want people to perceive you. It's really up to you. What kind of image would you like to project? What would be your ideal? What can you do to get closer to this ideal? Don't try to implement all the ideas that come through just yet, just look at them and think of what they require and their consequences.

Ask yourself, too, about your love life. What kind of love life would be your ideal? What can be done to get closer to it? The new Moon of the 9th is going to clarify all these issues for you.

One of the few areas of your life that moves forward right now is your inner spiritual life. Volunteering to help those in need, or service done for spiritual organizations, brings you great satisfaction.

Your financial affairs go surprisingly well this month. Your personal earnings are strong. Remember that your financial judgement will fluctuate with the phases of the Moon – the lord of your financial life. As the Moon waxes – from the 9th to the 23rd – your financial energy, enthusiasm and ability are strongest. When it wanes (from the 1st to the 9th and from the 23rd to the 30th) your financial energy will tend to be weaker.

Your 2nd House of Money is active and the Moon will wax as it moves through there on the 10th and 11th. Expect a boost in earnings on those days. Money comes to you through your dreams and intuitions and from spiritual organizations. After the 15th your financial opportunities come through neighbours. A sale in the neighbourhood brings extra funds. Your partner's earnings seem delayed; this could cause him or her to be less generous towards you.

Your love life seems on hold. This is not a good month to rush into a marriage or make any long-term love decisions.

July

Best Days Overall: 5th, 6th, 14th, 15th, 23rd, 24th

Most Stressful Days Overall: 12th, 13th, 19th, 20th, 25th, 26th

Best Days for Love: 8th, 9th, 10th, 11th, 12th, 16th, 17th, 18th, 19th, 20th, 21st, 22nd, 25th, 26th, 30th, 31st

Best Days for Money: 7th, 8th, 9th, 16th, 17th, 25th, 26th, 27th, 28th, 29th

Though your health and vitality are not affected, the psychological atmosphere right now is not very comfortable for you, Gemini. Looking at your chart, 50 per cent of the planets are in Water signs and 40 per cent are in retrograde motion. In addition, 70 to 80 per cent of the planets are in negative, receptive signs. Mercury, your ruling planet, is in moody, emotional Cancer. With you being a talkative extrovert by nature, you feel a stranger in a strange land right now. People are not keen on thinking or talking right now. Nor are they keen on doing. They are only interested in feeling and in understanding *why* they feel as they do. It seems to you – and you are right – that they take refuge in the past rather than look forward to the future.

You will save yourself a lot of heartache if you understand that moods are not logical – at least, not in the way you perceive logic. Moods create their own logic. You will get further this period if you don't listen too much to *what* is being said but to *where* the statement comes from psychologically. When a person is in a certain mood, factual, objective reality is often ignored. Only the mood is real for him or her and he or she speaks from that place. Thus, if you observe the mood rather than the objective statement you will avoid needless arguments and misunderstandings. This perception is important to your financial success this period. People will buy or not buy according to their mood at the moment. People are much less scientific in their shopping habits. Thus if you can find customers in the right mood, you will make the sale. If you catch them in the wrong mood – no matter what you are selling – they will not buy.

This moodiness affects your love life as well – though it is picking up this month – as Jupiter starts moving forward again. Don't expect logic from your beloved and don't insist – not right now, anyway – that he or she conforms to some objective system of rationality. Discern the mood and act accordingly.

Avoid making plans or important decisions when you are tired or feeling depressed. Wait till your mood changes.

August

> Best Days Overall: 1st, 2nd, 3rd, 11th, 12th, 19th, 20th

> Most Stressful Days Overall: 8th, 9th, 15th, 16th, 21st, 22nd, 23rd

> Best Days for Love: 4th, 5th, 11th, 12th, 13th, 14th, 15th, 16th, 19th, 20th, 21st, 22nd, 23rd, 29th, 30th, 31st

> Best Days for Money: 4th, 5th, 6th, 7th, 13th, 14th, 15th, 16th, 21st, 22nd, 23rd, 26th, 27th, 31st

Though most of the people around you are lethargic, introverted and content to stay at home, you seem full of energy and passion right now. You assert yourself and your positions with unusual force. You are accused of being combative. You have some trouble – though you perhaps don't feel this – seeing other people's positions on things. Your fire and passion overwhelm any other opinion.

Your health is excellent until the 23rd, after which you should rest and relax more. Adequate sexual expression, romantic harmony and eliminating impurities from your system are important keys to good health this period.

Financially the month starts off slow but picks up as you go along. The new Moon of the 7th creates new enthusiasm for money-making – especially in sales, marketing, advertising and communications. After the 16th, friends are making extraordinary efforts – working hard and aggressively – on your financial behalf. The Moon, your money planet, visits your 2nd House of Money twice this month – which equals a cosmic bonus to your income. Lump sums come to you on the 13th and 14th through partners, friends and co-workers. Extra money made by working overtime also seems likely on those days.

Your love life is also much improved now. Jupiter, your love planet, moves forward in the sign of Scorpio. Your social charisma is strong and you have your social confidence back. A current relationship moves forward. Friends conspire to promote true love. Singles find love at the workplace. After the 23rd, neighbours also promote romance. The transformation of your social sphere progresses. You are fearless in eliminating false friends and lukewarm loves from your life. You want – and will get – total devotion and loyalty.

After the 23rd, your focus shifts to home and family. There is a need to explore the past – especially your childhood – so that you can understand the present. Any psychological therapies you indulge in go well. Your ability to speak to people's feelings – rather than just to their intellects – is greatly enhanced.

September

Best Days Overall: 7th, 8th, 15th, 16th, 25th, 26th

Most Stressful Days Overall: 5th, 6th, 11th, 12th, 18th, 19th

Best Days for Love: 1st, 8th, 9th, 10th, 11th, 12th, 18th, 19th, 28th, 29th

Best Days for Money: 1st, 5th, 6th, 9th, 10th, 13th, 14th, 18th, 19th, 24th, 25th, 26th, 28th, 29th

With most of the planets in the western half of your solar chart this month you have ample opportunity to exercise your diplomatic and communication skills. You will need them, for in order to succeed this month you need the co-operation of others – and in order to get this co-operation you must explain and sell your ideas.

This is not a period for over-asserting your will, Gemini. You are much better off behaving as if the interests and needs of others were your own. Put their interests first and your own will come to pass in due course.

Your health is excellent – in fact you will hear good news on the health front this period. A long-standing problem gets resolved happily and harmoniously. In spite of this, your vitality is not what it should be until the 23rd. Rest and relax more. Conserve energy by refraining from needless, unnecessary speech. You'll be amazed at how your vitality improves. After the 23rd your vitality returns in great abundance.

Until the 23rd, the demands of home and family dominate your attention. People from your past come back – briefly – into your life. Your parents need and give love and support. This is a good period to delve into your deeper feelings and moods. Housecleaning and repairs also go well right now. The simple pleasures of home and hearth are particularly attractive now. Though you have ample opportunities to go out and enjoy yourself, you prefer staying home. This will change after the 23rd as your zest for personal pleasure intensifies.

Your attempts at purifying your family relationship may cause you to be overly analytical about it. So long as your criticism is constructive and goal-orientated you will make progress. If your criticism turns destructive you will have major problems with members of your household.

Perhaps the most interesting thing going on right now has to do with your work situation. This seems unusually happy and fulfilling. You are easily and effortlessly productive. You take great joy in your work – receiving great personal satisfaction. Who would think that work could ever be so enjoyable? The workplace is the source and site of major romance for you. If you are single, a marriage is likely. Co-workers conspire to foster true love.

October

Best Days Overall: 4th, 5th, 13th, 14th, 22nd, 23rd, 24th

Most Stressful Days Overall: 2nd, 3rd, 8th, 9th, 15th, 16th, 30th, 31st

Best Days for Love: 6th, 7th, 8th, 9th, 15th, 16th, 25th, 26th

Best Days for Money: 4th, 5th, 6th, 7th, 13th, 14th, 15th, 16th, 24th, 25th, 26th

Love, pleasure and work are the dominant activities this month, Gemini, and all are favourable. This is a happy and pleasure-filled month for you. You are wrapped up in other people, adapting to their needs and enjoying yourself immensely in the process. The fact that 80 to 90 per cent of the planets are in the western hemisphere of your solar horoscope – a devastation for other signs – is for you just another opportunity to exercise your genius – your ability to adapt.

Perhaps the greatest danger of all this socializing is that you can lose your own centre. In your zeal to find favour with others – people-pleasing – you can lose sight of who you really are. By letting others define who you are you give up the power to define yourself. Thus your ego and self-esteem become totally at the mercy of your social circle. Happily this situation is only temporary. And the ego lessons you learn will serve you in good stead later on.

Your work life is active and happy. Your role at work is expanding and co-workers are amiable and charming. Love meets you at the workplace.

Speculations are favourable until the 13th. Your ability to attract outside capital to your business or pet project advances this month as Uranus and Neptune both start going forward in your 8th House of Elimination, Transformation and Other People's Money. Your partner's income becomes more regular. Payments due you from insurance settlements, litigation or royalties start to come. Your ability to pay off debts is stronger now. Also keep in mind that, with the unusual amount of power in the sign of Scorpio, the mood of the rich is to invest – and they are particularly interested in reforming idle or unprofitable companies. Profit-making opportunities may come to you through health and service industries.

Your health continues to be good. The health of your partner is basically good, though there will be a downturn in his or her energy after the 13th. Mercury, your ruling planet, goes retrograde from the 9th to the 30th. Use this period to review and revise your goals.

November

Best Days Overall: 1st, 2nd, 9th, 10th, 19th, 20th, 28th, 29th

Most Stressful Days Overall: 5th, 6th, 11th,
12th, 26th, 27th

Best Days for Love: 3rd, 4th, 5th, 6th,
11th, 12th, 21st, 22nd, 30th

Best Days for Money: 3rd, 4th, 11th, 12th,
21st, 22nd, 24th, 25th, 30th

With so much power in Scorpio this month, be careful that you don't get perceived as someone with a flighty, superficial, light-weight mind. It is best to eliminate unnecessary speech and gossip, as people are feeling more serious this month and are not amused by them. Speak only after you've thought through what you want to say and get to the point quickly.

The solar eclipse of the 3rd occurs in your 6th House of Health and Work. This denotes upheavals and shake-ups in the workplace. But with so many powerful benefits congregated there, these shake-ups benefit you and enhance your position. The workplace becomes – over the next six months – happier and more favourable for you. Political operators in the office are flushed out and their opposition to you nullified.

The lunar eclipse of the 18th brings long-term changes in your spiritual life. A temporary eruption in a spiritual or charitable organization you belong to clears the air. Secret, covert enemies are exposed so that you can deal with them. They were not really dangerous to you – only in that they were secret were they dangerous. Rejoice as you discover them. A health problem for your partner comes to the foreground so that it can be dealt with.

The overwhelming dominance of planets is still in the western half of your chart, so you are still wrapped up with other people, their needs and their conditions. You have to put your own interests and desires in second place – temporarily. The positive side of this is a tremendous surge in your popularity – you receive more invitations to parties and functions – and a general increase in your circle of friends. Love is blooming. A neighbour who also works with you is a strong romantic prospect right now. The lunar eclipse of the 18th affects Jupiter, your love planet. This means that many of you will experience a break-up and/or will remarry. The eclipse supplies the necessary boost – the jolt – that makes things happen.

December

Best Days Overall: 6th, 7th, 16th, 17th, 25th, 26th

Most Stressful Days Overall: 2nd, 3rd, 8th, 9th, 10th, 23rd, 24th, 30th

Best Days for Love: 1st, 2nd, 3rd, 8th, 9th, 10th, 11th, 19th, 20th, 21st, 22nd, 28th, 29th, 30th

Best Days for Money: 1st, 2nd, 3rd, 11th, 12th, 19th, 20th, 21st, 22nd, 24th, 30th

The positive changes going on in your love and social life are really the major concern for this month and for the coming year. Jupiter, your lord of love, moves into his own sign and House on the 9th and stays there for the next year. This is wonderful social news, for Jupiter is very comfortable in his own sign of Sagittarius and is thus going to operate unusually powerfully on your behalf.

Also, most of the planets are in the western hemisphere of your solar chart. So you are still wrapped up in other people's affairs and in conditions that others have created. Usually this is not a comfortable position to be in, as it leaves you dependent on others' good graces for any success or achievement. But with Jupiter doing his thing you have their good graces, they create success for you. You are relieved of the feeling of being on your own and relying only on your own resources. You have the resources of friends, partners and lovers available to you.

Mercury, your planetary lord is also moving through your 7th House of Love and Marriage most of the month. This further emphasizes your social life. There is much love – both romantic and platonic – in your life. Your social confidence is very strong and your personal judgement is good. You make good decisions about love during this period. A current relationship might not go over well with your family, but this conflict is short term. If you really love this person your family will accept him or her over time.

This is a month of parties, social functions and romance. Creativity and the arts in general also call upon you. You appreciate fine art more than you usually do. Your aesthetic sense is enhanced.

Rest and relax more until the 22nd. By all means fulfil the needs of friends and lovers, but don't overdo it. Fulfil what you are able to fulfil and let the rest go. Your health improves dramatically after the 22nd.

Cancer

♋

THE CRAB
Birthdays from
21st June
to 20th July

Personality Profile

CANCER AT A GLANCE

Element – Water

Ruling planet – Moon
  Health planet – Jupiter
  Love planet – Saturn
  Money planet – Sun
  Planet of home and family life – Venus

Colours – blue, puce, silver

Colours that promote love, romance and social harmony – black, indigo

Colours that promote earning power – gold, orange

Gems – moonstone, pearl

Metal – silver

Scents – jasmine, sandalwood

Quality – cardinal (= activity)

Quality most needed for balance – mood control

Strongest virtues – emotional sensitivity, tenacity, the urge to nurture

Deepest need – a harmonious home and family life

Characteristics to avoid – over-sensitivity, negative moods

Signs of greatest overall compatibility – Scorpio, Pisces

Signs of greatest overall incompatibility – Aries, Libra, Capricorn

Sign most helpful to career – Aries

Sign most helpful for emotional support – Libra

Sign most helpful financially – Leo

Sign best for marriage and/or partnerships – Capricorn

Sign most helpful for creative projects – Scorpio

Best sign to have fun with – Scorpio

Signs most helpful in spiritual matters – Gemini, Pisces

Best day of the week – Monday

CANCER

Understanding the Cancer Personality

In the sign of Cancer the heavens are developing the feeling side of things. This is what a true Cancerian is all about – feelings. Where Aries will tend to err on the side of action, Taurus on the side of inaction and Gemini on the side of thinking, Cancer will tend to err on the side of feeling.

The Cancerian tends to mistrust logic. Perhaps rightfully so. For them it is not enough for an argument or a project to be logical – it must *feel* right as well. If it doesn't feel right a Cancerian will reject it or chafe under it. The phrase 'follow your heart' could have been coined by a Cancerian, because it describes exactly the Cancerian attitude towards life.

The power to feel is a more direct – more immediate – method of knowing than thinking is. Thinking is indirect. Thinking about a thing never touches the thing itself. Feeling is a faculty that contacts the thing or issue in question directly. We actually touch and experience it. Feeling is almost like another sense that humans possess, a psychic sense. Since the realities that we come in contact with during our lifetime are often painful and even destructive, it is not surprising that the Cancerian chooses to erect barriers of defence – a shell – to protect his or her vulnerable, sensitive nature. To Cancerians this is only common sense.

If Cancerians are in the presence of people they don't know or in a hostile environment, up goes the shell and they feel protected. Other people often complain about this, but one must question their motives. Why does this shell disturb them? Is it perhaps because they would like to sting and feel frustrated that they can't? If your intentions are honourable and you are patient, have no fear. The shell will go down and you will be accepted as part of the Cancerian's circle of family and friends.

Thought processes are generally analytic and separative. In order to think clearly we must make distinctions, separations, comparisons and the like. But feeling is unifying and integrative. To think clearly about something you have to distance yourself from that object. But to feel something you must get close to it. Once a Cancerian has accepted you as a friend he or she will hang on. You will have to be really bad to lose the friendship of a Cancerian. If you are related to Cancerians they will never let you go no matter what you do. They will always try to maintain some kind of connection even in the most extreme circumstances.

Finance

The Cancer-born has a deep sense of what other people feel about things and why they feel as they do. This faculty is a great asset in the workplace and in the business world. Of course it is also indispensable in raising a family and building a home, but it has its uses in business. Cancerians often attain great wealth in a family type of business. Even if the business is not a family operation, they will treat it as one. If the Cancerian works for somebody else then the boss is the parent figure and the fellow employees are brothers and sisters. If a Cancerian is him- or herself the boss, then all the workers are the children. Cancerians like the feeling of being the source of provisions for others. They enjoy knowing that others derive their sustenance because of what they do. It is another form of nurturing.

With Leo on their solar 2nd House (of Money) cusp, Cancerians are often lucky speculators especially with residential property or hotels and restaurants. Resort hotels and nightclubs are also profitable for the Cancerian. Waterside properties allure them. Though they are basically good family people they sometimes like to earn their livelihood in glamorous ways.

The Sun as Cancer's money planet represents an important financial message: in financial matters they need to be less moody, more stable and fixed. They cannot allow their moods – which are here today and gone tomorrow – to get in the way of their business life. They need to develop their self-esteem and self-worth more if they are to realize their greatest financial potential.

Career and Public Image

Aries rules the 10th solar House (of Career) cusp of Cancer, which indicates that Cancerians long to start their own business, to be more active publicly and politically and to be more independent. Family responsibilities and a fear of hurting other people's feelings – or getting hurt themselves – often inhibit them from attaining these goals. However, this is what they want and long to do.

Cancerians like their bosses and leaders to act freely and to be a bit self-willed. They can deal with that in a superior. Cancerians expect their leaders to be fighters – warriors – in their defence. A boss has to be a bit of a 'warlord' in order to be credible to a Cancerian.

When the Cancerian is in the position of boss or superior he or she behaves very much like a 'warlord'. Of course the wars they wage are not egocentric but in defence of those under their care. If they lack some of this warrior instinct – independence and pioneering spirit – Cancerians will have extreme difficulty in attaining their highest career goals. They will be hampered in their attempts to lead others.

Since they are so parental Cancerians like to work with children and that is why they make great educators and teachers.

Love and Relationships

Like the Taurus, the Cancerian likes committed relationships. They function best when the relationship is clearly defined and everyone knows his role. When they marry it's usually for life. They are extremely loyal to their beloved. But there is a deep little secret that most Cancerians will never admit to: commitment or partnership is really a chore and a duty to them. They enter into it because they know of no other way to create the family that they desire. Union is just a way – a means to an end – rather than an end in itself. The family is the ultimate end for them.

If you are in love with a Cancerian you must tread lightly on his or her feelings. It will take you a good deal of time to realize how deep and sensitive Cancerians can be. The smallest negativity upsets them. Your tone of voice, your irritation, a look in your eye or an expression on your face can cause great distress for the Cancerian. Your smallest gesture is registered by them and reacted to. This can be hard to get used to, but stick by your love – Cancerians make great partners once you learn how to deal with them. Your Cancerian lover will react not so much to what you say but to how you are actually feeling at the moment.

Home and Domestic Life

This is where Cancerians really excel. The home environment and the family that they create is their own personal work of art. They strive to make it a thing of beauty that will outlast them. Very often they succeed.

Cancerians feel very close to their family, their relatives and especially their mothers. These bonds last throughout their lives and mature as they grow older. They are very fond of those members of their family who become successful and they are also very attached to family heirlooms and mementos. Cancerians also love children and like to provide them with all the things they need and want. With their nurturing, feeling nature Cancerians make very good parents – especially the Cancerian woman, who is the mother *par excellence* of the zodiac.

As a parent the Cancerian's attitude is 'my children right or wrong.' Unconditional devotion is the order of the day. No matter what a family member does, the Cancerian will eventually forgive him or her, because 'you are, after all, family.' The preservation of the institution – the tradition – of the family is one of the Cancerian's main reasons for living. They have many lessons to teach others about this.

Being such family-orientated people the Cancerian home is always clean, orderly and comfortable. They like old-fashioned furnishings but they also like to have all the new comforts available today. Cancerians love to have family and friends over, to organize parties and to entertain at home – they make great hosts.

Horoscope for 1994

Major Trends

1993 was a stressful year for you, Cancer, but the celestial powers have heard your groans and 1994 is much easier and happier.

Your health and vitality are the first and major areas of improvement. Perhaps even more important, however, is the new sense of optimism and the fun that come into your life this year. Where last year you were concerned with family and domestic issues, this year you are concerned with which theatre outing or party to attend. Where last year you were doing a cosmic juggling act between your duties to your partner and your duties to your family, this year you are hard at work deciding which foreign paradise you want to fly to.

Your newfound playfulness is having a positive effect on a current marriage or relationship. If it hasn't deteriorated past the point of no return there is a good chance of salvation here. Your *joie de vivre* is also increasing your social charisma. This is based on the ancient principle, 'smile and the world smiles with you.' Your sense of play is making you more creative. Your ability to relate to children is very much increased.

Naturally, the coming year – though happy – is not *all* fun and games. Many of you are furthering your education these days and working quite hard at it. The going is sometimes tough. High marks are not handed you on a plate – you have to work for them. You are seeing how hard intellectual work can be – very often it is easier to dig ditches than to master a complex subject.

Health

Your health is vastly – radically – improved over 1993. In 1993 you had four of the major, long-term planets in stressful aspect to you. In 1994 two of these – Jupiter and Saturn – move into harmonious aspects to you. You will feel this change 'in your bones'.

Though your 6th House of Health is not particularly prominent for most of the year, Jupiter (your health planet) is quite stimulated this year. You will be very much focused on health concerns, but the outcome is favourable.

Jupiter's close proximity to Pluto in Scorpio for most of the year shows how your good health can be maintained: there is a need for physical and psychological purity. A refinement of your diet is very much in order. Eat healthier and less toxic foods. Health regimes that cleanse the system are also called for this year, as is purifying your general emotional state. Refrain, as much as possible, from indulging in negative – highly toxic – emotions such as fear, depression, anger and grief. Keep your emotions positive. Feelings are the food of the astral (emotional) body – keep your astral diet as well as your physical diet wholesome. If you stick to these regimes – under the supervision of someone qualified, please – you will wake up one day with a totally transformed body.

Jupiter's position in your 5th House of Fun and Creativity represents another cosmic health message: the optimism you feel – your playful urges – are important in maintaining good health. Avoid getting too serious about things. Make fun an integral part of your life. The expression of repressed creative urges – by painting, making music and dancing – will not only be fun but will also improve your emotional and physical well-being.

Your best overall health periods this year will be from 18th February to 20th March, 21st June to 22nd July and 23rd October to 22nd November.

Your most stressful overall health periods will be from 1st to 20th January, 21st March to 20th April, 22nd September to 22nd October and 21st to 30th December.

Home and Domestic Life

As a Cancer you will always be concerned with your home, family and children. This is you – your nature. But this year you seem less concerned with home than you were last year. This is because you probably did everything that needed to be done there last year – when Jupiter activated your domestic concerns. Many of you moved or expanded your residence last year. All of you improved substantially – in one way or another – the quality of your domestic situation. This year you can relax.

Though your domestic situation is basically stable you are more involved with children this year. Those of you of childbearing age – male or female – are much more fertile this year. You enjoy children more and have a knack for getting on with them. You know how to enter their universe of play and wonder. Both you and they derive great joy from this interaction. Those of you who have older children will hear good news from them. Their lives are going well – taking a turn for the better.

Venus rules your domestic situation. Her movements, positions and aspects shape to a great extent the way in which you experience this area of your life. Because Venus moves rather speedily through the zodiac – her movements parallel those of the Sun – there will be periods when domestic concerns are more (or less) important, easy (or less easy) to handle. These are short-term trends and you can read about them in the month-by-month forecasts.

Home and family issues will tend to be most active from

21st June to 22nd July, 7th August to 7th September and 22nd September to 23rd October.

Love and Social Life

For some years now you have been experimenting with relationships. This is true whether you are married or single. Marrieds are experimenting within their relationship, while singles are experimenting with different types of people. This is all part of the great celestial plan of your life.

Basically you are seeking – and being led to – a perfect, ideal love. Many of you are still seeking it and each experiment – successful or unsuccessful, hurtful or rapturous – brings you closer to the real thing. Some of you, unfortunately, are learning what real love is through the long, tedious process of trial and error. You don't know or are not sure of what it is yet, but you are learning what it is *not*. The upheavals and sudden changes that occur in your relationships can be quite bewildering. It's as if the tried and true ways of relating are no longer valid and you must step into the great unknown and discover things anew, for yourself.

Basically you are staid and conservative in your love and social life. By nature you dislike change and experimentation. Left to your own devices, you probably would not dissolve an unsatisfactory relationship. You would linger and languish in it endlessly. Under normal circumstances it would take major pain to make you dissolve an established marriage or love affair. Thus the cosmos is doing the job for you. It abruptly – often shockingly, like a bolt of lightning – destroys what is not right for you.

Whereas in the past few years the adjustments tended to be disruptive, this year they are more constructive. Singles suddenly find that special someone – out of the blue – when least expected. Those already in a committed relationship suddenly find out the 'right way' to enhance it.

Those of you who have already found your true love need

not worry about the changes and upheavals in your life. They will only make what you have better. Enjoy the changes. A new rapture is being brought to you. New dimensions of relating are being revealed.

With Saturn, your lord of love, making a major, long-term move into your 9th House of Religion and Philosophy, many of you are now attracted to foreign, highly educated and cultured people. You are seeing that religious and philosophical harmony is important in a relationship. Many ailing relationships can be healed by resolving religious issues this year. Religious intolerance will kill even the best of relationships.

Perhaps the most positive trend in love is that you are finally having some fun with your lover this year. Romance is coming back to the relationship. You are not taking each other for granted anymore. You are going out more, enjoying shared activities. You and your partner are more light-hearted and carefree.

Your love life is so good, romantic opportunities are so abundant, that singles feel confused about whether to settle down or not. This is understandable when there are so many fish in the sea. But marriage is definitely on the cards over the long term.

Married people will discover that constructive experimentation in physical intimacy will strengthen the relationship. Shared mystical and religious experiences will also strengthen the bonds between you.

Singles will find romantic opportunities at schools, colleges, religious institutions – church 'do's and the like – and in foreign lands. The attraction is most definitely to the foreign, the unconventional, creative and spiritual. The more exotic your partner, the better you like him or her.

Your best overall periods for social activities and romance will be from 18th February to 20th March, 21st June to 22nd July and 23rd October to 22nd November.

Career and Finance

As mentioned, this is basically a fun, social year, not really a serious career and work year. Of course this doesn't mean that you neglect this part of your life completely, just that the cosmos is not emphasizing it. It is giving you a free hand in shaping your career. It neither impels you in one direction nor does it obstruct you.

You feel that there are other things to life than just work and professional status this year. What good are these things if there is no fun? You're going to take your happiness when and where you can find it and let the chips fall where they may. Interestingly, there are rises and promotions coming your way, but they happen almost by themselves and you don't seem overly impressed one way or another.

Nevertheless you are going to be financially secure this year. First off, you become an unusually lucky speculator. Your light-heartedness and freedom from recent stresses allows your intuitive side to come into play. When you are calm and at peace you have a knack for seeing what will (and won't) work. Follow your intuition.

Secondly, your partner's economic burden is lifted this year. Your partner's financial experimentation starts to pay off. Thirdly, because your self-esteem and self-worth are increased, you tend to earn more. You are perceived as more valuable. Fourthly, profit opportunities arise – almost spontaneously – as a result of your creative activities.

Self-improvement

The greatest potential for improvement this year lies in your relationship and in your educational status. The former can be improved by positive experimentation and a willingness to suffer a few failures. Remember, even failed experiments are useful in that you will learn what doesn't work. Chances are that you will have more successes this year than failures – and these will lead you into new areas of happiness.

Your educational status is going improve. Saturn, the great

taskmaster, is seeing to it. Higher education, religious and philosophical training are very much called for now. Don't expect a 'quickie' success; be willing to give these things all the time and attention they need. If you do so, the rewards will be great later on down the road.

When you study, stress quality rather than quantity. That is, one hour of quality – focused – study is worth more than ten hours of superficial thinking. Study in a relaxed state, rhythmically. Play quiet, soothing music in the background – avoid loud, dissonant, clashing sounds. Create a pleasant aroma around yourself – light some incense as you study. Try as much as possible to enjoy the process.

Read a book for an hour and then let it go. Take notes. Really try to understand what you've read. Don't take the attitude that you just want to be able to pass your exam. What you really want is total comprehension of the subject in question. Many short study sessions are more effective than a few long ones.

When you read, it's a good idea to skim quickly through the entire book first. Write down any questions that spring to mind. It is normal that there will be details you don't understand. Then – after a break, or the next day – start reading the book more deeply – chapter by chapter. Write down a paragraph that summarizes the essence of each chapter. Then, summarize your paragraph into one 'key word'. Do this for all the chapters. There is no rush. After a few days, reread the book again, quickly. Rest assured, there is little that you won't understand after you've completed this studying process.

Month-by-month Forecasts

January

Best Days Overall: 6th, 7th, 15th, 16th,
25th, 26th

Most Stressful Days Overall: 4th, 5th, 10th,
11th, 17th, 18th, 19th, 31st

Best Days for Love: 2nd, 3rd, 4th, 5th,
10th, 11th, 12th, 13th, 14th, 22nd, 23rd,
31st

Best Days for Money: 1st, 2nd, 3rd, 6th,
7th, 10th, 11th, 15th, 16th, 22nd, 23rd,
25th, 26th, 27th, 28th, 31st

The major focus this month is unquestionably the enormous planetary power in your 7th House of Love and Marriage. The fast-moving planets – the Sun, Mars, Mercury and Venus – are triggering the long-term, slow-moving planets into intense and volatile activity. Not only is your social agenda unusually hectic and exciting this month, but major long-term shifts in a current relationship or serious relationship are taking place. You would have to be superhuman to avoid feeling a little confused on a social level – for you are meeting so many new friends and receiving so many new romantic opportunities. Those of you involved in an unsatisfactory relationship will find that your partner – sensing the inevitable – becomes suddenly more amenable and flexible.

What to do, what to do? The new Moon of the 11th is going to clarify all of these social issues for you. By the time it reaches its peak on the 27th you will know where things stand with your partner and which love prospect is best for you. The cosmos, in its Infinite wisdom, presents you with so many options that you have no reason not to be honest with yourself and with others. You can have your ideal love – so why not go for it?

All of this power in the 7th House of Love and Marriage – between 60 and 70 per cent of the planets – makes you more concerned with the needs of other people this month. You see the claims of friendship and love as your duty – your divine mission. This sensitivity to others enhances your social popularity still further. All of this is well and good, only remember your limits. You can't help the whole world and you can't fulfil every friend's need. Do what you are able to do and leave the rest.

Healthwise and energywise January is stressful – especially until the 20th. In your zeal to help others don't forget to help yourself – you need more rest and relaxation this month. Your health and vitality will improve after the 20th, by which time you will be back to your normal superabundant state of vitality.

All of this power in Capricorn – though stressful – has its good points. It forces you to be more adaptable, more flexible in handling situations. For this is a month when you don't create situations but must respond to situations that others create. Your normal ability to control conditions and circumstances is much weakened now. In the East this is called Karma; in the West we call it faith.

February

Best Days Overall: 2nd, 3rd, 11th, 12th, 21st, 22nd

Most Stressful Days Overall: 1st, 7th, 8th, 14th, 15th, 27th, 28th

Best Days for Love: 1st, 2nd, 3rd, 7th, 8th, 9th, 10th, 11th, 12th, 21st, 22nd

Best Days for Money: 1st, 2nd, 3rd, 9th, 10th, 11th, 12th, 21st, 22nd

Though the strong Aquarian energies flowing in right now are not your favourite – they make people too abstract, too theoretical and mental for your taste – your health and self-esteem will not be affected. Your health will be wonderful all month, but especially after the 18th. Life-force itself is the magic elixir, stronger than any medicine, that cures whatever ails us – whether it be physical, financial or emotional. You will see this for yourself, dramatically, after the 18th.

For the better part of the month your 8th House of Elimination and Transformation is highly activated. Thus, there is a need to eliminate the unnecessary from your life – whether it be excess weight, false friends, incorrect ideas or needless work. After the unbelievably hectic social month you had in January a little paring down of your social agenda is called for.

This paring down is short-lived, however. By the 18th, your social life goes back into full swing – as expansive and as happy as ever.

Your partner's income is turbulent right now, reaching wild highs and lows. His or her generosity towards you reflects this: one day lord or lady bountiful, the next tight as a drum. You are doing a lot to help your partner's income, but be careful not to harm your own personal work goals. You run the danger of doing so much for your partner that you have trouble completing your own work. Keep a balance. Bosses and superiors at work seem overly aggressive. Don't give them further excuses to be so.

Though you are an unusually lucky speculator, avoid speculations until the 18th. Afterwards your magic touch returns.

Confusion about issues of physical intimacy are highlighted in your February solar horoscope. You seem unclear about whether intimacy is mere pleasure or power – or some combination of both. The new Moon of the 11th is going to give you all the clarification you need.

March

Best Days Overall: 1st, 2nd, 10th, 11th, 12th, 20th, 21st, 22nd, 29th, 30th

Most Stressful Days Overall: 6th, 7th, 13th, 14th, 27th, 28th

Best Days for Love: 1st, 2nd, 6th, 7th, 10th, 11th, 12th, 13th, 14th, 20th, 21st, 22nd, 23rd, 24th, 31st

Best Days for Money: 1st, 2nd, 10th, 11th, 12th, 20th, 21st, 22nd, 23rd, 24th, 29th, 30th, 31st

Not all the signs feel as comfortable as you do with all the power held in Water signs this month. You positively revel in it. The general mood of sensitivity and moodiness fits right in with your own psychological disposition. You don't need to do anything special to be appreciated this period, Cancer. Just be who you are. Your natural sensitivity, psychological insight and values are very much in vogue. Your health, self-esteem, self-worth and overall vitality are strong. All of this will naturally improve your earnings and romantic life.

This is also very much a fun, 'up' kind of period for you – especially until the 20th. Theatre, concerts, travel and entertainments are very prominent in your solar horoscope. And though you are still very much involved in furthering your career and increasing your professional status, the whole process seems a big game that you can thoroughly enjoy.

Educational opportunities pertaining to your career are offered you now and you should grab them. Your company offers seminars or says it will pay to have you attend. This is good and will further your career. A foreign journey is both pleasurable and boosts your public prestige.

Finances definitely take a back seat to career issues this month. Well-meaning elders or bosses are trying to guide your financial life but you might feel that they're overly controlling. Developments in foreign countries affect your investments or earning ability positively, without any effort on your part. Financial opportunities come from or through higher education, the travel industry, book publishing and religious institutions. Speculations are basically favourable but you could meet with delays in getting paid.

Saturn, your love planet, is highly stimulated and favourably aspected until the 20th. Expect increased romantic opportunities. Your social charisma is particularly strong and altruistic. Your 'ideal love' is very probably the one you know right now. Attractive and highly cultured foreigners are in your life now. Foreign travel promotes a current relationship.

April

Best Days Overall: 7th, 8th, 17th, 18th, 25th, 26th

Most Stressful Days Overall: 2nd, 3rd, 9th, 10th, 23rd, 24th, 30th

Best Days for Love: 2nd, 3rd, 7th, 8th, 12th, 13th, 17th, 18th, 21st, 22nd, 25th, 26th, 30th

Best Days for Money: 1st, 7th, 9th, 10th, 11th, 17th, 18th, 19th, 20th, 21st, 25th, 26th, 30th

The power in Aries, along with 70 to 80 per cent of the planets in the top hemisphere of your solar horoscope, emphasizes strongly career issues, ambitions and the urge for high professional status. So strong is this urge within you now that even family issues – your usual dominant interest – takes a back seat. Happily your family seems supportive of your ambitions and liberates you from many domestic cares. Your partner and/or a current love is not so understanding and feels neglected. Keeping the balance between career and relationship is just as much a challenge as the various power struggles going on in your climb to higher status.

You are making great progress in your career. Seldom are you this aggressive. Any opposition to your advancement is simply overwhelmed. Some of the things you have to do are messy, but you seem willing to do them. You have to make people redundant or purge the office of undesirable elements. You have to fight some battles on the company's behalf. But you're ready to take on all comers. Your public persona is martial. A current lawsuit – involving your company – is awkward but will work out in your favour.

With all this work in your life it is unlikely that you will get all the rest and relaxation you need. Learn to make your rest periods count by learning how to relax consciously. A few hours of conscious relaxation can often take the place of a full night's sleep. There are many audio and video tapes on the market that teach this relaxation method.

Your health and vitality will improve dramatically after the 20th when your career stabilizes somewhat. The general energy will be less go-go-go.

Earnings are strong all month. Elders, parents and professional superiors are helping you to attain financial goals. Rises in salary are likely – corporate perks are given that increase your income indirectly.

As mentioned, your love life is volatile – exciting, but volatile. Sudden break-ups and equally sudden make-ups are likely. The problem is that your partner feels neglected.

May

>Best Days Overall: 4th, 5th, 14th, 15th, 23rd, 24th, 31st

>Most Stressful Days Overall: 6th, 7th, 8th, 21st, 22nd, 27th, 28th

Best Days for Love: 1st, 2nd, 3rd, 4th, 5th, 11th, 12th, 13th, 14th, 15th, 23rd, 24th, 27th, 28th, 31st

Best Days for Money: 4th, 5th, 9th, 10th, 14th, 15th, 16th, 17th, 19th, 20th, 21st, 23rd, 24th, 29th, 30th, 31st

You are still unusually martial and militant in your career. You are ready to defend your position – and the company's – with power and determination. So strong is your force that even partners – who might feel neglected now – back away from any conflict.

But it's not all work right now. Your social life – especially platonic relationships – is very prominent in your horoscope all month. Friends are helping you make your fondest wishes come true. And those that won't or can't help you will be exposed as false friends with the coming of the solar eclipse of the 10th. A definite shake-up in your friendships and other areas of your life is occurring. A fond wish is shattered so that a better one – even fonder – can come to pass. A social organization you belong to threatens to pass from the scene. The solar eclipse will also produce some temporary financial upheavals – perhaps due to a friendship. But these upheavals won't have a long-term effect.

The eclipse of the 25th is a lunar eclipse which should be taken more seriously. The Moon, after all, is your ruling planet. This eclipse could affect your health negatively if you're not careful. Rest and relax more and avoid strenuous, taxing activities. Take a reduced schedule from the 24th to 26th.

Your romantic life is more harmonious before the 21st than afterwards. Though your lover seems cautious, your relationship is still solid. Friends are working to improve your love life and a current relationship. After the 21st this relationship gets tested. A neighbour is – or wants to be – romantically involved.

Finances seem relatively unimportant during this period – though, as mentioned, the solar eclipse is sure to trigger off some activity. Basically you have a free hand in shaping and pursuing your financial goals. Friendship seems more important than money right now. You choose true friendship over money any day. False friendship, on the other hand, is a different matter.

You become active in charitable and philanthropic pursuits after the 21st. You are generous to those in need. This is a good subjective period in which to explore yourself on a psychological or spiritual level.

June

> Best Days Overall: 1st, 10th, 11th, 19th, 20th, 28th, 29th
>
> Most Stressful Days Overall: 5th, 6th, 7th, 13th, 14th, 25th, 26th
>
> Best Days for Love: 1st, 10th, 11th, 19th, 20th, 21st, 22nd, 23rd, 24th, 28th, 29th, 30th
>
> Best Days for Money: 1st, 8th, 9th, 10th, 11th, 13th, 14th, 17th, 18th, 19th, 20th, 28th, 29th

You are always a subjective, inner-orientated, person Cancer, but now with so many planets in Water signs you are even more so. You usually feel quite good and comfortable in this type of cosmic environment, but right now it's all making you feel a bit strange. That is, even though you personally feel fine, confident and worthy, nothing seems to be happening.

The solution to this mystery is that, for starters, 60 per cent of the planets are moving backwards. This causes most of the people around you to feel stalled, blocked, immobile – perhaps frustrated. Secondly, the power in your 12th House of Spiritual Wisdom until the 21st makes you want to withdraw even further from people and into yourself. This might be just the right thing to do. The doors of the great within are always open. And planetary retrogrades are always a good time for subjective, inner work – work that involves planning rather than execution.

So, your path is clear. Review the past year, see where you've come from and where you want to go. Acknowledge past mistakes and resolve to correct them. Let the deep wisdom within you be your guide. It speaks with many voices – the horoscope is just one of these.

People are emotional and moody now and that suits you just fine. This is something you can understand and deal with. Your normal sensitivities are even greater this period than usual; little things can upset you if you're not careful. It's OK to be moody so long as you keep these moods positive and constructive. Only bad moods cause problems.

Your love life, which overall is positive, now seems on hold. Both you and a current love seem indecisive, cautious and unable to decide where to go next. With so many planets in your own sign this month your sex appeal is strong. Singles attract love easily right now. At issue is knowing what you want. Social experimentation now will probably take you backwards rather than forwards.

Finances are a bright spot this month. Your self-esteem is good so earnings are naturally improved. The Sun, lord of your finances, never goes retrograde, so you are achieving financial goals. Venus moving into your 2nd House of Money on the 15th makes earning pleasurable, creative and easy. Look for a net increase in your wealth by the end of the month.

July

      Best Days Overall: 7th, 8th, 9th, 16th,
      17th, 25th, 26th

CANCER

This is a happy and healthy month for you, Cancer –
perhaps the high point of your year. Enjoy.

The psychological atmosphere of the month, which so
devastates, depresses and confuses others, is comfortable
and pleasant for you. You know very well how to handle the
moodiness, the emotionalism, the apparent irrationality and
hyper-sensitivity of those around you. You are a master of
these things. The subjectivity and introversion of the period
is also very comfortable for you. Your virtues are highlighted
and appreciated by others. You know instinctively how to
discern the mood of the moment and use it to your
advantage. Where others are drowning in a sea of emotion
you are swimming very surely. Your levels of self-esteem,
self-worth and self-confidence are high. Your health is
excellent and you make great psychological strides.

The focus on the past during this period is also right up
your street. History, personal and national, is one of your
main interests. Your ability to penetrate the inner world of
feeling – always a formidable talent – is now even more so.
The cosmos adds its energy to your own and you are thus
able to penetrate inner realms that were inaccessible
previously.

Moreover, you are in the position of healer and counsellor
right now, as others turn to you for guidance and
understanding. Your ability to navigate in the sea of emotion
gives you power to help others steer clear of inner whirlpools
and reefs. Children and family members in particular benefit

from your help. You are going to hear a lot of talk about family problems, and since you have already gone through these things you will be the perfect guide.

Finances are excellent, but love issues are delayed. Though you have no trouble attracting others, that special someone in your life needs more time and patience on your part.

August

Best Days Overall: 4th, 5th, 13th, 14th, 21st, 22nd, 23rd, 31st

Most Stressful Days Overall: 11th, 12th, 17th, 18th, 24th, 25th

Best Days for Love: 4th, 5th, 11th, 12th, 13th, 14th, 17th, 18th, 19th, 20th, 21st, 22nd, 23rd, 29th, 30th, 31st

Best Days for Money: 4th, 5th, 6th, 7th, 13th, 14th, 15th, 16th, 21st, 22nd, 23rd, 26th, 27th, 31st

This is a very powerful financial month for you, Cancer. Enjoy.

The new Moon of the 7th occurs in your 2nd House of Money, marking the beginning of a new financial cycle. Many formerly confusing areas about earnings are going to be made more clear. This is a month in which you will acquire high-priced possessions. You make more and you spend more. Money comes to you in pleasurable and easy ways – and since it comes so easily you feel that you can spend it easily. Overspending is a real danger. You are willing to gamble and take risks. Of itself this is good, for no one ever got rich without taking some risks. But you should calculate your risks and don't wager more than you can afford to lose – either at the track or casino or on the stock-market.

Men – and especially authority figures – are working

powerfully on your financial behalf. The Sun, your money planet, moves through his own domain this month, putting your financial life in 'divine' order. Until the 23rd sports, entertainment and art industries are good investments. After the 23rd money comes through neighbours, sales, marketing, advertising and public relations ventures. Financial opportunities emerge in the fields of health care, pharmaceuticals and bio-technology.

Your love life is still on hold; more patience is called for. Don't make any rash decisions now – either to commit to or break up a relationship. Take a 'wait and see' attitude to love. Singles find abundant love opportunities in their neighbourhood and through family members. Love is close to home.

Your health, if anything, is too good. You have a surplus of energy that you don't know what to do with – especially after the 16th. You seem restless, over-active and prone to go far out of your usual orbit in the pursuit of career success. Your personal magnetism is so strong that few are willing to oppose your interests. However, over-asserting your personal – and career – goals can cause some problems with your partner. Do your best to see his or her position.

September

Best Days Overall: 1st, 9th, 10th, 18th, 19th, 28th, 29th

Most Stressful Days Overall: 7th, 8th, 13th, 14th, 20th, 21st

Best Days for Love: 1st, 8th, 9th, 10th, 13th, 14th, 18th, 19th, 28th, 29th

Best Days for Money: 1st, 3rd, 4th, 5th, 6th, 9th, 10th, 13th, 14th, 18th, 19th, 24th, 25th, 26th, 28th, 29th

In certain respects you confront may of the same challenges that Ariens are facing right now – though things are easier for you than for the Ariens. With Mars moving through your own sign you are very Aries-like: you are action- and results-orientated. You tend to want things in a hurry and you assert your will forcefully. You are quite strident and militant these days and want to create your own circumstances and conditions. Yet with 80 to 90 per cent of the planetary power in the western half of your solar chart you find yourself in situations not of your making. Moreover, you find that everything you want to do seems dependent on the grace of other people. This is especially irksome at this time, as you feel really independent – or in need of being independent.

Don't allow yourself to wallow in feelings of frustration – you will get nowhere. Force yourself – and this will be a challenge – to see other people's viewpoints and to harmonize with them – you can then enlist their co-operation. Put other people's needs before your own right now and your success is assured. Some people will no doubt take advantage of your empathy, but this will teach you about their character for future reference. However, others will reciprocate – and this will more than make up for the discomfort of being taken advantage of.

Aside from this challenge you are in a fun-filled and happy period. Finances are becoming ever more favourable – and next month will be even better. Speculations are auspicious. Your self-esteem and self-confidence are strong. Others appreciate your sensitivity and psychological insight. The dominance of the Water Element this month is very comfortable for you and fosters love and money. Big romance is in your life, though you should not make any serious commitments just yet. The cosmos gives you many romantic options this month – either for fun and games or for profound relationships. The choice is yours.

Your health is excellent all month, but rest and relax more after the 23rd.

October

Best Days Overall: 6th, 7th, 15th, 16th, 25th, 26th

Most Stressful Days Overall: 4th, 5th, 10th, 11th, 17th, 18th, 19th

Best Days for Love: 6th, 7th, 10th, 11th, 15th, 16th, 25th, 26th

Best Days for Money: 1st, 4th, 5th, 6th, 7th, 13th, 14th, 15th, 16th, 24th, 25th, 26th

What a banner month this is, Cancer! A life-time peak. The celestial powers are setting you loose to play, and they are paying all the bills.

Your dominant interests this month are family, children and fun. Family issues – which to some people are onerous – are for you a pleasure. You are psychologically geared for them and – of all the zodiac types – most able to handle them. In spite of a conflict between your partner and other family members, this is a happy month. The conflict doesn't seem to affect you personally as it is more between them. Moreover, the new Moon of the 5th – a particularly powerful one – is going to bring you all the information you need to handle family disputes and responsibilities.

You are an incredibly lucky speculator right now. You prosper in enjoyable ways. You earn money both at work and (perhaps even more) in your leisure time. Creative projects are fun and profitable. Those of you involved in the entertainment business will certainly find employment this month – this is the month for the lucky break. Artists will make big sales.

Love is the major headline this month. Those of you who are married are having more fun with your partner than you've had in a long time. Romance is back. Singles have abundant romantic opportunities – some serious and some not so serious. Commitment should perhaps wait for a while, as Venus goes retrograde on the 13th. But you seem to be in control as far as love is concerned. The decision whether to keep a current affair just fun and games or to take it further is up to you. Next month's new Moon will clarify these issues.

Though this is a month for parties and entertainment, earnings are going to sky-rocket after the 23rd. You are in the right place at the right time. You seem able to do more work with less effort and so you earn more.

November

Best Days Overall: 3rd, 4th, 11th, 12th, 21st, 22nd, 30th

Most Stressful Days Overall: 1st, 2nd, 7th, 8th, 14th, 15th, 28th, 29th

Best Days for Love: 3rd, 4th, 7th, 8th, 11th, 12th, 21st, 22nd, 30th

Best Days for Money: 3rd, 4th, 11th, 12th, 21st, 22nd, 24th, 25th, 30th

You should be thankful that there are two eclipses this period to liven things up and jolt you out of a euphoria that threatens to keep you stagnant. Too much good – and the aspects are very good for you – can make things very boring. The solar and lunar eclipse are important to you. The solar eclipse of the 3rd affects your money planet, the Sun. The lunar eclipse of the 18th affects your ruling planet, the Moon. Be sure to rest and relax more on these days and take a reduced schedule, especially on the 18th.

The sale of your present residence is favourable and profitable, especially since the eclipse will flush out false buyers. Though your earnings are very strong this month, the solar eclipse brings with it a short-term financial upheaval –

a sudden expense for your home or children – that forces you to go out and earn more. With the monetary aspects so good for you, however, this added expense will turn out to be one of the luckiest financial breaks you've ever had. Good luck masquerades in strange disguises sometimes.

Similarly, a humiliating experience with a friend or with some group that you belong to around the 18th shakes you into positive action regarding your image and personal appearance.

Aside from these temporary bumps in the road, life is good. Speculations are still favourable – though avoid any gambling on the 3rd. Your ability to sense a winner, whether it be a stock, commodity, business investment or horse, is uncanny. So long as you are calm, not upset or depressed, you can go to the bank on your intuition.

Your creativity is wonderful. Your imagination is rich and full of marketable images. In fact, the imagination is your secret gold-mine right now.

After the 22nd you are still, as you were last month, hard at playing – but the demands of work become more important. Money comes to you through increased effort and service to others.

Your health is excellent all month.

Your love and social life is very much improved over the way it's been the past few months. A current relationship moves forward again. Marital relations improve. You and your lover have more fun together.

December

Best Days Overall: 1st, 8th, 9th, 10th, 19th, 20th, 28th

Most Stressful Days Overall: 4th, 5th, 11th, 12th, 25th, 26th

Best Days for Love: 1st, 4th, 5th, 8th, 9th, 10th, 19th, 20th, 28th, 29th

Best Days for Money: 1st, 2nd, 3rd, 11th,
12th, 21st, 22nd, 23rd, 24th, 30th

For the past year you've been developing your sense of play
and creativity – just for its own sake. You've had a light-
hearted attitude to life. All this was wonderful. Now, with
Jupiter moving into your 6th House of Work you need to
bring some of that creativity and light-heartedness to your
work. This doesn't mean that you should treat your work
lightly, but rather that you instil it with some fun, make it
enjoyable. Do your job more creatively and you'll become
more productive.

Those of you in your own businesses are going to hire more
employees and otherwise expand the workplace this month.
You are fortunate in attracting the right employees as well.
Those of you who work for others are going to become more
productive and thus increase your earnings. All of you are
concerned with practical service to others. Service to others
takes on religious overtones now and for the long term.

The new Moon's lunar movement of the 2nd is what's
known as a Super Moon. This highly unusual event occurs
when the Moon is at its closest to Earth – its *perigee* position.
Thus it's going to be particularly powerful in clarifying your
work and employee matters. Everything you need to know
is close at hand and clearly revealed.

Sales and marketing activities are prominent in this
month's horoscope. You go to unusual lengths – way beyond
your normal bounds – to make that sale or find those
prospects. You are this keen in your charitable activities as
well. You break out of the normal pattern in your giving and
your volunteer work.

Your love life becomes unusually exciting after the 22nd.
Romance is unconventional, experimental and titillating.
Affections can change suddenly; the ways your lover
expresses love change without warning. You will be kept on
your toes. It would be most unwise to take a current love for
granted right now.

On the positive side, your lover is supportive financially. Earning opportunities come from within your social sphere. Remember to take a more social attitude with business associates and sales prospects.

After the 22nd, you are partying and attending social functions. This is always the time of the year for parties, but in your case you are attending more than usual. Be sure to rest and relax more after the 22nd (that is, between parties!).

Leo

♌

THE LION
Birthdays from
21st July
to 21st August

Personality Profile

LEO AT A GLANCE

Element – Fire

Ruling planet – Sun
  Health planet – Saturn
  Love planet – Uranus
  Money planet – Mercury

Colours – gold, orange, red

Colours that promote love, romance and social harmony – black, indigo, ultramarine blue

Colours that promote earning power – yellow, yellow-orange

Gems – amber, chrysolite, yellow diamond

LEO

Metal – gold

Scents – bergamot, frankincense, musk, neroli

Quality – fixed (= stability)

Quality most needed for balance – humility

Strongest virtues – leadership ability, self-esteem and confidence, generosity, creativity, love of joy

Deepest needs – fun, elation, the need to shine

Characteristics to avoid – arrogance, vanity, bossiness

Signs of greatest overall compatibility – Aries, Sagittarius

Signs of greatest overall incompatibility – Taurus, Scorpio, Aquarius

Sign most helpful to career – Taurus

Sign most helpful for emotional support – Scorpio

Sign most helpful financially – Virgo

Sign best for marriage and/or partnerships – Aquarius

Sign most helpful for creative projects – Sagittarius

Best sign to have fun with – Sagittarius

Signs most helpful in spiritual matters – Aries, Cancer

Best day of the week – Sunday

Understanding the Leo Personality

When you think of Leo, think of royalty – that way you'll get an idea of what the Leo character is all about and why they are the way they are. It is true that for various reasons some Leo-born are not always expressing this quality, but even if they are not they would like to do so.

A monarch rules not by example (as does Aries) or by consensus (as do Capricorn and Aquarius) but by personal will. Will is law. Personal taste becomes the style that is imitated by all subjects. A monarch is somehow larger than life. This is how a Leo desires to be.

When you dispute the personal will of a Leo it is serious business. He or she takes it as a personal affront, an insult. Leos will let you know that their will carries authority and that to disobey it is demeaning and disrespectful.

A Leo is king (or queen) of his or her personal domain. Subordinates, friends and family are the loyal and trusted subjects. Leos rule with benevolent grace and in the best interests of others. Leos have a powerful presence; indeed, they are powerful people. They seem to attract attention in any social gathering. They stand out because they are stars in their domain. Leos feel that, like the Sun, they were made to shine and rule. Leos feel that they were born to special privilege and royal prerogatives – and most of them attain this status, at least to some degree.

The Sun is the ruler of this sign and when you think of sunshine it is very difficult to feel unhealthy or depressed. Somehow the light of the Sun is the very antithesis of illness and apathy. Leos love life. They also love to have fun; they love drama, music, theatre and amusements of all sorts. These are the things that give joy to life. If – even in their best interest – you try to deprive Leos of their pleasures, good food, drink and entertainment, you run the serious risk of depriving them of the will to live. To them life without joy is no life at all.

Leos epitomize humanity's will to power. But power in and

of itself – regardless of what some people say – is neither good nor evil. Only when power is abused does it become evil. Without power even good things can't come to pass. Leos realize this and are uniquely qualified to wield power. Of all the signs, they do it most naturally. Capricorn, the other power sign of the zodiac, is a better manager and administrator than Leo – much better. But Leo outshines Capricorn in personal grace and presence. Leo loves power where Capricorn assumes power out of a sense of duty.

Finance

Leos are great leaders but not necessarily good managers. They are better at handling the overall picture than the nitty-gritty details of business. If they have good managers working for them they can become exceptional executives. They have vision and a lot of creativity.

Leos love wealth for the pleasures it can bring. They love an opulent lifestyle, pomp and glamour. Even when they are not wealthy they live as if they were. This is why many fall into debt, from which it is sometimes difficult to emerge.

Leos, like Pisceans, are generous to a fault. Very often they want to acquire wealth solely so that they can help others economically. Wealth to Leo buys services and managerial ability. It creates jobs for others and improves the general well-being of those around them. Therefore – to a Leo – wealth is good. Wealth is to be enjoyed to the fullest. Money is not to be left to gather dust in a mouldy bank vault but to be enjoyed, spread around, used. So Leos can be quite reckless in their spending.

With the sign of Virgo on Leo's 2nd House (of Money) cusp, Leo needs to develop some of Virgo's traits of analysis, discrimination and purity when it comes to money matters. They must learn to be more careful with the details of finance (or to hire people to do this for them). They have to be more cost-conscious in their spending habits. Basically, they need to manage their money better. Leos tend to chafe under financial constraints, yet these constraints can help Leos reach their highest financial potential.

Leos like it when their friends and family know that they can depend on them for financial support. They don't mind – even enjoy – lending money, but they are careful that they are not being taken advantage of. From their 'regal throne' Leos like to bestow gifts and presents upon their family and friends and then enjoy the good feelings these gifts bring to everybody. Leos love financial speculations and – when the celestial influences are right – are often lucky.

Career and Public Image

Leos like to be perceived as wealthy, for in today's world wealth often equals power. When they attain wealth they love having a large house with lots of land and animals.

At their jobs Leos excel in positions of authority and power. They are good at making decisions – on a grand level – but they prefer to leave the small details for others to take care of. Leos are well respected by their colleagues and subordinates, mainly because they have a knack for understanding and relating to those around them. Leos usually strive for the top positions even if they have to start at the bottom and work hard to get there. As might be expected of such a charismatic sign, Leos are always trying to improve their work situation. They do so in order to have a better chance of advancing to the top.

On the other hand, Leos do not like to be bossed around or told what to do. Perhaps this is why they aspire so for the top – where they can be the decision-makers and needn't take orders from others.

Leos never doubt their success and focus all their attention and efforts on achieving it. Another great Leo characteristic is that – just as good monarchs – they do not attempt to abuse their power or the success they achieve. If they do so this is not wilful or intentional. Usually they like to share their wealth and try to make everyone around them join in their success.

Leos are – and like to be perceived as – hard-working, well-established individuals. It is definitely true that they are capable of hard work and often manage great things. But don't forget that deep down inside Leos really are fun-lovers.

Love and Relationships

Generally, Leos are not the marrying kind. To them relationships are good while they are pleasurable. When the relationship ceases to be pleasurable a true Leo will want out. They always want to have the freedom to leave. That is why Leos excel at love affairs rather than commitment. Once married, however, Leo is faithful – even if some Leos have a tendency to marry more than once in their lifetime. If you are in love with a Leo, just show him or her a good time. Travel, go to casinos and clubs, theatres and discos. Wine and dine your Leo love – it's expensive but worth it and you'll have fun.

Leos generally have an active love life and are demonstrative in their affections. They love to be with other optimistic and fun-loving types like themselves, but wind up settling with someone more serious, intellectual and unconventional. The partner of a Leo tends to be more political and socially conscious than he or she is and more libertarian. When you marry a Leo, mastering the freedom-loving tendencies of your partner will definitely become a life-long challenge – but be careful that Leo doesn't master you.

Aquarius sits on Leo's 7th House (of Love) cusp. Thus if Leos want to realize their highest love and social potential they need to develop a more egalitarian, Aquarian perspective on others. This is not easy for Leo, for 'the king' finds his equals only among other 'kings'. But perhaps this is the solution to Leo's social challenge – to be 'a king among kings'. It's all right to be royal, but realize the nobility in others.

Home and Domestic Life

Although Leos are great entertainers and love having people over, sometimes this is all show. Only very few close friends will get to see the real side of a Leo's daily lifestyle. To a Leo the home is a place of comfort, recreation and transformation; a secret private retreat – a castle. Leos like to spend money, show off a bit, entertain and have fun. They enjoy the latest furnishings, clothes and gadgets – all things fit for kings.

Leos are fiercely loyal to their family and of course expect the same from them. They love their children almost to a fault; they have to be careful they don't spoil them too much. They also must try to avoid attempting to make individual family members over in their own image. Leos should keep in mind that others also have the need to be their own individuals. That is why Leos have to be extra careful about being over-bossy or over-domineering in the home.

Horoscope for 1994

Major Trends

1993 was a stressful year on many levels, Leo, but it was also constructive. You were forced to create a working balance between your interests and those of your partner and between your duties to him or her and your obligations to the rest of your family. Tensions were high all year long.

Happily, 1994 is going to be much easier. Saturn, which has been opposing you for the past two to three years, is now moving away from its stressful aspect. Your health and vitality will be the first areas to improve. Then you will note growth in your sense of self-esteem and self-worth. Marriage and partnership issues seem resolved and finally laid to rest; you are free at last to make that move into your dream house or to create your dream house from your existing residence.

Psychological therapies dominate your interest for most of the year – and it is well that they do. You always knew that you were the most interesting person in your world – and you are certainly right about this. But this year you get to see why.

A Leo who can't shine is one of the most miserable creatures in existence. This state ranks in severity with the misery of the Virgo who is unemployed or the Libra who is romantically uninvolved. You've had some rough going the past two to three years. This year your light does shine. Actually it has always shone, only now the bushel under which it was hidden has been taken away.

Health

Your health and vitality are going to be vastly improved in 1994 to what they were in 1993. Yet you still seem occupied with them. This has been a long-term trend and will continue for a few more years.

You still seem willing to explore all kinds of different avenues in your search for the 'perfect body, the perfect diet, the perfect regime'. This is all to the good, for you are gaining a lot of knowledge of this area. Over the past few years you have probably left no stone unturned – no fad not followed – no vitamin or miracle cure unexplored. You are probably attributing your greater sense of well-being to your latest health craze – and, though some of these things have no doubt done you some good – the truth is that you feel better because you have more energy available. Think of a rubber ball that has been squeezed. What happens when you release the pressure on it? It just snaps back to its natural state automatically. Something negative and unnatural was taken away. This is your situation this year, Leo.

By all means continue your experimentation and exploration. You are being led to a deeper, more cosmic understanding of the laws of health and dis-ease. You are – and have been – seeing the spiritual causes of dis-ease. If you have not yet been led to these depths you will be this year. There are many reasons for this. Uranus and Neptune in your 6th House of Health are helping you rethink your conventional notions about good health. Ultimately, they will lead you to your ideal body. Those who perceive the correct way to work on this will be spared much trial and error. Saturn, your lord of health, moves into spiritual Pisces this year, showing you that you must work spiritually on your health if you want to get long-term results.

Foot reflexology is a particularly powerful health preventive this year, Leo – for the Pisces sign rules the feet and your health lord is in that sign.

The fact that your health lord is in your 8th House of Elimination and Transformation shows that sexual balance – neither too much nor too little – is an important key to good health (your normal tendency is to overdo it). Your partner's income and generosity also – curiously enough – affect your health. Debts, financial burdens and trying too hard to collect money owed you are additional sources of stress – if you allow them to be. Do what you can do comfortably and then let go and relax.

Your best overall health periods this year will be from 20th March to 20th April, 23rd July to 23rd August and 22nd November to 21st December.

Your most stressful overall health periods will tend to be from 20th January to 18th February, 21st April to 20th May and 23rd October to 21st November. Be sure to rest and relax more during these periods.

Home and Domestic Life

Home, family and psychological issues have been important in your horoscope for many years now, Leo, but this year they take on a new and added significance.

For the past few years now all the dark family secrets have been coming to the surface. The blacker side of your own nature – especially as experienced in childhood – has been coming up as well. Your family is not what you thought it was, nor are you what you thought yourself to be. Some family relationships have been little more than covert struggles for power. No one denies that it is natural for humans to group themselves into families – Nature ordains it, it is a mechanism for survival. But you have seen that this institution – which in essence is benevolent – can sometimes be corrupt or be misused. Family, which should make life more abundant, can sometimes be an obstacle to one's highest aspirations. What should be a safe haven in which to develop one's highest life capacities can become a trap from which there is no escape.

It is just as well that the celestial powers have revealed this truth, however painful, to you. For unless you see things clearly, you will not be able to go further in your development. Don't think that you have been singled out to be saddled with a dysfunctional family. Many, many others are also so burdened. But at least you are closer to your liberation than many others. You have seen what is and, once you have seen it, you are in a position to do something constructive about it.

Happily, this year your family situation takes a decided turn for the better. The whole family pattern, which has really been unravelling of late, renews and regenerates. There are two basic scenarios – with some minor variations – this year. First, you will probably break with those family members with whom no possibility of harmony exists. Concurrently, a new and more harmonious family is created. This new family could very well be one of blood. That is, you may have children and thus create your own family. This is very likely. Alternatively you may create (or discover) your true spiritual family. They have always been with you on another dimension – even before you were born! Still others of you might find that your whole family situation is so utterly resolved and transformed – through psychological or spiritual therapy – that it is like having a new one.

In short, negative, troublesome family members fade out

of your life this year, one way or another, and new people who are like family to you come into the picture. A move to a larger, more opulent home is also quite likely, or you might decide to raze your present residence and rebuild where you are. Your living space, one way or another, will increase. New – and very flash – items for the home are coming to you. Your family circle increases. Male or female, you are more fertile this year.

Now that the less happy side of family life has been revealed to you, you can avoid making the same mistakes twice. Your new family situation is going to be more supportive – in more enlightened ways – than you ever dreamed possible.

Love and Social Life

Much of the conflict between your partner and family is resolving itself this year. This will ease tensions in your relationship. So, your love life is infinitely more stable this year than last.

Keep in mind that Uranus, your love planet, has been moving through your 6th House of Health, Work and Service for some years now. It has been governing your love life under the powerful influence of Neptune. This has been a long-term trend and will continue for some years to come.

You have been more idealistic and freedom-conscious in your relationships. Overly structured, regimented relationships have turned you off. All of this is understandable. But now you are seeing that a relationship with no structure is as bad as one with too much. Your ideal relationship will not be one without limits but one with freedom within certain (agreed upon) boundaries.

You are looking for the ideal romance. The vision of this is opening up to you. Many of you have found it already and many of you will find it this year, for Uranus, your love planet, is more beneficially stimulated this year than it has been for quite a few years.

You have always liked an independent, freedom-loving and brilliant partner. But of late you want someone spiritual and creative as well. You want and need a spiritual connection, a common metaphysical purpose with your prospective partner. If you can find this with your current love, all is well and good. If you can't, your present relationship is in trouble.

Many of you want a merging that is so close, so intimate that all physical and ego differences are annihilated. 'I and my Love are One.' This is a natural desire. Only realize that this kind of bonding is only possible on a spiritual level and not in the mundane reality. So become one with your love spiritually; merge totally on that level. On the physical level, recognize and love the differences and distinctions between you. This is the key to a healthy, happy love life.

Those of you involved with Leos this year ought to know that – for some time now – practical service has been seen by him or her as the highest form of love. Show love by doing practical things for your Leo love. Your Leo love will reciprocate. Leo also feels an unusual need for glamour both in a partner and in friendships.

Career and Finance

Your earning power is basically stable this year, Leo. Your 2nd House of Money is not unduly activated and seems relatively unimportant. This should be considered a good sign, since only when something goes amiss do we need to pay attention to it. The cosmos is neither helping nor hindering your financial goals.

Keep in mind that speedy Mercury is your Money Planet. When it moves fast and receives good aspects your earnings tend to increase and be earned rather easily. When Mercury moves slowly – or goes retrograde (backwards) – your earning power seems to diminish. There is less financial confidence during these periods and your financial judgement is apt to be unrealistic. You can track these short-term trends by reading your month-by-month forecasts.

The major financial herald in 1994 is Saturn's move from your 7th House of Love to your 8th House of Transformation. This affects you indirectly – it affects your partner. Your partner's income will diminish. Wild financial experiments don't turn out that well and your partner might be less generous with you than you might normally expect. You need to work harder to collect monies owed you. Creditors seem unsympathetic and hard-hearted. Debts are repaid this year, but only through hard work. Litigations with insurance companies, or over estates and inheritances, are delayed.

Yet, there is an up-side to all this. Your family – which has been unsupportive of your partner – now makes an about-face and provides financial opportunities for him or her. Your own newfound psychological awareness also enhances his or her income. Basically, your partner needs to be cautioned against taking undue risks. All financial risks should be calculated ones. The long-term view must be kept in mind if your partner is to succeed. He or she must cut costs and manage present resources more effectively. But rest assured, because Saturn is eminently fair. When Saturn bestows the gift of abundance, it is abundance that endures over the long term.

You seem more concerned with building a harmonious emotional base – having personal happiness – than in attaining career success this year. You are right to feel this way. For, without a stable emotional base – a happy, harmonious home – career success is much more difficult to attain. The higher you intend to climb in your business or profession, the deeper, more solid must be your emotional roots. Like the foundation of a building, your domestic situation needs to be strong enough to bear the weight of your career aspirations.

Self-improvement

This is a year for psychological awareness. Standard psychological therapies – those that deal with your early life, your parents, siblings and early relationships – are very much in order now. You have the capacity to attain great understanding here – to clean out a lot of useless baggage. Your ability to understand your own feelings – and those of others – becomes a great tool for achieving your aims this year. Especially so in terms of creating a stable home and enhancing your partner's income. You learn much this year from studying children. Observe little children and you will understand 'the child within'. And conversely, when you understand your child within you are better able to handle children.

Month-by-month Forecasts

January

Best Days Overall: 1st, 8th, 9th, 17th, 18th, 19th, 27th, 28th

Most Stressful Days Overall: 6th, 7th, 12th, 13th, 14th, 20th, 21st

Best Days for Love: 2nd, 3rd, 10th, 11th, 12th, 13th, 14th, 20th, 21st, 22nd, 23rd, 29th, 30th, 31st

Best Days for Money: 2nd, 3rd, 6th, 7th, 10th, 11th, 15th, 16th, 22nd, 23rd, 25th, 26th, 29th, 30th

Up to 90 and sometimes 100 per cent of the planets are in the western hemisphere of your solar horoscope this month, Leo. This is quite unusual. It shows that you are almost totally absorbed by others – by the demands of relationships – to the neglect of your own self-interest. You are not too comfortable with this. You like having your own way, to create your own conditions, circumstances and situations. Adapting to conditions created by others or otherwise outside your personal control makes you feel less powerful – less sunny. Yet, sometimes great life lessons are learned in this way. For one thing, you learn flexibility. And, by meeting the needs of others you clear up old personal and karmic debts. If this kind of thing were to carry on too long it would be quite an ordeal for you, but happily it's only for the short term.

Until the 20th you seem caught up with work duties, both for your employer and for others in general. The call of duty is so strong that even your mighty will cannot fight it. You are called upon to help friends or associates who are under the weather and who cannot help themselves. You need to manage the details of your own life and theirs as well – and how you hate details! Yet, you gain a certain satisfaction from handling all this. As you serve now so shall you be served in the future.

Your social agenda is hectic the entire month, but after the 20th it heats up even more. Invitations to parties, social events and fund-raisers multiply. Romantic opportunities are superabundant. You have an understandable need to break loose and party after so much work and regimentation. But you find that social commitments are as much duties – can be just as onerous – as work. Try to be more selective.

On the health front, things are a bit stressful. Until the 20th you feel more psychologically stressed. There's a feeling of frustration as the enormous power in the sign of Capricorn and the Element of Earth – between 60 to 70 per cent of the total planetary power – makes people unduly slow, cautious, restrained, prudent and practical. This doesn't sit well with your fiery, passionate nature. Like Aries, you like action *now*. You can't understand all this focus on trivial practical details. To make things worse, others view your Leo courage and passion as rash foolhardiness.

After the 20th the stress is more physical. Definitely try to rest and relax more the entire month. Wear your colours, scents and metal. Listen to the demands of your body. If you have no energy or are ailing, you certainly can't do the altruistic work of helping others.

February

> Best Days Overall: 4th, 5th, 14th, 15th, 23rd, 24th
>
> Most Stressful Days Overall: 2nd, 3rd, 9th, 10th, 16th, 17th
>
> Best Days for Love: 1st, 7th, 8th, 9th, 10th, 11th, 12th, 16th, 17th, 21st, 22nd, 25th, 26th
>
> Best Days for Money: 2nd, 3rd, 10th, 11th, 12th, 19th, 20th, 21st, 22nd, 25th, 26th, 27th, 28th

Except for the Moon, all the long- and short-term planets are still concentrated in the western hemisphere of your solar horoscope, Leo. You are cleaning up past situations and reacting and responding to conditions that already exist. You seem unable to create the new atmosphere that you want to create. You are not comfortable with this; you see it as a limitation on your freedom. But dealing with these things will clear the ground for a truer, happier freedom later on in the year. Sometimes we have to take life as we find it, we can't deal the cards ourselves but must work with the cards dealt to us. Your challenge now is not to create some absolute nirvana, but to make the best of what you've got. If you do so, you can consider yourself successful – you have passed the test – and will be ready to move on.

Until the 18th your health and vitality are not what they should be, so be sure to rest and relax more. Social demands – filling the needs of others as well as those of your family – can be quite draining. Remember that you are not called to give more than you are physically or materially able to give. Rest when you're tired.

The situation at home seems stressful. The demands of your lover conflict with those of the rest of your family and household. Give each its due. Walk the middle path. Chances are that you can't satisfy everybody and have everyone's universal approval, but you can do what is right in your own eyes. This will ultimately see you through. Conflicts quiet down after the 18th.

The retrograde of Mercury, your money planet on the 11th shows a need for caution in all communication affairs and projects, especially those that involve finances. Financial deals and any long-term purchases or commitments should be reviewed more carefully from the 11th onwards. It is better to delay signing any contracts or making any major investment until Mercury goes direct, next month. Be especially careful about how you communicate with your friends or with a political or social organization you belong to. Take the time to make sure that they get the true message and not some garbled distortion. Conflicts are likely to arise from these misunderstandings. You've got enough real challenges to deal with without adding this kind of blunder to your list.

March

Best Days Overall: 4th, 5th, 13th, 14th, 23rd, 24th, 31st

Most Stressful Days Overall: 1st, 2nd, 8th, 9th, 15th, 16th, 17th, 29th, 30th

Best Days for Love: 1st, 2nd, 6th, 7th, 8th, 9th, 13th, 14th, 15th, 16th, 17th, 23rd, 24th, 25th, 26th, 31st

LEO

Best Days for Money: 1st, 2nd, 8th, 9th,
10th, 11th, 12th, 20th, 21st, 22nd, 25th,
26th, 29th, 30th

With 50 to 60 per cent of the planetary power in emotional Water signs, people's general psychology is emotional, sensitive, introverted and psychic. Though there are aspects of this mood that you like – it stimulates your natural creativity – you basically feel out of tune. It is hard for you to understand all this subjectivity – everyone keeping everything inside. With you things are just the opposite: you say what you think, you express what you feel and to hell with the consequences. Be careful not to be perceived as insensitive right now. Watch the tone of your voice when you speak as it could come across as harsh or cruel. Dealings with your family, which seem better than last month, could erupt over sensitive issues.

This is a good month to do those home repair projects, search for a new home, redecorate and the like. If you don't try to rush things and are willing to put up with a few delays, these projects should work very well this month. Psychological therapy – explorations into moods and feelings – also goes well.

Finances are going to improve considerably this month as Mercury starts to go direct on the 5th. This boosts your financial confidence and judgement. Until the 18th money comes through social connections and through the generosity of your partner. Your partner, by the way, can expect increased earnings this period. You are a factor in this. After the 14th, lump sum amounts may come from insurance companies, stock transactions and/or dividends. Debts are easily incurred this period – be careful. If you have a legitimate business venture, investors are more easily lured after the 14th.

You seem voluntarily to limit yourself socially until the 20th. This could be due to a feeling of isolation or because you want to focus your energies on one person. Until the 20th

157

you are attracted to older, more established people. You enjoy their benevolent control. After the 20th, you are more attracted to younger people – perhaps foreigners – active, energetic types.

Your health is wonderful all month, but especially after the 20th. Spring fever really inspires you.

April

Best Days Overall: 1st, 9th, 10th, 19th, 20th, 27th, 28th

Most Stressful Days Overall: 4th, 5th, 12th, 13th, 25th, 26th

Best Days for Love: 2nd, 3rd, 4th, 5th, 12th, 13th, 21st, 22nd, 30th

Best Days for Money: 7th, 8th, 9th, 10th, 17th, 18th, 19th, 20th, 21st, 22nd, 25th, 26th, 30th

Though domestic and family issues are prominent and favourable the entire year, for this month they take a back seat to career and worldly issues. Domestic expansions are on hold for a while, as are psychological therapies. This is basically good. It gives you a break so that you can concentrate on the outer world – your career and educational interests. In truth, you are more comfortable dealing with these issues than with family ones. You like being out there expressing yourself and building up your public persona. The considerable power in Aries makes you shine again. Your ego and self-esteem are strong. You shine in educational settings and, after the 20th, you shine in your career.

Your health is excellent until the 20th. After that career pressures – which are basically favourable – can force you to overwork and deplete yourself. You need to meet both the amount of energy your body needs to function effectively and the energy demands made in fulfilling your ambitions. Don't give too much to either. Keep your ambitions within your physical scope.

Career issues go well all month. No matter how you feel subjectively it's nice to have the appreciation of superiors and the public in general. Honours come to you this period. Rises, promotions and corporate perks come your way. Venus, the lord of your career activities is in her own House this month and thus acts powerfully on your behalf. You have great charisma. You socialize with the right people – people who can help you ascend. Women are particularly helpful careerwise.

Finances also go well. Your money planet (Mercury) moves speedily forward, heralding great financial confidence and ease. Again, these financial breaks come through your career and people at the top, through a rise in salary or a new perk.

Love is volatile and unstable until the 20th. After that it looks pleasant indeed. The workplace is the likely meeting ground for romance. People involved in your career are interested in you romantically. It all seems congenial right now.

May

Best Days Overall: 6th, 7th, 8th, 16th, 17th, 25th, 26th

Most Stressful Days Overall: 1st, 2nd, 3rd, 9th, 10th, 23rd, 24th, 29th, 30th

Best Days for Love: 1st, 3rd, 9th, 10th, 11th, 12th, 13th, 19th, 20th, 23rd, 24th, 27th, 29th, 30th, 31st

Best Days for Money: 4th, 5th, 11th, 12th, 13th, 14th, 15th, 19th, 20th, 21st, 22nd, 23rd, 24th, 31st

Career issues and attaining your public and professional ambitions are paramount the entire month, Leo. The work you are doing is not in vain and not hopeless.

The solar eclipse of the 10th is an important event for you both personally and professionally. It's going to produce long-term career changes. A shake-up of the corporate hierarchy is likely and it will work out in your favour if you are patient. An elder or figure of authority passes from your life.

Your health and vitality will be considerably lower on the 10th, so be sure to rest and relax more. Remember that the planet being eclipsed is the Sun – your ruling planet. Your self-image will also change for the better as repressed feelings and undesirable personal habits go by the board.

The lunar eclipse of the 25th seems much more harmonious to you than the solar one. Unless you have important Natal planets in Sagittarius (which can only be ascertained by a study of the particular day and time of your birth within the sign of Leo), chances are that you won't feel it. But whether you feel it or not there will be long-term changes in your creative life and in your relationship with a child.

Career pursuits are taxing you until the 21st, so rest and relax more. Try to handle only priorities. Chances are that you cannot avoid a power struggle with others involved in your designs. So, other areas of life will have to be toned down. A lot is at stake now in your career – prestige, position and money.

Finances are good all month. You are going way out of your normal orbit in the pursuit of profit. You seem willing to do anything and go anywhere. Your financial confidence and judgement are sound. Earning opportunities come from friends, groups and spiritual activities. Powerful 'money magic' is revealed to you towards the end of the month.

June

Best Days Overall: 3rd, 4th, 13th, 14th, 21st, 22nd, 30th

Most Stressful Days Overall: 5th, 6th, 7th, 19th, 20th, 25th, 26th

Best Days for Love: 1st, 5th, 6th, 7th, 10th, 11th, 15th, 16th, 21st, 22nd, 23rd, 24th, 25th, 26th, 30th

Best Days for Money: 1st, 10th, 11th, 15th, 16th, 19th, 20th, 28th, 29th

You will probably chafe at the advice given here, Leo, but you need to hear it anyway. The theme for this month is caution, caution, *caution*; patience, patience and more *patience*. Your hot, fiery nature doesn't like this – but even your immense personal power is not going to speed things up right now. Let go. Do what can be done and leave the rest. Powers above your will are at work. 60 per cent of the planets – including your love and money planets – are moving backwards. There is a need for review and re-evaluation, for perfecting, improving and correcting most of the departments of life. This is true for most other people as well. So, just because you think you're ready to sign that contract, make that investment or schedule that wedding – others may not be so sure. They need to think things over. Previously hidden factors come to light that make a re-evaluation necessary. Co-operate with this process.

This is an introverted month. The power in your 12th House of Spiritual Wisdom and Charity further emphasizes this trait. Psychologically this is uncomfortable for you as you are an extrovert. But a short period of introversion, of studying your inner thoughts, feelings, motivations – of reviewing your life, especially the past year – won't harm you.

This is a good month for studying psychic and spiritual subjects, for joining spiritual organizations, for getting involved in psychology or seeing a therapist and for charitable, voluntary activities. It is also good for socializing with groups and with platonic friends – friends of the mind rather than friends of the heart. They have much to teach you.

In romance and finance just try to stay afloat and relax. Do whatever constructive things you can but don't worry or fret. Most of what you fear won't happen. When the planets go direct again the whole picture changes almost of itself.

July

> Best Days Overall: 1st, 10th, 11th, 19th, 20th, 27th, 28th, 29th
>
> Most Stressful Days Overall: 2nd, 3rd, 4th, 16th, 17th, 23rd, 24th, 30th, 31st
>
> Best Days for Love: 1st, 2nd, 3rd, 4th, 10th, 11th, 12th, 13th, 21st, 22nd, 23rd, 24th, 30th, 31st
>
> Best Days for Money: 7th, 8th, 9th, 12th, 13th, 16th, 17th, 25th, 26th

Though your health and vitality are not affected this month – in fact they are rather excellent – you still don't feel yourself. You feel moody, subjective, drawn to the past and to inner spiritual concerns. This is not you and you know it.

There are various reasons for this. Two powerful planets are energizing your 12th House of Spiritual Wisdom and Charity. Emotional Water signs control 50 per cent of the planetary power; 40 per cent of the planets are moving backwards. Also, 70 to 80 per cent of the planets are in introverted signs. You feel you are drowning in a sea of emotion and you need to explore this in order to solve it.

Though you want to go out and have fun, others prefer to be couch potatoes. People are more concerned with feeling than with doing. If you can become more aware of their moods you will find it easier to navigate this sea of feeling. Social and/or financial rebuffs – there will be a few – have nothing to do with you personally but with the atmosphere of the time. Discern the atmosphere and you can transform rebuffs into acceptance. Make another offer at a later time.

You must continue to be aware of the hyper-sensitivity of those around you. If you behave in your normal brash, blunt, fiery style people will consider you insensitive – or even cruel. Make special efforts to be aware of other people's feelings. What to you is harmless could be devastating to another.

Though a current relationship seems to be going backwards it is not your fault but the state of your partner. You have no trouble attracting others as your personal magnetism and charisma are strong. You can be a force for good this period by lifting the depression felt by your partner and those around you. Only be careful that you yourself don't get sucked into it. You can only heal the emotions of those people who choose to be healed. You can only uplift those who want to be uplifted. Don't force it.

Finances are unusually good this period as elders, parents and bosses conspire to support you and provide you with earning opportunities.

August

Best Days Overall: 6th, 7th, 15th, 16th, 24th, 25th

Most Stressful Days Overall: 13th, 14th, 19th, 20th, 26th, 27th

Best Days for Love: 8th, 9th, 11th, 12th, 17th, 18th, 19th, 20th, 29th, 30th

Best Days for Money: 4th, 5th, 6th, 7th, 8th, 9th, 13th, 14th, 15th, 16th, 18th, 21st, 22nd, 23rd, 26th, 27th, 31st

Though the forces of subjectivity and introversion are still overwhelming this month, things are a bit easier than they were last month, Leo. For one thing, more – but not all – of the planets are moving forward now, reducing the sense of delay and frustration around you. The Sun's movement through your own sign of Leo also promotes a more fun-loving attitude in the people around you. There is definitely more optimism around now than there has been in the last two months.

Your health and self-esteem are improved. For the Sun, your ruling planet acts especially powerfully while in Leo. Your ability to assert yourself and your desires is enhanced. You have greater ease in getting your way right now. Personal pleasures are increased.

Though your health is good all month you can enhance your sense of well-being by eliminating impurities from your system, taking special care of your spine, posture and feet and maintaining a balanced sex life (that is, neither too much nor too little!).

Your self-assertion can cause some conflict with children and members of your household. Patience and compromise are the answers. There is always a middle way where everyone gains and no one loses. Look for it.

Finances are steadily improving. There is no question that money issues are very important this month – more so than usual. Mercury, your money planet moves forward speedily, showing great financial confidence and ease. Until the 3rd, profit ideas come through dreams, psychics and intuition. After the 3rd you must put these ideas into practice. You must do the leg work – make the moves – necessary to manifest the ideas. Your physical appearance – the projection of the right image – become unusually important in financial success. Dress for success after the 3rd.

Until the 18th you can be overly optimistic and overly generous in money matters. The danger is that you might overspend on unnecessary items. After the 18th, when Mercury moves into his own sign of Virgo, your financial judgement becomes rational, sound and down-to-earth. Hold off on buying luxury items until this time, when you will be a more shrewd and more careful shopper.

Though you must tread cautiously in love matters now, after the 23rd there is greater harmony with a current love. Abundant love opportunities come through the pursuit of your earnings and with those involved in your work and finances.

September

Best Days Overall: 3rd, 4th, 11th, 12th, 20th, 21st, 30th

Most Stressful Days Overall: 9th, 10th, 15th, 16th, 22nd, 23rd, 24th

Best Days for Love: 5th, 6th, 8th, 9th, 13th, 14th, 15th, 16th, 18th, 19th, 22nd, 23rd, 24th, 28th, 29th

Best Days for Money: 1st, 5th, 6th, 7th, 8th, 9th, 10th, 15th, 16th, 18th, 19th, 26th, 27th, 28th, 29th

From 80 to 90 per cent of the planets are clustered at the bottom half of your solar horoscope chart this month, Leo. In addition, 50 to 60 per cent of them are in the Element of Water. This fosters emotional and domestic concerns. The need for emotional harmony and personal happiness far outweighs the need for 'outer' success. You won't regret a business deal that you missed, but you will regret not spending time with your family.

This area of life is not only intensely active but also very favourable and happy. You are amazed at how fulfilling family life can be – since you are by nature an outer-orientated person. This is the time to build a deep, powerful and stable home base upon which you can build your career later on. The higher your career aspirations, the deeper and more stable must be your family support. This month work at getting that family support. You will be successful.

Your family circle expands greatly this month. This will happen either through births or new relationships. You meet new people who are emotionally supportive and who are like family to you. Your ability to give and receive emotional support is greatly increased. People's moods are optimistic now.

A move to a larger, more opulent home is very likely. A renovation/expansion of your present home is an alternative scenario. Parties and entertaining from home boost your public and professional standing. Always a lover of night-life, Leo, this month you see that you can have as much fun at home as you do hitting the clubs. Major improvements of the home – furniture and items that make living more comfortable – are coming to you this month. Get rid of the old and unnecessary stuff first.

Those of you involved in psychological therapy or counselling, or those who are studying to be therapists will achieve unusual success this month. Major psychological breakthroughs are likely.

Earnings are strong as there is great emotional support for your financial goals. After the 4th, community involvement – and local businesses – bring financial opportunities.

October

Best Days Overall: 1st, 8th, 9th, 17th, 18th, 19th, 27th, 28th

Most Stressful Days Overall: 6th, 7th, 13th, 14th, 20th, 21st

Best Days for Love: 2nd, 3rd, 6th, 7th, 10th, 11th, 13th, 14th, 15th, 16th, 20th, 21st, 25th, 26th, 30th, 31st

LEO

Best Days for Money: 2nd, 3rd, 6th, 7th, 13th, 14th, 15th, 16th, 22nd, 23rd, 24th, 25th, 26th, 30th, 31st

Most of the planetary power this month is concentrated in the western and bottom half of your solar chart, Leo. This means that your life revolves around the quest for emotional harmony and personal happiness. The need to deal with family issues and domestic affairs – issues not of your making – is also paramount. Perhaps what is most uncomfortable for you at this time is the lack of independence that you feel. Your destiny seems wrapped up in your family and their good graces. After the 23rd you try to assert your authority at home, but diplomacy and kindness win more battles. An unusual amount of activity – visitors, house-guests and entertaining – takes place in your home.

The trend towards a move or expansion of your current residence continues this month – perhaps even more strongly than last month. But other people have decided the move for you, others have done the redecorating for you. You must adapt to their tastes.

Until the 23rd, your pursuit of intellectual interests is powerful. Sales, marketing and writing activities are prominent, but with Mercury and Venus going retrograde this month progress is not what it should be. You just need to be more patient and more careful about communicating. Don't take things for granted. For example, don't assume that others understand the intent of your message; make yourself quite clear. It might be a good idea to have your phones, faxes, computers, copiers, modems and the like checked before the 9th – just to be sure that they don't decide to play you up.

Definitely rest and relax more after the 23rd. Physically and psychologically the month is uncomfortable for you. There is so much Water energy in the cosmos now that you feel your fire sputtering out. People around you seem unduly pessimistic, moody and hyper-sensitive. Your normal flamboyant style seems loud and cruel to them. Make sure to engage in adequate – but not too much – physical exercise. This will help detach you from emotional issues and bring you back into your body.

Be patient in finances as Mercury goes retrograde from the 9th to the 30th. Avoid, if possible, any major purchases, investments or financial commitments during this period.

November

Best Days Overall: 5th, 6th, 14th, 15th, 24th, 25th

Most Stressful Days Overall: 3rd, 4th, 9th, 10th, 16th, 17th, 30th

Best Days for Love: 3rd, 4th, 7th, 8th, 9th, 11th, 12th, 16th, 17th, 21st, 22nd, 26th, 27th, 30th

Best Days for Money: 1st, 2nd, 3rd, 4th, 9th, 10th, 11th, 12th, 21st, 22nd, 26th, 27th, 30th

Definitely rest and relax more this month, Leo. The seriousness and intensity of the current atmosphere is stressful and alien to your nature. Your fun, light-hearted attitude to life is not much appreciated now, as people are concerned with more serious subjects. Even the most talented entertainer cannot please an audience that is unwilling to be pleased. People are concerned with death, the after-life, revolution and major changes. Two eclipses this month bring these subjects even more to the fore.

The solar eclipse of the 3rd is a significant one for you, Leo, as the Sun, your ruling planet, is the one that gets eclipsed. Changes in your self-image and personal appearance take place. All Leos will be affected, but those born in July will feel it most. A major change in family relations takes place. Family upheavals clear the decks for future harmony, but in the meantime, duck. Be sure to take an even more relaxed schedule on the day of the eclipse.

The lunar eclipse of the 18th is less serious for you. Only those of you born in mid-August will feel it. It announces long-term career changes and a temporary upheaval with a parent or superior. Your conception of what your life's work is gets tested. If it doesn't survive the test you have some re-evaluating to do.

In general you are overly concerned with family and domestic matters. With most of the planets at the bottom half of your solar chart you are still concerned with building a stable home base and getting emotional support for your goals. You also give more emotional support to others – which can be quite draining.

In spite of any discomfort you feel, your earnings are quite strong. With Mercury moving forward on the 10th, stalled financial projects go forward again. Payments that were due you start to come through. Your family supports you financially, though there is a price to pay for this support.

December

Best Days Overall: 2nd, 3rd, 11th, 12th, 21st, 22nd, 30th

Most Stressful Days Overall: 1st, 6th, 7th, 13th, 14th, 15th, 28th

Best Days for Love: 1st, 4th, 5th, 6th, 7th, 8th, 9th, 10th, 13th, 14th, 15th, 19th, 20th, 23rd, 24th, 28th, 29th

Best Days for Money: 1st, 2nd, 3rd, 11th, 12th, 21st, 22nd, 23rd, 24th, 30th

You're brimming with health and vitality this month, Leo. You exude strength, confidence and power. You can feel conditions changing for the better and a new sense of optimism comes into your life. Whatever needed to be done in the home has been done – aside from a few odds and ends. You are now ready to play.

Jupiter's move into your 5th House of Fun, Entertainment and Creativity this month initiates a cycle of play and enjoyment for you. You are a 5th-House personality to begin with and now that your own 5th House gets activated – the fun never stops.

Your normal gambling instincts are further enhanced this month, and with good reason. You are an unusually lucky speculator now. You will also win a contest of some sort this month. You excel in sports, dancing, exercise and creative pursuits as well.

But all is not fun and games. The demands of the workplace become insistent after the 22nd. Work is hectic, changeable and volatile, yet there is a degree of excitement and challenge there. After the 19th, money is earned through work and practical service to others rather than through luck. A foreign business trip is likely after the 12th.

You are probably unaware of how strong and aggressive you are in financial matters. You win every conflict of wills. You go after the possessions that you want and you get them. You are financially fearless – though perhaps a bit impulsive. Your business sense sharpens after the 19th. Before that you seem too reckless – too optimistic – in business matters. It's perfectly fine to be a risk-taker when there is so much power in your 5th House, but you tend not to hedge your bets. After the 19th you become more cautious.

Your love life too becomes more active, dynamic and volatile after the 22nd. Almost anything can happen in love then. There is very little stability in your love life just now – you can fall in and out of love quickly and suddenly. You break up and make up with equal ease. You have a taste for the unconventional and mysterious in love. The workplace is the scene of romance.

Virgo

♍

THE VIRGIN
Birthdays from
22nd August
to 22nd September

Personality Profile

VIRGO AT A GLANCE

Element – Earth

Ruling planet – Mercury
  Career planet – Mercury
  Health planet – Uranus
  Money planet – Venus
  Planet of family and home life – Jupiter

Colours – earth tones, ochre, orange, yellow

Colour that promotes love, romance and social harmony – aqua blue

Colour that promotes earning power – jade green

Gems – agate, hyacinth

Metal – quicksilver

Scents – lavender, lilac, lily of the valley, storax

Quality – mutable (= flexibility)

Quality most needed for balance – seeing the big picture

Strongest virtues – mental agility, analytical skills, ability to pay attention to detail, healing powers

Deepest needs – to be useful and productive

Characteristic to avoid – destructive criticism

Signs of greatest overall compatibility – Taurus, Capricorn

Signs of greatest overall incompatibility – Gemini, Sagittarius, Pisces

Sign most helpful to career – Gemini

Sign most helpful for emotional support – Sagittarius

Sign most helpful financially – Libra

Sign best for marriage and/or partnerships – Pisces

Sign most helpful for creative projects – Capricorn

Best sign to have fun with – Capricorn

Signs most helpful in spiritual matters – Taurus, Leo

Best day of the week – Wednesday

Understanding the Virgo Personality

The virgin is a particularly fitting symbol for those people born under the sign of Virgo. If you meditate on the image of the virgin you will get a good understanding of the essence of the Virgo type. The virgin, of course, is a symbol of purity and innocence – not naïve, but pure. A virginal object has not been touched. A virgin field is land that is true to itself, the way it has always been. The same is true of virgin forest. Pristine. Unaltered.

Apply the idea of purity to the thought processes, emotional life, physical body and activities and projects of the everyday world, and you can see how Virgos approach life. Virgos desire the pure expression of the ideal in their mind, body and affairs. If they find impurities they will attempt to clear them away.

Impurities are the beginning of disorder, unhappiness and uneasiness. The job of the Virgo is to eject all impurities and keep only that which the body and mind can use and assimilate.

The secrets of good health are here revealed: 90 per cent of the art of staying well is maintaining a pure mind, pure emotions and pure body. When you introduce more impurities than your mind and body can deal with, you will have what is known as dis-ease. It is no wonder that Virgos make great doctors, nurses, healers and dietitians. They have an innate understanding of good health and they realize that good health is more than just physical. In all aspects of life, if you want a project to be successful it must be kept as pure as possible. It must be protected against the adverse elements that will try to undermine it. This is the secret behind Virgo's awesome technical proficiency.

We could talk about Virgo's analytical powers – which are substantial. We could talk about their perfectionism and their almost superhuman attention to detail. But we would be missing the point. All of these virtues are manifestations of a Virgo's desire for purity and perfection – a world without Virgos would have ruined itself long ago.

A vice is nothing more than a virtue turned inside out, a virtue that is misapplied or used in the wrong context. Virgos' apparent vices come from their inherent virtue. Their analytical powers, which should be used for healing, helping or perfecting a project in the world sometimes get misapplied and turned against people. Their critical faculties, which should be used constructively to perfect a project, can sometimes be used destructively to harm or wound. Their urge to perfection can become worry and lack of confidence; their natural humility can become self-denial and self-abasement. When Virgos turn negative they are apt to turn their devastating criticism on themselves, sowing the seeds of self-destruction.

Finance

Virgos have all the attitudes that create wealth. They are hard-working, industrious, efficient, organized, thrifty, productive and eager to serve. A developed Virgo is every employer's dream. But until Virgos master some of the social graces of Libra they won't even come close to their full financial potential. Purity and perfectionism, if not handled correctly or gracefully, can be very trying to others. Friction in human relationships can be devastating not only to your pet projects but – indirectly – to your wallet as well.

Virgos are quite interested in their financial security. Being hard-working, they know the true value of money. They don't like to take risks with their money, preferring to save for their retirement or for a rainy day. Virgos usually make prudent, calculated investments that involve a minimum of risk. These investments and savings usually work out well, helping them achieve the financial security they seek. The rich or even not so rich Virgos also like to help their friends in need.

VIRGO

Career and Public Image

Virgos reach their full potential when they can communicate their knowledge in such a way that others can understand it. In order to get their ideas across better Virgos need to develop greater verbal skills and more non-judgemental ways of expressing themselves. Virgos look up to teachers and communicators; they like their bosses to be good communicators. Virgos will probably not respect a superior who is not their intellectual equal – no matter how much money or power that superior has. Virgos themselves like to be perceived by others as educated and intellectual.

The natural humility of Virgos often inhibits them from great ambitions, from acquiring name and fame. Virgos should indulge in a little more self-promotion if they are going to reach their career ambitions. They need to push themselves with the same ardour that they would use to foster others.

At work Virgos like to stay active. They are willing to learn any type of job as long as it serves their ultimate goal of financial security. Virgos may change several occupations during their professional lives, until they find the one they really enjoy. Virgos work well with other people, are not afraid to work hard and always fulfil their responsibilities.

Love and Relationships

If you are an analyser or a critic you must, out of necessity, narrow your scope. You have to focus on a part and not the whole; this can create a temporary narrow-mindedness. Virgos don't like this kind of person. They like their partners to be broad-minded, with depth and vision. Virgos seek to get this broad-minded quality from their partners since sometimes they lack it themselves.

Virgos are perfectionists in love just as they are in other areas of life. They need partners who are tolerant, open-minded and easy-going. If you are in love with a Virgo don't waste time on impractical romantic gestures. Do practical and useful things for him or her – this is what will be appreciated and what will be done for you.

Virgos express their love through practical and useful gestures, so don't be put off because your Virgo partner doesn't say 'I love you' day-in and day-out. Virgos are not that type. If they love you, they will demonstrate it in practical ways. They will always be there for you; they will show an interest in your health and finances; they will fix your sink or repair your radio. Virgos deem these actions to be superior to sending flowers, chocolates or St Valentine's Day cards.

In love affairs Virgos are not particularly passionate or spontaneous. If you are in love with a Virgo, don't take this personally. It doesn't mean that you are not alluring enough or that your Virgo partner doesn't love or like you. It's just the way Virgos are. What they lack in passion they make up for in dedication and loyalty.

Home and Domestic Life

It goes without saying that the home of a Virgo will be spotless, sanitized and orderly. Everything will be in its right place – and don't you dare move anything around! For Virgos to find domestic bliss, however, they need to ease up a bit in the home, to allow their partner and kids more freedom and be more generous and open-minded. Family members are not to be analysed under a microscope, they are individuals with their own virtues to express.

With these small difficulties resolved, Virgos like to stay in and entertain at home. They make good hosts and they like to keep their friends and families happy and entertained at family gatherings and social affairs. Virgos love children, but they are strict – at times – since they want to make sure their children are brought up with the right sense of family and values.

Horoscope for 1994

Major Trends

1993 was a work and finance year, a serious year. If the truth be told, this is just the way you like it, Virgo. But this year the emphasis is less on money and work goals and more on relationships and communication. Since by nature you are a more work-orientated person, you find this need to involve yourself in relationships and the mysteries of good communication a little uncomfortable. However, these are the skills that your solar horoscope shows need to be developed and refined this year. You might as well get on with it.

Your intellectual and educational interests are very much expanded this year over last year. You seem quite concerned with reaching people in a deep rather than superficial way. Educational opportunities are offering themselves to you: by all means take them.

This is a year of much local, short-distance travel. Travel within your own country is called for and seems pleasurable. You will be running around your neighbourhood more, as well, getting involved with local and community projects.

Health

Your health is always a concern to you, Virgo. Even the healthiest Virgo is always on the alert for the slightest sign of dysfunction. This trait may even compel some people (and some astrologers) to label you a 'hypochondriac'. But this is not strictly true. You are just more attuned to health issues and have greater sensitivity to your health than most. In this regard you are like the mechanic who hears things in a motor that others don't hear. He or she is alerted to problems long before they are actually manifest. What some people label a flaw is really an expression of your particular genius.

Saturn's move into Pisces on 29th January is a stressful one for you. Your vitality is not as strong as you are accustomed to. But this is not an indication of a health problem. All the other major planets are still in harmonious aspect, so the forces arrayed for you are much stronger than those arrayed against you. But chances are you will be attuned to this slight disharmony and run around to every doctor, chiropractor or healer in town.

This syndrome is reinforced by the closeness of Uranus – your health planet – to Neptune. Your perfectionism in health matters is thus increased even more, because you have a vision of what your body could and should be. You feel the need to explore new avenues and techniques of healing. You search continually for the perfect regime, diet and physical fitness programme. In short, you are looking to achieve the perfect body. This body, by the way, *does* exist, on a spiritual level. You can make it manifest by meditating on its perfection. This will lead you to that regime, diet or programme that will suit your needs for a given time. Just be aware that there is no such thing as an absolutely perfect regime. Even the best needs to be modified at different times and for different circumstances. You must be more spiritually attuned.

By all means continue your experimentation – hopefully under qualified supervision – in health matters. You are being led to deeper knowledge.

Uranus and Neptune in Capricorn also represents a specific health message for you, Virgo: take particular care of your spine and feet. Also, develop creative, artistic outlets for the release of your pent-up emotions. The need to express yourself creatively is a long-term trend.

Your best health periods this year will be from 1st to 20th January, 20th April to 20th May, 23rd August to 22nd September and 21st to 31st December.

Your most stressful periods healthwise will tend to be from 18th February to 20th March, 21st May to 21st June and 22nd November to 20th December. Be sure to rest and relax more during these periods.

VIRGO

Home and Domestic Life

Though your 4th House of Home and Domestic Life is not particularly active for most of the year, your domestic planet (Jupiter) *is* quite stimulated. You are going to be unusually involved with the family and with domestic issues in general.

This year you are more concerned with brothers, sisters and in-laws. Dealings with them have been messy of late – the secret 'dirt' in your relationships has been coming out. Long-repressed negative feelings come out for resolution. In the past few years these emerging feelings have got quite vicious. Happily, this year there are opportunities either to repair these relationships or to forge new ones – with those who are not 'brothers and sisters' by birth, but by choice.

You know very well how to communicate on an intellectual level. This year, the challenge is to communicate on an *emotional* level – to get your point across on highly-charged issues with those you are connected to emotionally. Your solar horoscope can offer some important communication tips: first off, say less but make it to the point. Avoid extraneous issues that will confuse the listener or touch sensitive nerves. If you are going to communicate effectively with your family you will – almost inevitably – step on a few toes. The idea is to reduce this. Only discuss emotional matters when absolutely necessary – and do so with a calm state of mind. Being overly diplomatic might not be effective – be blunt and direct, but not hurtful.

Major renovations are going on both in your neighbourhood and in your home. But these are happy events. Streets are being widened; the borders of your community are being pushed back. Your community might absorb or be absorbed by a larger town and be enlarged in this way.

You may inherit a family member's home – not necessarily by his or her death. He or she might move and let you take over. By the end of the year your home is going to be a much happier place.

Love and Social Life

For a few years now you've been highly experimental in your love and social relationships. You've pursued everyone but a traditional kind of partner. The more unconventional your partner and the resulting relationship, the better you liked it. This was because many of the same urges that were at play in your health concerns were at play in your love life. Your solar horoscope shows an intimate connection between these two areas of your life. You want good health and the perfect body in order to attract the perfect love. Conversely, you want the perfect love in order to feel more healthy – more whole as a person.

Yes, you've been partying for a long time. Many of you didn't care whether or not you settled down. The search for love was more fun than actually finding it. But this year your attitude shifts. You seem more serious about love. Short-term love affairs – though they may still be plentiful in your life – no longer satisfy as they once did. A past relationship didn't work out that well and it hurt. You want something more steady, more secure. You still want someone unconventional and original, but not too much so. A little tradition, a little commitment, a little taking of responsibility are what you find endearing right now.

If you are still holding some unrealistic attitudes towards love, they will disappear this year. Your social sphere will contract as you begin to re-order and restructure this area of life. You simply can't meet every social obligation. You are forced to set some voluntary limits. Your ability to forgive will also get tested; it is wise that you learn how to do this.

Usually, Saturn moving through one's 7th House of Love and Relationships is considered a stern, stressful aspect. If you do the re-ordering that Saturn demands of you, however, its presence in this House can *lead* to a relationship or marriage – and a long-lasting one at that.

What does the solar horoscope tell us about your partner? As mentioned, he or she needs to be original and unconventional. But he or she should also be older and more settled than you. You've had enough of freedom and now seem to welcome someone more controlling – someone who takes charge. Issues of emotional security are important this year. A marriage or relationship will certainly narrow your social scope – but in a positive way.

Career and Finance

1993 was a banner financial year. Meeting your financial goals was an important priority and for the most part you succeeded. In 1994 mere money-making takes a back seat to other issues.

It was never ordained by Nature that you spend all of your time and attention on making money. Out of the 12 Houses in a horoscope, only four deal with career, job and financial issues; just one third of the total circle of life. There are times, of course, when we need to focus on these things – just as there are times when we need to strengthen the other parts of our lives.

The work you did in 1993 has given you enough. Of course you still need to work and earn your living, but you can 'coast' now. You are well enough off financially to give this area a minimum of attention.

Mercury is both your personal and career lord. It is quite unusual to have the same planet perform both functions. This shows that your health, self-esteem and self-confidence are vital to your success in attaining career goals. This is true to a certain extent for everyone else, but for you (and Gemini) the connection is more dramatic.

The movements, speed, positions and aspects of Mercury will illuminate the current state of your career matters (and self-esteem). But Mercury is a fleet and often erratic planet. Its velocity fluctuates greatly. Three times a year it actually goes backwards. Mercury also tends to be unduly affected – more so than other planets – by other planetary influences. All this accounts for the varied and fluctuating state of your career and ambitions. When Mercury moves in high gear you achieve career goals easily. You are confident and bold. When Mercury slows down, you become more cautious. When it goes backwards you feel that you've lost rather than gained status. Professional projects are delayed. When it receives good aspects career matters go well. When it receives stressful aspects you need to work that much harder, perhaps having to overcome unusual resistance in order to achieve your goals. Short-term fluctuations are described in the month-by-month forecasts – be sure to read them.

Self-improvement

Three areas of your life are undergoing radical change this year, Virgo: your creative impulse, intellectuality and affections.

Your creativity has been developing and changing for many years now. This will and should continue.

Your intellectual life – your ability to learn, communicate, teach, etc. – is expanding rapidly this year as well. This will happen almost by itself – for this area is a source of great joy to you. Philosophers have long maintained that the pleasures of the mind are stronger and more enduring than the pleasures of the senses. This year you will have ample opportunity to test this. If you co-operate with this trend your progress will be further enhanced. By all means follow up on the educational opportunities that will be coming to you. Get involved in community and civic affairs as well – there are secret rewards to be gained. On a more mundane level, invest in better and more modern communication equipment. This is the year to buy that new phone system, computer or word processor. Good, affordable deals will come up. You might even receive these things as gifts.

The third area of life that will be improved – perhaps uncomfortably at first – is your love and/or social life. Friendships will be tested. Some of your so-called heart friends will fail the test and you will feel disappointed. No human being can love you with the perfect, unconditional love you so ardently desire. People can only love as people, with all their flaws and imperfections. Become more realistic in love. Forgive human frailties and move on to the new and the better.

Month-by-month Forecasts

January

Best Days Overall: 2nd, 3rd, 10th, 11th, 20th, 21st, 29th, 30th

Most Stressful Days Overall: 8th, 9th, 15th, 16th, 22nd, 23rd

Best Days for Love: 2nd, 3rd, 10th, 11th, 15th, 16th, 20th, 21st, 22nd, 23rd, 29th, 30th, 31st

Best Days for Money: 2nd, 3rd, 4th, 5th, 6th, 7th, 10th, 15th, 16th, 22nd, 23rd, 25th, 26th, 31st

Other signs may chafe and feel frustrated under the tremendous Capricorn energy that everyone is feeling this month, but not you, Virgo. It just goes to prove the old axiom that 'One man's meat is another man's poison.' You feel very comfortable. In fact this is one of your happiest months in a happy year. The urge to work, duty and responsibility – the serious, sober side of life – which this Capricorn energy produces is very pleasant for you. Right up your street. Your health and self-esteem are unusually high as others recognize and appreciate your virtues. Practical, productive, detail-orientated people like yourself are in fashion now.

Your earnings are going to improve in various ways. First

off, you have so much extra energy that you can do more, achieve more, work harder and thus earn more. Secondly, with all this power in your 5th House of Creativity and Speculations – between 60 and 70 per cent of the total planetary power this month – you become a very lucky speculator. This speculative acumen need not manifest as mere winnings at the casino or track but as fortuitous investments and windfall earnings from a creative project. Third, as mentioned earlier, because you are perceived as a more valuable person – your skills fit right in with what is needed right now – employers are likely to compete for your services, offering you all kinds of financial inducements and the like. No need to pretend to be what you are not, Virgo, just be yourself and you'll shine.

Your love life is particularly interesting as your 5th House also governs love affairs. The problem is that with so many love affairs open to you now you would be less than human if you were not tempted and a current romance could be jeopardized. Many of you will marry this year, but this month you want fun and games with as little commitment as possible. The lover with whom you can have the most fun is the lover who will conquer you.

You have so much energy this month that you seem well able to work hard and play hard. You don't at all mind burning the candle at both ends. This is OK in the short term, but next month you'll have to slow down.

February

Best Days Overall: 7th, 8th, 16th, 17th, 25th, 26th

Most Stressful Days Overall: 4th, 5th, 11th, 12th, 18th, 19th, 20th

Best Days for Love: 1st, 7th, 8th, 9th, 10th, 11th, 12th, 16th, 17th, 21st, 22nd, 25th, 26th

VIRGO

Best Days for Money: 1st, 2nd, 3rd, 9th,
10th, 11th, 12th, 21st, 22nd, 27th, 28th

Mercury, your ruling planet, goes retrograde on the 11th and stays that way for the rest of the month. You have gone through this sort of thing many times before, Virgo. You know that it causes delays and distortions in communications. You know that it makes you feel that you are going backwards instead of forwards in your life, that you find it more difficult to assert yourself and get your way. This particular retrograde seems even more severe than usual. It affects both your health and your ability to communicate.

Take the time to make sure that others understand what you say. Make sure you understand what is really being said to you as well. Don't be afraid to ask questions and nail down details. Don't take action if there is doubt or uncertainty about a situation. This is especially crucial with regard to co-workers or work assignments. Get the facts. Healthwise, definitely rest and relax more. Enjoy the opportunity to work inwardly and subjectively on your goals. This can be a rewarding and productive period if you take the proper precautions.

Though you like to work, the demands of the workplace seem unusually great, even for you. Moreover, when you get home there is more work to do – repairs, renovations and the like.

By the 18th of the month you are ready for a little fun and the cosmos is going to give it to you. Your social and love life becomes unusually active. Neighbours entertain at home. You are invited to parties and charitable functions.

A truer, more refined kind of love comes into your life. Marrieds will become more altruistic within their relationship. Singles meet that special someone. You seem ready to sacrifice your own personal interests and comfort for the sake of true love. There is no question that this attitude will attract both real love and exploiters into your life. But you – more than almost any other sign – are capable of discernment. And this discernment is your only protection right now.

March

> Best Days Overall: 6th, 7th, 15th, 16th, 17th, 25th, 26th
>
> Most Stressful Days Overall: 4th, 5th, 10th, 11th, 12th, 18th, 19th, 31st
>
> Best Days for Love: 1st, 2nd, 6th, 7th, 10th, 11th, 14th, 15th, 16th, 17th, 23rd, 24th, 25th, 26th, 31st
>
> Best Days for Money: 1st, 2nd, 10th, 11th, 14th, 20th, 21st, 22nd, 23rd, 24th, 27th, 28th, 29th, 30th, 31st

All this Water energy in your sign – between 50 and 60 per cent of the planets – is not your style, Virgo. It seems that no one is interested in thinking clearly, analysing things and just doing what needs to be done. They prefer to emote, to moan and groan about things rather than do something constructive about them. Your usual honest, intellectual appraisal of things is suddenly considered insensitive and cruel. Criticism is dangerous now as it is sure to alienate others. They are much too sensitive.

However, the power in Pisces has got some very good news for you. This kind of energy is perfect for your love life. The climate for romance is wonderful. You can safely lose yourself in good feeling for a while. You and your partner seem ready to sacrifice all for your relationship. Your social charisma is powerful and gets more powerful as the month progresses. This is a month where you are concerned more with the needs of your lover than with your own. Social popularity is important to you and you seem willing to compromise your personal and political positions for the sake of social harmony. Singles are dating a lot of different people – all of whom seem wonderful. Those within a serious relationship are socializing with various types of people. Variety is fun but can be confusing. The new Moon of the 12th is going to clarify your social life and help you choose Mr or Ms Right from all the different prospects.

Your health could be a bit better, but improvement begins on the 5th when Mercury starts to go direct. This strengthens your self-esteem and vitality. By the 20th most of the major planetary stress has been lifted from you.

With Venus, your money planet in Pisces until the 8th your earning power is strong. Venus functions very powerfully in Pisces. It enhances your financial intuition and transforms money-making into something pleasurable. Until the 8th money is earned effortlessly. Your partner and other social connections provide you with golden financial opportunities. When Venus goes into Aries on the 8th you become more aggressive in your pursuit of financial goals – perhaps even a little rash. You have an uncanny knack for making money for others – and partners will be generous with you.

April

Best Days Overall: 2nd, 3rd, 12th, 13th, 21st, 22nd, 30th

Most Stressful Days Overall: 1st, 7th, 8th, 14th, 15th, 27th, 28th

Best Days for Love: 2nd, 3rd, 7th, 8th, 12th, 13th, 21st, 22nd, 30th

Best Days for Money: 2nd, 3rd, 7th, 8th, 12th, 13th, 17th, 18th, 21st, 22nd, 23rd, 24th, 25th, 26th

Hot, fiery, passionate energies of Aries dominate the cosmos right now. Though your health is not affected you are not entirely comfortable with this. People are too action-orientated, too hot-tempered, too apt to fly off the handle for your taste. Your cool, practical, matter-of-fact quality seems out of step with those around you. But this condition is only temporary. By the 20th the planetary power moves into Taurus, a practical Earth sign very harmonious to your nature. In the meantime it won't hurt you to catch a little of the Spring fever that's manifest all around you.

Until the 14th your social life is unusually active. You are not usually this aggressive – even rash – in love. Singles tend to jump into relationships without thinking – and jump out of them just as fast. You show a fickleness in love during this period. You are madly in love one day and out of love the next. If you set your sights on someone you have difficulty taking no for an answer. You sweep the object of your affection off his or her feet.

This is a month for eliminating the unnecessary from your life. The new Moon of the 11th will show you what to eliminate and how.

Finances are good all month. Your personal earnings are greater than usual and money is earned pleasurably and with ease. Financial opportunities come from religious institutions, foreign affairs, book publishing and institutions of higher learning. Speculations are favourable. Your partner's income is greatly enhanced all month – though his or her earnings will fluctuate from very high to average. Your partner is also rashly generous towards you.

Mercury, your ruling planet zips along quite speedily, showing that you achieve goals quickly and confidently. Your self-esteem and self-worth are strong – and get stronger after the 20th.

With most of the planets in the western hemisphere of your chart, you are still adapting to situations rather than creating them. You feel less free than usual but you seem to be adapting quite well and easily. Later on in the year you will start to create your own situations.

May

Best Days Overall: 9th, 10th, 19th, 20th, 27th, 28th

Most Stressful Days Overall: 4th, 5th, 11th, 12th, 13th, 25th, 26th, 31st

Best Days for Love: 1st, 2nd, 3rd, 4th, 5th, 9th, 10th, 11th, 12th, 13th, 19th, 20th, 23rd, 24th, 27th, 28th, 31st

Best Days for Money: 1st, 2nd, 3rd, 4th, 5th, 11th, 12th, 13th, 14th, 15th, 21st, 22nd, 23rd, 24th, 31st

The two eclipses this month signify dramatic changes on a world level and in the people around you. The solar eclipse of the 10th seems kind to you. The upheavals around you create opportunities for you. They produce religious and philosophical changes in you that are pleasant and profitable. Shocking developments in foreign countries benefit you. A religious conversion is happening. All of this will lead to new opportunities for career advancement after the 21st.

The lunar eclipse of the 25th is the more serious one as far as you're concerned. All Virgos will feel it, those with birthdays in August most dramatically. Definitely rest and relax more and take a reduced schedule from the 24th through the 26th. Don't hide out at home, but do avoid activities that are strenuous and taxing. Schedule them for another time.

The eclipse of the 25th occurs in your 4th House of Home and Family. A major upheaval in the home leads to better domestic conditions later on. For many of you this signals a move or major repair job. Unresolved emotional issues – resentments between family members – are likely to come up as well. Emotional support that you thought was there is not, but you discover new support. It is a good idea to get

189

in touch with your parents (or those who are like parents to you) during this eclipse period.

Your health and vitality are wonderful until the 21st. After that rest and relax more. Career ambitions are forcing you to work harder than normal. Pace yourself. You make a lot of progress in your career after the 21st. Your spiritual mission for the year is being revealed to you.

Your social agenda is much quieter now than it's been. Love is pleasant and stable until the 21st. But don't get lulled into a false sense of security with a current love – when you start focusing more on your career after the 21st you'll hear his or her howls of complaint. Don't let your beloved think that your career comes first.

Earnings increase because of a pay rise or the largesse of superiors. They may offer you not only cold cash but perks as well. Your professional standing definitely aids your wallet.

June

Best Days Overall: 5th, 6th, 7th, 15th, 16th, 23rd, 24th

Most Stressful Days Overall: 1st, 8th, 9th, 21st, 22nd, 28th, 29th

Best Days for Love: 1st, 5th, 6th, 7th, 10th, 11th, 15th, 16th, 21st, 22nd, 23rd, 24th, 28th, 29th, 30th

Best Days for Money: 1st, 10th, 11th, 17th, 18th, 19th, 20th, 21st, 22nd, 28th, 29th

In spite of the fact that you feel that you're going backwards instead of forwards this month, career progress is being made behind the scenes, invisibly. You are highly thought of in the right places regardless of what you may think or feel at the moment.

Definitely continue to rest and relax more until the 21st. The stressful aspects to your Natal Sun and the retrograde of your ruling planet tend to lower your vitality. Your energy will start to come back after the 21st. In the meantime handle only priorities and coast along as much as possible.

Lack of confidence and lower self-esteem are hampering your earning efforts until the 15th. Friends are helpful and supportive, however, so things are not as bad as they might be. After the 15th your financial intuition gets stronger. Profitable ideas – practical methods of procedure – are revealed to you in dreams, visions and through psychics and astrologers. You take a more spiritual approach to money and so you are supplied with some almost by supernatural means – in miraculous ways. Your generosity to those in need opens the floodgates of abundance. Intuition – if it is real intuition and not just wish-fulfilment or fantasy – is the short-cut to success.

As for many other signs of the zodiac right now, your love life is on hold, Virgo. Everyone seems confused as to what he or she wants. Everyone is re-thinking and re-evaluating love needs and social goals. Relationship break-ups could happen now through no fault of your own. But don't worry, as over the long term romance is positive.

This is a period when you enjoy being at home with your family and emotional support system. All the power is in Water signs for most of the month, indicating that you would benefit from psychological therapies and from investigating your inner world. People from your early childhood are coming back into your life right now. Unresolved issues will now come up for review.

July

> Best Days Overall: 2nd, 3rd, 4th, 12th, 13th, 21st, 22nd, 30th, 31st
>
> Most Stressful Days Overall: 5th, 6th, 19th, 20th, 25th, 26th

Best Days for Love: 1st, 2nd, 3rd, 4th,
10th, 11th, 12th, 13th, 21st, 22nd, 25th,
26th, 30th, 31st

Best Days for Money: 1st, 7th, 8th, 9th,
10th, 11th, 12th, 14th, 15th, 16th, 17th,
21st, 22nd, 25th, 26th, 30th, 31st

All the power in Water signs this month is going to make you more aware of the feeling side of things, Virgo. Don't believe that understanding emotions will hamper your practicality. On the contrary, this understanding will make you more practical – in the long run – than you already are.

This is a beautiful period in which to explore the power of mood. Observe the difference in your work – in terms of both quantity and quality. Note how well work goes when you are in the right mood – enthusiastic, optimistic and harmonious. Watch what happens to your productivity when you feel depressed. Watch how certain thoughts and images either uplift or dishearten you. You can get a real and powerful grasp on life by appreciating these things.

You must guard against your tendency to criticize and nit-pick. Destructive criticism is always dangerous even when the aspects are good. Now, when the aspects are so emotional, even positive criticism is not taken well – never mind the destructive sort. Be very gentle in the way you talk to others. People around you are hyper-sensitive and easily hurt. Why create problems for yourself?

Your health is very much improved over last month. Mercury's direct motion on the 3rd brings back your confidence and optimism. Relationships with friends – which have been sticky of late – start improving. The need to impress a new love causes you to make drastic changes to your appearance and image. Love, in general, requires a lot of patience now.

Your practical, analytic nature can be a real force for good at this time. You can dispel gloom and doom in those around you by showing them a practical way out. Depression ensues when there seems to be no practical solution to a problem. Come up with a practical solution and depression will disappear.

Your financial intuition – as well as generosity – is very strong all month. Many financial impasses can be overcome by creating new wealth rather than relying on the fixed income you get from your job.

August

Best Days Overall: 8th, 9th, 17th, 18th, 26th, 27th

Most Stressful Days Overall: 1st, 2nd, 3rd, 15th, 16th, 21st, 22nd, 23rd, 29th, 30th

Best Days for Love: 8th, 9th, 11th, 12th, 17th, 18th, 19th, 20th, 21st, 22nd, 23rd, 26th, 27th, 29th, 30th

Best Days for Money: 4th, 5th, 11th, 12th, 13th, 14th, 19th, 20th, 21st, 22nd, 23rd, 29th, 30th, 31st

Though the inner-orientated, subjective energies of the cosmos are still overwhelming you, you now become a bit more extroverted in this period of introversion. Your spiritual life is active, dynamic and creative. You are involved in charitable and philanthropic activities. Your dream life is dynamic and creative ideas percolate constantly from the depths of your unconscious. Prayer groups and healing circles attract you.

With your ruling planet, Mercury, and the Sun both moving through your 12th House of Spiritual Wisdom much illumination is coming to you. It will probably take you some time to digest it all. The new Moon of the 7th also occurs in this House, bringing further clarification as the month progresses. You become aware of secret invisible support.

Your spiritual guides are revealed to you. Though you seem modest and humble on the outside, you know you are 'royalty' on the inside. Your self-esteem and self-worth are strong. This will inevitably translate into higher earnings and greater personal attractiveness.

The fact that your love life seems to go backwards or seems stalled has nothing to do with your personal appeal or attractiveness. Much of it has to do with your partner's inner doubts and fears. Time alone can resolve this. Give your partner all the space he or she needs. Singles are meeting many new romantic prospects this period – especially after the 23rd. But these relationships need time to develop. This is not a time for love at first sight.

Your earnings increase after the 7th as Venus moves into her own sign (Libra) and House and brings order to them. She operates most powerfully, bringing you both money and pleasure. Though generally speculations are favourable this year, right now it is best to avoid them. You have to juggle your personal financial goals with the needs of children and partners. Your focus on money can make them feel neglected or deprived. They expect you to enhance their income as well. Good career progress is made with the help of partners. Jewellery, cosmetics and fashion are profitable industries during this period.

Your health is excellent all month.

September

Best Days Overall: 5th, 6th, 13th, 14th, 22nd, 23rd, 24th

Most Stressful Days Overall: 11th, 12th, 18th, 19th, 25th, 26th

Best Days for Love: 5th, 6th, 8th, 9th, 13th, 14th, 18th, 19th, 22nd, 23rd, 24th, 28th, 29th

VIRGO

Best Days for Money: 1st, 7th, 8th, 9th, 10th, 18th, 19th, 28th, 29th

Planetary power this month is congregated at the bottom half of your solar horoscope chart, Virgo. This trend will continue for the next few months or so. This means that the cosmos impels you to take care of emotional issues before you attempt the career heights.

Personal happiness and harmony take precedence over your need for glory, honour and public recognition. What good is the adulation of thousands when you feel out of sorts with yourself?

Most of the planets are in the eastern segment of your chart as well. Thus you have an unusual ability to create your own conditions and circumstances. You have greater free-will this month. Begin by determining what you need and what makes you happy and build from there.

With the Sun moving through your own sign until the 23rd, your health, self-confidence and self-esteem are vigorous. You assert yourself – and you should assert yourself – with greater force. Make your needs known and they will be fulfilled.

Your earnings are very much increased this month. The time you spend making money, however, can make your friends and your lover feel neglected. Be careful. Try to keep a balance. Try also not to neglect your own creative side or your children in your rush for gold.

Community activities are highlighted this month. You are learning that there is as much fun to be had close to home as there is exploring exotic lands and climes. Community work improves your domestic life, earnings, love life and self-esteem. Local businesses and organizations bring you financial opportunities. Classes you've been attending supply you with important financial contacts. Your intellectual interest blossoms. Local, domestic travel is happy and profitable. High-tech communication equipment – and perhaps a new car – may come to you.

October

Best Days Overall: 2nd, 3rd, 10th, 11th,
20th, 21st, 30th, 31st

Most Stressful Days Overall: 8th, 9th, 15th,
16th, 22nd, 23rd, 24th

Best Days for Love: 2nd, 3rd, 6th, 7th,
10th, 11th, 15th, 16th, 20th, 21st, 25th,
26th, 30th, 31st

Best Days for Money: 4th, 5th, 6th, 7th,
15th, 16th, 25th, 26th

Finances and intellectual interests are the dominant activities this month, Virgo. Earnings are basically strong and you are acquiring new and expensive possessions. You are willing to go to extraordinary lengths in the pursuit of profit – way out of your normal orbit. But your earning power is hampered by the retrograde of Venus, your money planet, from the 13th onwards. Certain deals may have to be redone. Payments due to you could be delayed for a time, although you will receive them eventually. With Mercury going retrograde as well, you need to rethink, review and perhaps revise both financial and career goals. This is especially important now since you are, in effect, creating your own conditions and circumstances – and must bear the responsibility for what you create.

Though Mercury going retrograde makes you less assertive and more introverted, your health is excellent all month.

Your educational and other intellectual interests are also made more complicated by the retrograde of Mercury. Administrative foul-ups – the breakdown of communication equipment and the like – are more likely now than usual. There's not much you can do about administrative foul-ups, but you can have any personal communication equipment checked and serviced now. You can also avoid major mailings and media activities during this Mercury retrograde period.

Happily, your love and social life is starting to pick up. A current relationship is moving forward again. Neighbours and siblings are promoting your love life and introducing you to new people. Singles find love in adult education classes, in their local neighbourhood and with neighbours. But a marriage should not be scheduled now – especially not after the 13th. Wait until Venus starts to move forward.

A move or expansion of your home is likely now and seems very happy. Psychological therapies go especially well; there is the likelihood of a major breakthrough and change of your emotional patterns. Someone from your early childhood has passed on.

November

Best Days Overall: 7th, 8th, 16th, 17th, 26th, 27th

Most Stressful Days Overall: 5th, 6th, 11th, 12th, 19th, 20th

Best Days for Love: 3rd, 4th, 7th, 8th, 11th, 12th, 16th, 17th, 21st, 22nd, 26th, 27th, 30th

Best Days for Money: 1st, 2nd, 3rd, 4th, 11th, 12th, 21st, 22nd, 28th, 29th, 30th

Finances, education and community interests dominate your attention for most of this month. Though this is a tumultuous month for many people and for the world at large, you pass through unscathed and happy.

Your health, self-esteem and self-confidence are strong all month. With Mercury moving speedily forward you know how you want to build and your clearheadedness enables you to make rapid progress.

Money dominates your attention until the 10th, but caution is necessary as Venus is still retrograde. Major financial commitments and purchases should be avoided until the 23rd. In the meantime prepare the way for future earnings and purchases by doing all the preliminary work. Income from interest is very much increased, though you may have to change banks or accounts to get it.

Intellectual and educational interests are moving forward briskly this month. A shake-up benefits you. Blockages to your intellectual progress are being removed – perhaps dramatically. The solar eclipse of the 3rd is causing this. This eclipse will test – once again – the quality of your telephone and communication equipment.

With Mercury, your ruling planet joining the major line-up of planets in the sign of Scorpio you will be concerned with personal pleasure and eliminating impurities from your body and negative character traits from your mind. You are in a period of self-reformation. You have unique opportunities to re-invent yourself – for the better – at this time.

Your love life is very much improved this month. Delays and blockages affecting a current relationship or your social progress are being removed. You make new contacts. Love is happy and optimistic. A current lover, older than you, gives in to your need for good times. Your partner's self-esteem is increased, and when he or she feels good, you are treated better. Your partner needs to be concerned with the financial tricks of his or her siblings. He or she also needs to take a reduced schedule during the solar eclipse of the 3rd.

December

> Best Days Overall: 4th, 5th, 13th, 14th, 15th, 23rd, 24th
>
> Most Stressful Days Overall: 2nd, 3rd, 8th, 9th, 10th, 16th, 17th, 30th

VIRGO

Best Days for Love: 1st, 4th, 5th, 8th, 9th, 10th, 13th, 14th, 15th, 19th, 20th, 23rd, 24th, 28th, 29th

Best Days for Money: 1st, 8th, 9th, 10th, 11th, 12th, 19th, 20th, 21st, 22nd, 25th, 26th, 28th, 29th, 30th

Though your health is basically excellent you should rest and relax more until the 22nd. Domestic responsibilities and overblown emotional reactions can tax your physical strength. Many of you are thinking of moving to a bigger home because of new additions to the family – either through births or new relationships. Your household has grown or is about to grow and you need more space. The new Moon of the 2nd – a 'Super Moon' occurring at the Moon's closest distance to the Earth – is going to clarify all emotional and domestic issues.

Everything you need to know about taking the next step is being shown to you – in dreams, visions and through psychics. This is the month – and the trend continues next year – for stabilizing your home base and attaining personal and emotional harmony. Career issues can safely be put on hold for a while.

This is the season for parties and entertainment, for you even more so than usual. Your social agenda, love life and outings (concert- and theatre-going, etc.) are more glamorous than even you are used to. Enjoy – there is much in your life to celebrate.

Your health is excellent, especially after the 22nd. You have so much energy that you don't know what to do with it all. You might try putting some of it into sports and exercise. Your capacity for both work and play – burning the candle at both ends – is greatly enhanced after the 22nd. It won't be this way forever, but for now make the most of it.

A current serious relationship becomes less gloomy and more fun-filled as your lover catches the spirit of the season.

By now you have learned that in love, as in anything else, it's quality and not quantity that counts. You're definitely finding older, more established people attractive. You admire their experience and the obstacles they've overcome, their stability and depth. And – though you probably don't like to admit this – you like the guidance and control they offer you.

Finances are excellent. You are probably too generous in your gift-giving but you receive large and generous gifts in return. As you give so do you get. Sales and marketing activities bring profits. When you sell, speak to the deepest emotions of the customer and not so much to the intellect.

Libra

♎

THE SCALES
*Birthdays from
23rd September
to 22nd October*

Personality Profile

LIBRA AT A GLANCE

Element – Air

Ruling planet – Venus
  Career planet – Moon
  Health planet – Neptune
  Love planet – Mars
  Planet of home and family life – Saturn

Colours – blue, jade green

*Colours that promote love, romance and social
harmony* – carmine, red, scarlet

Colours that promote earning power –
burgundy, red-violet, violet

201

Gems – carnelian, chrysolite, coral, emerald, jade, opal, quartz, white marble

Metal – copper

Scents – almond, rose, vanilla, violet

Quality – cardinal (= activity)

Qualities most needed for balance – a sense of self, self-reliance, independence

Strongest virtues – social grace, charm, tact, diplomacy

Deepest needs – love, romance, social harmony

Characteristic to avoid – violating what is right in order to be socially accepted

Signs of greatest overall compatibility – Gemini, Aquarius

Signs of greatest overall incompatibility – Aries, Cancer, Capricorn

Sign most helpful to career – Cancer

Sign most helpful for emotional support – Capricorn

Sign most helpful financially – Scorpio

Sign best for marriage and/or partnerships – Aries

Sign most helpful for creative projects – Aquarius

Best sign to have fun with – Aquarius

Signs most helpful in spiritual matters – Gemini, Virgo

Best day of the week – Friday

LIBRA

Understanding the Libra Personality

In the sign of Libra the universal mind – the soul – expresses its genius of relationship, that is, its power to harmonize diverse elements in a unified, organic way. Libra is the soul's power to express beauty in all of its forms. And where is beauty if not within relationships? Beauty doesn't exist in isolation. Beauty arises out of comparison – out of the just relationship of different parts. Without a fair and harmonious relationship there is no beauty, whether it be in art, manners, ideas or the social or political forum.

There are two faculties humans have that exalt them above the animal kingdom. The first is their rational faculty, as expressed in the signs of Gemini and Aquarius. The second is their aesthetic faculty, exemplified by Libra. Without an aesthetic sense we would be little more than intelligent barbarians. Libra is the civilizing instinct or urge of the soul.

Beauty is the essence of what Librans are all about. They are here to beautify the world. We could discuss Librans' social grace, their sense of balance and fair play, their ability to see and love another person's point of view – but we would be missing their central asset: their desire for beauty.

No one – no matter how alone he or she seems to be – exists in isolation. The universe is one vast collaboration of beings. Librans, more than most, understand this and understand the spiritual laws that make relationships bearable and enjoyable.

So, a Libra is always the unconscious (and in some cases conscious) civilizer, harmonizer and artist. This is a Libra's deepest urge and greatest genius. Librans love instinctively to bring people together and they are uniquely qualified to do so. They have a knack for seeing what unites people – the things that attract and bind rather than separate individuals.

Finance

In financial matters Librans can seem frivolous and illogical to others. This is because Librans appear to be more concerned with earning money for others than for themselves. But there is a logic to this financial attitude. Librans know that everything and everyone is connected and that it is impossible to help another prosper without also prospering yourself. Since enhancing their partner's income and position tends to strengthen their relationship, Librans choose to do so. What could be more fun than building a relationship? You will rarely find a Libra enriching him- or herself at someone else's expense.

Scorpio is the ruler of Libra's solar 2nd House of Money, giving Libra unusual insight into financial matters and the power to focus on these matters in a way that disguises a seeming indifference. In fact, many other signs come to Librans for financial advice and guidance.

Given their social graces, Librans often spend great sums of money on entertaining and organizing social events. They also like to help others when they are in need. Librans would go out of their way to help a friend in dire straits, even if they have to borrow from others to do so. However, Librans are also very careful to pay back any debts they owe and like to make sure they never have to be reminded to do so.

Career and Public Image

Publicly, Librans like to appear as nurturers. Their friends and acquaintances are their family and they wield political power in parental ways. They also like bosses who are paternal or maternal.

The Sign of Cancer is on Libra's 10th House (of Career) cusp; the Moon is Libra's career planet. The Moon is by far the speediest, most changeable planet in the horoscope. It alone among all the planets travels through the entire zodiac – all twelve signs and houses – every month. This is an important key to the way in which Librans approach their careers and also to some of the things they need to do to maximize their career potential. The Moon is the planet of moods and feelings – and Librans need a career where they have free expression for their emotions. This is why so many Librans are involved in the creative arts. Libra's ambitions wax and wane like the Moon. They tend to wield power according to their mood.

The Moon 'rules' the masses – and that is why Libra's highest goal is to achieve a mass kind of acclaim and popularity. Famous Librans cultivate the public as other people cultivate a lover or friend. Librans can be very flexible – and often fickle – in their career and ambitions. On the other hand, they can achieve their ends in a great variety of ways. They are not stuck in one attitude or one way of doing things.

Love and Relationships

Librans express their true genius in love. In love you could not find a partner more romantic, more seductive and more fair. If there is one thing that is sure to destroy a relationship – sure to block the love force from flowing – it is injustice or imbalance between the lover and the beloved. If one party is giving too much or taking too much, resentment is sure to surface at some time or other. Librans are careful about this. If anything, Librans might err on the side of giving more, but never of giving less.

If you are in love with a Libra make sure you keep the aura of romance alive. Do all the little things. Have candlelit dinners, travel to exotic places. Bring flowers and little gifts. Give things that are beautiful although not necessarily expensive. Send cards. Ring regularly even if you have nothing particular to say. The niceties are very important. Your relationship is a work of art: make it beautiful and your Libra lover will appreciate it. If you are creative about it, he or she will appreciate it even more; for this is how the Libra will behave towards you.

Librans like their partners to be aggressive and even a bit self-willed. They know that this is a quality that they sometimes lack and so they like to get it from their partners.

In relationships, however, Librans can be very aggressive – but always in a subtle and charming way! Gorbachev's 'charm offensive' and openness of the late 1980s (that revolutionized the then-Soviet Union) is typical of a Libra.

Librans are determined in their efforts to charm the object of their desire – and this determination can be very pleasant if you're on the receiving end.

Home and Domestic Life

Since Librans are such social creatures, they don't particularly like mundane domestic duties. They like a well-organized home, clean and neat with everything needful present, but housework is a chore and a burden. To them it is one of the unpleasant tasks in life that one must do in order to survive. The quicker one gets it over with, the better. If a Libra has enough money – and sometimes even if not – he or she will prefer to pay someone else to take care of the daily household chores. However, Librans like to do some gardening and they love flowers and plants in their home.

A Libra's home is modern and furnished in excellent taste. You will find many paintings and sculptures there. Since Librans like to be with friends and family, they like to entertain at home and they make great hosts.

Capricorn is on the cusp of Libra's 4th solar House of Home and Family. Saturn, the planet of law, order, limits and discipline, rules Libra's domestic affairs. If Librans want their home life to be supportive and happy, they need to develop some of the virtues of Saturn – order, organization and discipline. Librans, being so creative and so intensely in need of harmony, can tend to be too lax in the home and too permissive with their children. Too much of this is not always good; children need some freedom but also limits.

Horoscope for 1994

Major Trends

1993 was a year of great personal expansion. True, the expansion could have been easier and less turbulent, but it happened nevertheless. It was a year of personal pleasure and sensual indulgence. Because you *were* more, you earned more. Your horizons widened financially and personally. But 1993 was only the beginning. This trend will continue – and perhaps grow even stronger – in 1994.

1994 is basically a career and finance year, Libra – and a good one at that. Even this serious side of life can be fun if it is driven by your true will and is aligned with Nature's forces. Libra natives are not especially noted for working hard. On the contrary, they love beauty, ease and pleasure – which often prompts others to label them 'lazy'. Yet this year no one can accuse you of this. Your nose is to the grindstone and your eye is on your growing bank account.

You feel a little uncomfortable with all this work and all this money-making – it is not really your nature – yet this year you are impelled to these things. It's all part of the celestial plan. Your greatest happiness and fulfilment this year lie in increasing your earning power and acquiring those possessions that make life more enjoyable and worth living.

In 1993 you travelled; this year you stick closer to home. 1993 was a year of glory, honour and recognition – this year you are sated with these and have no special need for them.

Health

1993 – especially the first four months – was unusually stressful healthwise. As the year unfolded, your normal vitality began coming back. This positive trend will continue in 1994. Overall, there are no major health concerns this year.

However, your 1994 solar horoscope has a special health message for you, Libra: harmony at home and in the family and emotional well-being are particularly vital factors in maintaining your good health this year. This is, of course, true for most people, but it is more dramatically true for you in 1994. The reasons why are somewhat intricate, but it is worth looking into them.

Neptune, your health planet, governs your health from the 4th House of Family and Emotions. Saturn, the lord of your emotional and domestic life, moves into your 6th House of Health on 29th January and stays there for the next two to three years. Any way you look at your horoscope you get the same message: keep your mood positive. Avoid negative emotional states. If you are caught in a negative state express it – either with a therapist or friend – and get into the positive as quickly as possible. If you don't feel up to par physically, first check to see if there is some problem you have not noticed before with a family member. Correct that before you run to your doctor. Chances are that harmonizing your emotional sphere will clear up any physical problems very quickly. Even if you must see a health professional, this precaution will make his or her job much easier.

With both Saturn and Neptune so prominent in your health chart take special care of your feet, ankles and spine. Foot reflexology is an excellent way to keep your feet – as well as the rest of you – healthy. Take special care with the kind of shoes you wear – make sure they fit properly and are comfortable. Avoid shoes that throw you off balance or squeeze your feet – no matter how sexy they make you look.

Chiropractors specialize in keeping the spine fit – a healthy spine makes for a healthy body. Make sure that when you sit (at home or at work) your chair doesn't force you into slumping or an unnatural position. Choose a chair that supports your spine and keeps it erect. This is especially important for those of you who sit for prolonged periods. Increasing your intake of bitter herbs is called for as well. This will help you lose some of the weight you gained in 1993 and add something essential to your diet.

There is a wonderful sense of co-operation between your family and your health interests this year. Your family co-operates in your health regimes, and health regimes foster family unity and harmony. This is another sign of a good health year.

Your best overall health periods this year are from 20th January to 18th February, 20th May to 21st June and 22nd September to 23rd October.

Your most stressful overall health periods this year are from 1st to 19th January, 20th March to 20th April, 22nd June to 22nd July and 21st to 31st December.

Home and Domestic Life

Family and domestic issues have been important – emphasized in your chart – for some years now, Libra. This trend continues in 1994 and though it is still experimental, changeable and unstable, it is much happier overall than it was in 1993.

Basically you are being led – through trial and error, successful and unsuccessful experiments, bizarre and erratic happenings – to a realization of your vision of the perfect home, family and emotional support system. Many of you – after all these years – have already found this and are now enjoying them. The changes that are happening are pleasant to you and are making things even more perfect. Other Librans, probably the majority, are still seeking this perfection, still trying to work it all out.

You can see clearly that it is very difficult to build a successful career without a stable home base. The home is both the womb from which our public aspirations emanate and the foundation on which they rest. The home is the secret place – far from the glare of the public eye – where we can recharge and regenerate. Just as night precedes day, so does a stable home life precede career success.

Saturn will govern your domestic situation from your 6th

House of Health and Work this year – a major shift from 1993. Thus, for many of you home will serve as the place of work as well. In other words, many of you will be working from home.

The trend to move house a lot continues. Sudden opportunities to move will come up and you take them. It's as if you're trying out home after home (the way some people try out clothing) until you find the one that really works for you. Of late, every time you've thought you've found your dream house another and better one comes into view. The message of the stars is that settling in your dream house is a gradual process – often of trial and error.

What does your 1994 solar horoscope reveal about the kind of house you should have? Saturn, the lord of your home life, rules mountains and high places. It governs your home from the sign of Pisces, a Water sign. So the first indication is of a house in the mountains, or the countryside, that is near water – a lake or a stream. The planet Neptune has been a power in your 4th House of Home and Family for many years now. This further emphasizes the need to be near water.

The influences of mystical Neptune and Pisces on your domestic affairs show that you treat (or should treat) your home as a kind of a shrinem, a personal holy place, a power centre from which you can connect to higher, more refined energies. Uranus' influence on your home life (also for many years now) makes you want to combine this holiness with ultra-modern technology. You crave – and will get – every conceivable gadget to make life less of a chore. There is really no conflict between mystical attitudes and high tech – so long as you keep things in perspective. Technology is only meant to be humanity's servant, to liberate people from the mundane tasks so that they can focus on the essentials.

Uranus is also the ruler of the very ancient, so we can envision a home that has a beautiful blend of the antique and the modern. Your blending of all these elements is your personal work of art.

Love and Social Life

Your love and social life will always be important to you, Libra for this is what you are all about. This is your nature and the special gift that you bring to the world. But this year your social life seems less important than usual. It takes a back seat to your domestic, health and financial interests. Basically, the cosmos is neither helping you socially nor hindering you – you have a free hand this year.

It can be considered fortunate that you don't need to pay undue attention to your love life this year. It means that everything is stable and under control. Nothing is amiss so there is no need to over-emphasize social issues.

However, your 1994 solar horoscope does indicate certain trends. Mars is the planet that governs your love and social life. The movements and positions of Mars and aspects to it will demonstrate how you are experiencing these areas of life. Until 24th May, Mars moves along at high velocity – faster than usual. Thus your social life will be more active – faster-paced – than usual. Your social confidence, in general, is strong and social goals are achieved quickly. From 4th July to 4th October, Mars starts to slow down. Your social needs and agenda also slow down. You are more tentative, prudent and cautious in your love life. Your normal social aggressiveness is moderated.

In addition to Mars' velocity through the zodiac it must be mentioned that your 7th House of Love and Romance will be activated – over the short term – by various planets at different times of the year. These activations will also have the effect of intensifying your love life and giving it more prominence. Be sure to read your month-by-month forecasts, where these happenings are covered in more depth.

Your happiest and most active romantic period this year will be from 8th March to 24th May. Singles are most likely to find that special someone during this time. Those already in a steady relationship will be more romantic within it.

Career and Finance

Your financial life is perhaps the major highlight of your 1994 solar horoscope. It shows a banner financial and career year, Libra. Enjoy.

Though you will continue to relish high professional esteem, your main thrust is in personal earnings. You go for the gold rather than the glory.

The financial ordeals of the past are swallowed up in victory this year. Big money and great success are offered you. Many of you will receive large lump sums through inheritances. Many will find substantial financial opportunities in such fields as insurance, sales, marketing, advertising, travel, book publishing or the stock-and-bond markets. Many of you are going to earn a lot of cash by teaching companies – and/or individuals – to eliminate waste and otherwise cut costs and expenses. Aside from this you have a special knack for taking dead or dying companies – hopeless situations – and turning them round into something profitable. These are only some of the scenarios by which gold comes to you this year.

Before 1993, some of you felt as if you were dying as earners. Your normal way of earning your living – the way that made you feel financially secure – was taken from you. Your sense of financial security was under siege. In 1993 you felt the stirring of a new birth. This year you are truly reborn as an earner. From your new vantage point of success you can see clearly the loving, compassionate workings of the celestial powers. If your former ways of earning were not taken from you, you could not have received this new – and infinitely better – good. You have been well prepared to handle the demands of your present career.

Self-improvement

For those of you who didn't change careers or jobs during 1993, the workplace looks drab, dreary and depressing this year. It's all work, work, work. The staff at your company has been trimmed and the existing workload must be handled by fewer people. Perhaps you have moved into smaller working quarters as well, for your chart shows you feel cramped there. There is less freedom and greater regimentation at work. Yet you have something special and precious to contribute.

Rather than succumbing to the drabness of the work environment, exercise your special genius for making it more beautiful, more pleasurable, more harmonious – without sacrificing the quality or quantity of work. You Librans don't need anybody to tell you how to do this: you know all about it already. Nevertheless, here are just some suggestions: bring flowers to work; wear pleasing scents; socialize more with your fellow-workers; smooth over disputes; don't let the environment bring you down; put some sugar into what seems a basically bitter brew. You will, over time, create subtle but very real changes in the energy of your work environment. Further, you will see that, though people are only a part of this environment, they ultimately have dominion over it and can rise above any and every external factor.

Month-by-month Forecasts

January

Best Days Overall: 4th, 5th, 12th, 13th, 14th, 22nd, 23rd, 31st

Most Stressful Days Overall: 10th, 11th, 17th, 18th, 19th, 25th, 26th

Best Days for Love: 2nd, 3rd, 10th, 11th, 17th, 18th, 19th, 20th, 21st, 22nd, 23rd, 31st

Best Days for Money: 6th, 7th, 15th, 16th,
25th, 26th

Don't be overly concerned with a short-term drop in your
feelings of self-esteem and self-worth this month, Libra. You
are living in an unusual time. Many of the other signs of the
zodiac also feel uncomfortable beneath the tremendous
weight and burden of 60 to 70 per cent of the planets in the
sign of Capricorn. Refinement, pleasure and social niceties
are looked upon as mere frills for most of the month. People
value the qualities of duty, responsibility, managerial ability
and stoicism more. This kind of energy doesn't sit too well
with you psychologically or physically. You will get through
this brief 20-day span with flying colours, but be sure to rest
and relax more and deal only with real priorities.

You won't be able to avoid emotional outbursts or wild
mood swings – dealings with your family will probably
trigger these – but you can minimize their negative impact.
Rather than unload on unwilling family members, talk out
your feelings with a friend or counsellor. If there's no one to
talk to, write your feelings out on a piece of paper and then
throw the paper away. The important thing is to express your
inner turmoil in a way that harms no one. Avoid repressing
it.

This is a month where you can make great psychological
progress. You can come to grips with your moods and persis-
tent emotional habits. There are always secret benefits even
in the most trying times. The new Moon of the 11th will
show you why you feel as you do and what you can do about
it.

Your home and family are your major interest for most of
the month. A move, a major renovation and/or shift in your
domestic arrangements is going on. Someone is moving in
and someone is moving out. You are called on to sacrifice
your personal interests in favour of your family responsibilities. Even your partner or current love seems to support
the family rather than you. As trying as all this is

emotionally, it leads to considerable financial benefits. Your family compensates with financial support and earning opportunities. Expect your net worth to have increased by the time the month is over.

By the 20th your health, vitality and self-esteem are restored. This will happen gradually; every day you will feel more energetic and optimistic. By the end of the month you will be having fun again.

February

Best Days Overall: 1st, 9th, 10th, 18th, 19th, 20th, 27th, 28th

Most Stressful Days Overall: 7th, 8th, 14th, 15th, 21st, 22nd

Best Days for Love: 1st, 9th, 10th, 11th, 12th, 14th, 15th, 18th, 19th, 20th, 21st, 22nd, 27th, 28th

Best Days for Money: 2nd, 3rd, 11th, 12th, 21st, 22nd

The strong Aquarian energies coming through from the cosmos are very comfortable and harmonious for you, Libra. You like the cool, sociable, mental mood that people are projecting. The social graces – your true genius – are very much appreciated this month. Your feelings of self-esteem and self-worth are strong. Your health and vitality are excellent.

After the emotional turmoil of January this is a period for some fun. By all means go to parties, the theatre, sporting events and concerts. Enjoy yourself – only do be careful not to overspend on these things – something very easy for you to do. Though your urge to speculate – to go to casinos and racetracks – is strong, it would be better to delay these things until after the 18th. Speculations and earnings in general are more favourable then.

After the deep, serious emotions of January you are sated with emotional intensity – in love and in general. You long for the light touch. Light-heartedness turns you on. Singles don't seem too interested in commitment right now, preferring fun and games with their beloved. Long-term commitments can certainly develop from the relationships you are currently involved in, but you are content to wait and just enjoy. Those of you involved with a Libra can win his or her heart by showing him or her a good time – at least for now.

Although this is a great financial year, you tend to overspend in the short term. But by the 18th your financial worries and fears dissipate. So much of these things are psychological and not fundamental.

By the 18th you've had enough of fun and games and are ready to get back to serious work. The demands of the workplace become important and stimulate your urge to serve.

March

> Best Days Overall: 8th, 9th, 18th, 19th, 27th, 28th
>
> Most Stressful Days Overall: 6th, 7th, 13th, 14th, 20th, 21st, 22nd
>
> Best Days for Love: 1st, 2nd, 10th, 11th, 12th, 13th, 14th, 20th, 21st, 22nd, 23rd, 24th, 29th, 30th, 31st
>
> Best Days for Money: 1st, 2nd, 10th, 11th, 12th, 20th, 21st, 22nd, 29th, 30th

The power in Pisces for most of the month creates a romantic energy that you enjoy, Libra. It's not what you are used to, but you're quite willing to adapt. In romance you tend to be fair and just. You are generally sensitive to the fact that your relationship must be equal, that you and your lover should get what you give to it. But this month neither you nor your beloved is keeping accounts. Each seems willing to give all.

Romance is prominent in your chart all month, Libra, for when the Sun leaves romantic Pisces it moves into Aries – your 7th House of Love and Marriage. Venus, your ruling planet, is also moving through these two signs. Until the 8th you love selflessly. After that you become more assertive and want your own way. Still, your partner knows that you are basically thinking of his or her happiness. Until the 8th you want to serve your partner and he or she wants to serve you. After the 8th, you fancy a more equal partnership.

Romance will also be more stable before the 20th than afterwards. On the other hand, instability – and a little insecurity – tend to make things more exciting. It's hard to say which period you will like better.

Your health and vitality are wonderful until the 20th, but after this rest and relax more. You need to balance your social life with your domestic and family responsibilities. Don't let either your family or your current love feel neglected. This balancing act is tricky but you can manage it.

Though you are experiencing some delays in your financial projects, your financial life is nevertheless good. Delays are normal when you deal with big projects that involve many other people. Your solar horoscope indicates that you are involved in something big. A lot of progress is being made behind the scenes, progress you are not aware of. The aspects are so good that even delays work in your favour.

April

Best Days Overall: 4th, 5th, 14th, 15th, 23rd, 24th

Most Stressful Days Overall: 2nd, 3rd, 9th, 10th, 17th, 18th, 30th

Best Days for Love: 2nd, 3rd, 7th, 8th,

9th, 10th, 12th, 13th, 19th, 20th, 21st, 22nd, 27th, 28th

Best Days for Money: 7th, 8th, 17th, 18th, 25th, 26th

Aside from the power in Aries this month, between 70 and 80 per cent of the planets are concentrated in the western hemisphere of your solar horoscope, Libra. Many zodiac signs would feel very uncomfortable with this arrangement, but you handle it well. This concentration in one hemisphere shows that you are more concerned with others than with yourself and that you are forced to respond to situations that were created by others. You seem to have less freedom to create your own setting right now – you must deal with circumstances that are beyond your control. This state of play will change as the year progresses, but for right now your skill in handling these situations will make you grow as a person and help you to create better personal circumstances when your turn comes.

Handling the needs of others is your forte, Libra so this is a good month to exercise your genius. However, your health is not 100 per cent – especially until the 20th. Try to rest and relax more. Temper your generosity and concern for others with a respect for your physical limits and you'll get through this part of the month beautifully.

Your social life is the major highlight this period. Mars, your love planet joins the Sun in your 7th House of Love on the 14th. Mars is particularly powerful in Aries – so your love life is exciting and happy. Your normal social aggressiveness is very much enhanced. You know what you want in a lover and you go after it with courage. You sweep others off their feet. Male or female, you are the social initiator. Few people can resist your charm this month. The main challenge in love is not whether or not you attract others – this is a given – but the reaction of your family to your social flitting about. They are likely to resent your neglect of them (as they see it); perhaps they don't like the person you have chosen. It's up to you to keep a balance. You can't please everybody, but you can reduce the amount of resentment. These conflicts get easier after the 20th – though they don't go away completely.

Your personal earnings are a bit slower in coming this month as investments or financial deals are being re-evaluated and reviewed. But a partner's income is enhanced, as is his or her generosity towards you. Your ability to make money for others is strong and you benefit financially in an indirect way.

May

> Best Days Overall: 1st, 2nd, 3rd, 11th, 12th, 13th, 21st, 22nd, 29th, 30th
>
> Most Stressful Days Overall: 6th, 7th, 8th, 14th, 15th, 27th, 28th
>
> Best Days for Love: 1st, 2nd, 3rd, 6th, 7th, 8th, 11th, 12th, 13th, 16th, 17th, 23rd, 24th, 27th, 28th, 31st
>
> Best Days for Money: 4th, 5th, 14th, 15th, 23rd, 24th, 31st

Most of the planets are still concentrated in the western hemisphere of your solar horoscope, so you still need to deal with situations as they arise and not try to create new ones. You must also continue to put other people's needs before your own. This situation will begin to change by the end of the month, but for the better part of May it is the status quo.

Your health is very good all month and gets even better after the 21st. The two eclipses this month don't seem to affect you too severely. Unless you are someone with important Natal planets (particular to the exact date and time of your birth) in Taurus or Sagittarius, you should coast through them.

The solar eclipse of the 10th produces a short-term upheaval with a friend – he or she resents your career ambitions and feels that you put these ambitions before his or her interests. Your partner's goes through a minor crisis around the 10th, possibly affecting your own sense of wealth. But all this is short term and is totally over-shadowed by the major world events taking place.

The lunar eclipse of the 25th produces some long-term career changes for you. It forces you to make new and better plans by revealing some of the follies and false expectations of your present plans.

On the day of the lunar eclipse you should also get in touch with your mum, just to see how she is getting on.

Though the eclipses don't seem to affect you personally too much, they *do* affect the world and people around you. Thus, even though you are up to par, others might not be. It is best to avoid strenuous, taxing activities – especially if others are involved – around the days of these eclipses.

The short-term financial blow around the 10th – a sudden expense comes up – is not devastating and in fact spurs you on to greater and more powerful financial action. Use this month to prepare the way for the avalanche of earnings to come next month. If you have enough cash to handle this month's expenses don't worry about the future. Next month will take care of itself.

Your love life is active and happy all month. Don't let superficial financial concerns come between you and your beloved.

June

Best Days Overall: 8th, 9th, 17th, 18th, 25th, 26th

Most Stressful Days Overall: 3rd, 4th, 10th, 11th, 23rd, 24th, 30th

Best Days for Love: 1st, 3rd, 4th, 5th, 6th,

7th, 10th, 11th, 15th, 16th, 21st, 22nd,
23rd, 24th, 30th

Best Days for Money: 1st, 10th, 11th, 19th,
20th, 28th, 29th

With 60 per cent of the planets in retrograde (backward) motion this month, the pace of your life is considerably slower. Perhaps this is good. Life is more leisurely, more harmonious. Much of what happens this month depends on other people – it's out of your hands. These other people are re-assessing and reviewing things. The activity that goes on in your life is hidden, invisible and behind the scenes. But this makes it no less potent. At the right time, when the astrological aspects are right, these hidden processes will come to light – and you will 'suddenly' discover what has always been.

The planets are quite evenly dispersed in the different sectors of your solar horoscope so that your normal highly developed sense of balance is sharpened. You see things in clear perspective. The correct ratios and proportions of life are revealed – and you give to each area of life its due measure.

Even in love matters the pace has slowed. Mars, your love planet is one of the few planets that is still moving forward all month. But its velocity is slower and it is in the sign of Taurus, where its action becomes cautious. You seem content with the status quo in romance. You feel more possessive with your beloved. Finances are a temporary source of conflict, but this is short term. Your partner makes demands on your wallet that you find difficult to fulfil. Perhaps these demands induce financial fear and insecurity in you. No need to fear, great wealth is manifesting in your life. After the 21st your earnings soar – though you might experience a delayed reaction. The financial trend is definitely on the up.

Your health and self-esteem are strong until the 21st. After that rest and relax more. Domestic issues are in a state of limbo right now, so don't waste time trying to hasten things. Use your energy to promote your career which, as mentioned, takes an upturn after the 21st.

July

Best Days Overall: 5th, 6th, 14th, 15th, 23rd, 24th

Most Stressful Days Overall: 1st, 7th, 8th, 9th, 21st, 22nd, 27th, 28th, 29th

Best Days for Love: 1st, 4th, 5th, 10th, 11th, 12th, 14th, 15th, 21st, 22nd, 23rd, 24th, 27th, 28th, 29th, 30th, 31st

Best Days for Money: 7th, 8th, 9th, 16th, 17th, 25th, 26th

Dealings with your family and important domestic projects seem bogged down. The conflict between your domestic duties and career is also very dramatic most of this month. Keep the balance as best as you can: the conflict is short-lived and passes by the 23rd.

Happily, your career is moving forward this month. Career issues get progressively clearer after the new Moon of the 8th. Friends of the family and spiritual guides are helping things along.

The power in Water signs and the general atmosphere of subjectivity don't sit too well with you, Libra, neither physically nor psychologically. Be sure to rest and relax more. Don't allow yourself to feel frustrated at the general inactivity around you. People are lethargic and cautious, prudent and sensitive. Lovers want security and nurturing rather than passion or romance right now. Your partner feels some frustration. He or she wants to talk and communicate rationally, but the general mood favours emotion.

Finances are being boosted this month in a substantial way. Stalled projects are going forward – and there is a general air of wealth around you. The same people supporting your career are creating financial opportunities for you as well.

Your health improves after the 23rd, but the psychological malaise of the general populace lifts only slightly. It is best to use this month to understand moods and feelings – to help yourself grow psychologically. A deeper understanding of your own emotional and spiritual needs will help you cope with the emotions around you. Some spiritual self-analysis – but not self-criticism – is called for.

Opportunities for foreign travel start coming up this month. Your partner seems quite keen about them. Singles are attracted to highly educated, talkative, refined types. A love affair with a teacher or professor is likely – but this could be quite stormy. Avoid confrontations with your partner's family right now. They are too emotional to be reasoned with.

August

> Best Days Overall: 1st, 2nd, 3rd, 11th, 12th, 19th, 20th, 29th, 30th
>
> Most Stressful Days Overall: 4th, 5th, 17th, 18th, 24th, 25th, 31st
>
> Best Days for Love: 1st, 2nd, 3rd, 11th, 12th, 19th, 20th, 24th, 25th, 29th, 30th
>
> Best Days for Money: 4th, 5th, 13th, 14th, 21st, 22nd, 23rd, 31st

The planets are starting to shift this month from the western part of your chart to the eastern part. This is good news. It means that in spite of the general lethargy and introspection in the mass psychology you are getting more control over your life. You are coming to a stage now where you can create your own circumstances and conditions. You are more able to demand what you want from life and to get it. This ability is going to grow ever stronger in the coming months.

The conflict between what your family wants, what your career demands of you and what you want to do is very much heightened during this period. Again, the middle way is the answer. Don't neglect yourself or the true desires of your heart while tending to family and career responsibilities. Give to each what is necessary. It means a real juggling act, but you can do it.

In career matters you are going far beyond the call of duty to achieve success. Your partner, too, goes to extraordinary lengths to support your career. Perhaps this is why your partner feels neglected or unappreciated when you pursue personal interests. He or she feels 'I'm doing so much – making all these sacrifices – how can you ignore me this way – especially when I need you?'

Group activities are favourable and active. Group study seems especially satisfying. After the 3rd you may be called upon to speak to a group.

Singles find romantic opportunities in foreign countries or with foreigners until the 16th. After that you are more attracted to the rich, the powerful and people of high status. You prefer someone who can help your career regardless of whether your family approves or disapproves.

Your health is excellent all month. Finances improve after the 23rd.

September

Best Days Overall: 7th, 8th, 15th, 16th, 25th, 26th

Most Stressful Days Overall: 1st, 13th, 14th, 20th, 21st, 28th, 29th

Best Days for Love: 8th, 9th, 18th, 19th, 20th, 21st, 28th, 29th

Best Days for Money: 1st, 9th, 10th, 18th, 19th, 28th, 29th

There's a lot of good news for you this month, Libra. Enjoy. First off, the planets finally shift from the western half of your solar horoscope to the eastern half. This is good news because you have a new sense of freedom and independence. You have greater control over circumstances and finally get the opportunity to create the conditions you desire rather than have to adapt to preordained ones.

Secondly, the financial news is unusually good. Now and for the next few months you are hitting a peak – perhaps the highest of your lifetime.

It is well that you spend the early part of the month a bit reclusively. Prayer, meditation, charitable and philanthropic activities are very favourable. The psychological insights you gain will stand you in good stead when success really hits. The more you understand about yourself and the world, the better you will be able to put material success into its right perspective. Success is as capable of throwing you off balance as failure is.

Your health is going to be excellent all month but especially after the 23rd. To make your health and vitality even better, your solar horoscope suggests that you take special care of your knees, ankles and feet. Massage them regularly – especially if they feel sore. The Sun's movement into your own sign on the 23rd increases your personal charisma, magnetism and general vitality. You are assertive – but in your charming, endearing, Libra way. People are not offended by your self-assertiveness.

Your physical appearance shines; your friends keep saying how radiant you look. Your new assertion of your personal interests will naturally create short-term conflicts with family members, bosses, your lover and those involved in your career. These issues will probably come to a head around the 20th and 21st. You have been giving in to others for too long. Still, it is not wise to withdraw totally from family or career concerns. Keep a balance and leave yourself and your own needs very much in the picture. If others are realistic they will understand that you have legitimate needs.

In finance, your biggest challenge is finding out what to do with all your cash surplus. Where will you put it? A happy problem indeed. In love there is a need for compromise – and since you are the master of compromise, love should be blissful.

October

> Best Days Overall: 4th, 5th, 13th, 14th, 22nd, 23rd, 24th
>
> Most Stressful Days Overall: 10th, 11th, 17th, 18th, 19th, 25th, 26th
>
> Best Days for Love: 6th, 7th, 8th, 9th, 15th, 16th, 17th, 18th, 19th, 25th, 26th, 27th, 28th
>
> Best Days for Money: 6th, 7th, 15th, 16th, 25th, 26th

With 80 to 90 per cent of the planetary power in the eastern half of your solar horoscope you feel more independent than you've felt in a long time. You are in the driver's seat. You create conditions and circumstances. The world adapts to you rather than vice versa. Yet this new freedom brings with it responsibility – for you will have to live with whatever you create. The retrograde of Venus, your planetary ruler on the 13th will be a welcome opportunity to rethink and review your goals and plans. If this is done properly your creations will be more sound.

The retrograde of your planetary ruler makes you more introverted, subjective and cautious but it doesn't affect your health, which is excellent all month. Your self-esteem doesn't seem affected either, as the Sun moves over your own sign until the 23rd.

The big news this month is in your financial life, which can only be described as sensational. Substantial sums come to you. Whatever you touch turns to gold. So uncanny is your financial judgement these days that you need to revise your goals upward. You have definitely underestimated yourself. Use the retrograde of Venus to achieve this revision. So many earning opportunities are presented that you need time to sort them out.

This focus on earnings does seem to stress your love life, however. Your partner tends to feel neglected. The fact that your earnings tend to overshadow his or her earnings is perhaps another bone of contention. Both you and your partner need to downplay the passion and cultivate friendship. Friendship will put the earnings game in perspective.

Singles find superabundant love opportunities in groups they belong to and with those involved in their financial affairs. An innocent trip to the bank or the shopping mall can turn into a romantic adventure right now.

The retrograde of Mercury (from the 9th to the 30th) complicates travel and education issues. Be patient.

November

> Best Days Overall: 1st, 2nd, 9th, 10th, 19th, 20th, 28th, 29th

> Most Stressful Days Overall: 7th, 8th, 14th, 15th, 21st, 22nd

> Best Days for Love: 3rd, 4th, 5th, 6th, 11th, 12th, 14th, 15th, 21st, 22nd, 24th, 25th, 30th

> Best Days for Money: 3rd, 4th, 11th, 12th, 21st, 22nd, 30th

Nature's capacity for growth is awesome and nowhere can this be seen more clearly than in your financial life, Libra.

For two years or so this growth has been invisible but inexorable nonetheless. Now the wealth that's been building up is there for all to see.

Sudden financial upheavals are blessings in disguise right now (good fortune delights in disguise). If you understand that powerful forces are hard at work developing you in their own way, you will laugh at and perhaps even welcome these upheavals. See them as pointers to areas of weakness and do your best to strengthen yourself. The two eclipses this month are going to create the conditions for correction. Once you correct any mistakes your wealth will become greater than before.

You will earn more this month, but you will also spend more. You've probably taken on major long-term financial commitments and feel a little fearful about meeting them. Just remember that as long as you have enough for the obligations immediately at hand, you are wealthy. Tomorrow's obligations will take care of themselves. The greatest danger right now is to fall into plutocracy – the belief that material wealth is, of itself, power. You are learning that material wealth is merely the consequence – the effect – of right living and right thinking.

Financial confidence returns when Venus, your ruling planet, moves forward – on the 23rd.

The solar eclipse of the 3rd – a particularly powerful one – is the more serious one for you, Libra, as Venus is affected. Take a reduced schedule on that day. Stresses in a current relationship will need to be resolved one way or another. Money matters seem to be at the root of it all. Tensions in love will subside after the 22nd.

December

Best Days Overall: 6th, 7th, 16th, 17th, 25th, 26th

Most Stressful Days Overall: 4th, 5th, 11th, 12th, 19th, 20th

LIBRA

Best Days for Love: 1st, 2nd, 3rd, 8th, 9th, 10th, 11th, 12th, 13th, 14th, 19th, 20th, 23rd, 24th, 28th, 29th

Best Days for Money: 1st, 8th, 9th, 10th, 11th, 12th, 19th, 20th, 21st, 22nd, 27th, 28th, 30th

The direct motion of all the planets – an unusual occurrence – brings important progress. Your financial life goes forward and all the delayed deals, payments and projects start to move ahead now. Money is simply not a problem. You're getting ready to focus on the things that money can't buy – intellectual achievements, good relations with your neighbours, strong communication skills. The prospects for all of these aims are happy and favourable, not only for the coming month but for the coming year as well.

After the 22nd, family and domestic responsibilities start taking dominance. Where many zodiac types are partying and going out, you are spending more time at home with your family. As far as you're concerned this is the most exciting place to be right now. If you've observed yourself over this past year you'll no doubt have noticed the connection between family harmony and your health and vitality. This connection is important over the long term. Moreover, with 80 to 90 per cent of the planets at the bottom half of your chart you need to establish a stable home base and deeper emotional support before you can go further in your career. You need to establish and learn how to enter an 'emotional comfort zone' from which you can grow.

You seem overly – and unusually – active in charitable and philanthropic activities. You go to amazing lengths – far beyond the call of duty – to help those less fortunate and to help a ministerial organization.

Your love life seems under wraps and secretive. You are more sacrificing in love right now. You are ready to give up personal love in favour of a higher collective ideal. Your altruism is strong. Unconditional, spiritual love is what you crave, but this is difficult for mere humans to give. You feel that if you love unconditionally you should get the same in return. You will, but not necessarily from those whom you give it or from whom you desire it. Your partner seems more concerned about his or health than about you – this is temporary. By the 22nd love stabilizes.

Scorpio

♏

THE SCORPION
Birthdays from
23rd October
to 22nd November

Personality Profile

SCORPIO AT A GLANCE

Element – Water

Ruling planet – Pluto
  Money planet – Jupiter
  Planet of home and family life – Uranus

Colour – red-violet

Colour that promotes love, romance and social harmony – green

Colour that promotes earning power – blue

Gems – bloodstone, malachite, topaz

Metals – iron, radium, steel

Scents – cherry blossom, coconut, sandalwood, watermelon

Quality – fixed (= stability)

Quality most needed for balance – a wider view of things

Strongest virtues – loyalty, concentration, determination, courage, depth

Deepest needs – to penetrate and transform

Characteristics to avoid – jealousy, vindictiveness, fanaticism

Signs of greatest overall compatibility – Cancer, Pisces

Signs of greatest overall incompatibility – Taurus, Leo, Aquarius

Sign most helpful to career – Leo

Sign most helpful for emotional support – Aquarius

Sign most helpful financially – Sagittarius

Sign best for marriage and/or partnerships – Taurus

Sign most helpful for creative projects – Pisces

Best sign to have fun with – Pisces

Signs most helpful in spiritual matters – Cancer, Libra

Best day of the week – Tuesday

SCORPIO

Understanding the Scorpio Personality

The symbol of the Scorpio sign of the zodiac is the phoenix. If you meditate upon the legend of the phoenix you will begin to understand a Scorpio's character, his or her powers and abilities, interests and deepest urges.

The phoenix of mythology was a bird that could recreate and reproduce all by itself. It did so in a most intriguing way: it would seek a fire – usually in a religious temple – fly into it, consume itself in the flames and then emerge as a new bird. If this is not the ultimate, most profound transformation, then what is?

Transformation is what Scorpios are all about – in their minds, bodies, affairs and relationships (Scorpios are also society's transformers). To change something in a natural and not an artificial way involves a transformation from within. This type of change is a radical change as opposed to a mere cosmetic cover-up. Some people think that change means only changing their appearance, but this is not the kind of change that interests a Scorpio. Scorpios seek deep, fundamental change. Since real change always proceeds from within, a Scorpio is very interested in – and usually accustomed to – the inner, intimate and philosophical side of life.

Scorpios are people of depth and intellect. If you want to interest them you must present them with more than just a superficial image. You and your projects or business deals must have real substance behind them in order to become interesting to a Scorpio. If that is not the case he or she will find you out – and that will be the end of the story.

If we observe life, the processes of growth and decay, we see the transformative powers of Scorpio at work all the time. The caterpillar changes itself into a butterfly, the infant grows into a child and then an adult. To Scorpios this definite and perpetual transformation is not something to be feared. They see this as a normal part of life. This acceptance of transformation gives Scorpios the key to understanding the true meaning of life.

Scorpios' understanding of life (including life's weaknesses) makes them powerful warriors – in all senses of the word. Add to this their depth and penetration, their patience and endurance and you have a powerful personality. Scorpios have good, long memories and can be at times quite vindictive – they can wait years to get their revenge. As a friend, though, there is no one more loyal and true than a Scorpio. Few are willing to make the sacrifices that a Scorpio will make for a true friend.

The results of a transformation are quite obvious, although the process of transformation is invisible and secret. This is why Scorpios are considered secretive in nature. A seed will not grow properly if you keep digging it up and exposing it to the light of day. It must stay buried – invisible – until it starts to grow. In the same manner, Scorpios fear revealing too much about themselves or their hopes to other people. However, they will be more than happy to let you see the finished product – but only when it is finished. On the other hand, Scorpios like knowing everyone else's secrets as much as they dislike anyone knowing theirs.

Finance

Love, birth, life as well as death are Nature's most potent transformations and Scorpios are interested in all of these. In our society money is a transforming power, too, and a Scorpio is interested in money for that reason. To a Scorpio money is power, money causes change and money rules. It is the power of money that fascinates them. But Scorpios can be too materialistic if they are not careful. They can be overly awed by the power of money, to a point where they think that money rules the world.

Even the term *plutocrat* comes from Pluto, the ruler of the sign of Scorpio. Scorpios will – in one way or another – achieve the financial situation they strive for. When they do so they are careful in the way they handle their wealth. Part of this financial tightness is really a kind of honesty, for

Scorpios are usually involved with other people's money – as accountants, lawyers, stockbrokers or corporate managers – and when you handle other people's money you have to be more careful than when you handle your own.

In order to fulfil their financial goals Scorpios have important lessons to learn. They need to develop qualities that are not naturally in their natures, such as breadth of vision, optimism, faith, trust and above all, generosity. They need to see the wealth in Nature and in life as well as the more obvious forms of money and power. When they develop this generosity their financial potential reaches great heights, for Jupiter, the lord of opulence and good fortune, is Scorpio's money planet.

Career and Public Image

Scorpio's greatest aspiration in life is to be considered by society as a source of light and life. They want to be leaders, to be stars. But they follow a very different road to it than do Leos, the other stars of the zodiac. A Scorpio arrives at the goal secretly, without ostentation; a Leo pursues it openly. Scorpios seek the glamour and fun of the rich and the famous in a secretive, undisclosed manner.

Scorpios are by nature introverted and tend to avoid the limelight. But if they want to attain their highest career goals they need to open up a bit and to express themselves more. They need to stop hiding their light beneath a bushel and let it shine. Above all, they need to let go of any vindictiveness and small-mindedness. All their gifts and insights were given to them for one important reason – to serve life and to increase the joy of living for others.

Love and Relationships

Scorpio is another zodiac sign that likes committed, clearly defined, structured relationships. They are cautious about marriage but when they do commit to a relationship they tend to be faithful – and Heaven help the mate caught or even suspected of infidelity. The jealousy of the Scorpio is legendary. They can be so intense in their jealousy that even the thought or intention of infidelity will be detected and is likely to cause as much of a storm as if the act had actually occurred.

Scorpios tend to settle down with those who are wealthier than they are. They usually have enough intensity for two, so in their partners they seek someone pleasant, hardworking, amiable, stable and easy-going. They want someone they can lean on, someone loyal behind them as they fight the battles of life. To a Scorpio a partner, be it a lover or a friend, is a real partner – not an adversary. Most of all a Scorpio is looking for an ally, not a competitor.

If you are in love with a Scorpio you will need a lot of patience. It takes you a long time to get to know Scorpios, because they don't reveal themselves readily. But if you persist and your motives are honourable, you will gradually be allowed into a Scorpio's inner chambers of mind and heart.

Home and Domestic Life

Uranus is the ruler of Scorpio's 4th solar House of Home and Domestic Affairs. Uranus is the planet of science, technology, changes and democracy. This tells us a lot about a Scorpio's conduct in the home and what he or she needs in order to have a happy, harmonious home life.

Scorpios can sometimes bring their passion, intensity and wilfulness into the home and family, which is not always the place for these qualities. These virtues are good for the warrior and the transformer, but not so good for the nurturer and family person. Because of this (and also because of their need for change and transformation) the Scorpio may be prone to sudden changes of residence. If not carefully constrained, the sometimes inflexible Scorpio can produce turmoil and sudden upheavals within the family.

Scorpios need to develop some of the virtues of Aquarius in order to cope better with domestic matters. There is a need to build a team spirit at home, to treat family activities as truly group activities – family members should all have a say into what does and does not get done. For at times a Scorpio can be most dictatorial. When a Scorpio gets dictatorial it's much worse than if a Leo or Capricorn (the two other power signs in the zodiac) does. For the dictatorship of a Scorpio is applied with more zeal, passion, intensity and concentration than is true of either a Leo or Capricorn. Obviously this can be unbearable to his or her family members – especially if they are sensitive types.

In order for a Scorpio to get the full benefit of the emotional support that a family can give, he or she needs to release conservatism and be a bit more experimental, to explore new techniques in child-rearing, be more democratic with family members and try to manage more things by consensus than by autocratic edict.

Horoscope for 1994

Major Trends

1993 was a year of secret, inner expansion. You grew spiritually and emotionally, behind the scenes. You did a lot of charitable and philanthropic work and you got your rewards – intangibles such as wisdom, understanding and insight.

In 1994 these intangibles get processed and translated into concrete things. You will see the truth of the scriptural dictum that 'the Father who seeth in secret shall reward thee openly.'

Two important – and long-term – planetary moves are causing this. First off, Saturn, which has been in stressful aspect to you for the past two to three years, is now – as of 29th January, 1994 – moving into a harmonious aspect to you. Secondly, Jupiter (the great benefic of the heavens) stays in your own sign of Scorpio practically all year. This means a natural expansion of the self: of self-esteem, self-worth, self-confidence. It means also a widening of your sphere of personal power. On the purely mundane level it means that because you have *become* more, you earn more and get more glory and recognition. You are accepted – and approved of – on your own terms, without compromises.

Scorpios are usually serious people. Even when you have fun you take it very seriously. But happily in 1994 this seriousness is very much lightened. There is a general optimism and playfulness in your character now. You have a looser approach to life. Worries roll off you 'like water off a duck's back'. You foresee a rosy future ahead and you make the fortunate connections that need to be made. Without thinking about it consciously you find yourself always in the right place at the right time.

If anyone deserves a powerful period of good luck, you do, Scorpio. You have endured and overcome many trials and tribulations in the past few years.

Health

The first and most dramatic improvement in 1994 – as opposed to 1993 – is in your health. Your vitality, which has been lacklustre for the past few years, now becomes superabundant. There are all kinds of complex astrological reasons for this turnaround, but rest assured: you will have plenty of energy to attain any goal that you choose.

If there is a health danger at all it comes not from lack of vitality or an illness, but from over-indulgence in personal pleasure. In other words, from too much of a good thing. This is a year of great personal pleasure for you. All kinds of sensual delights are offering themselves to you. By all means indulge, but don't over-indulge. Both males and females are unusually fertile now. Be aware that extra weight gained from overeating could pose a health problem.

Overall, your 6th House of Health and Mars, its lord, are not especially activated this year, so your health forecast is basically good. You could say that 'no news is good news' so, except for the points mentioned above, you don't really need to pay special attention to your health this year.

Overall, your best health periods will be from 18th February to 20th March, 21st June to 22nd July and 23rd October to 22nd November.

Your most stressful health periods overall will be from 20th January to 17th February, 20th April to 20th May and 23rd July to 23rd August.

Home and Domestic Life

Uranus (lord of your domestic and family situation) has been – for years now – conjoined with Neptune. Saturn, too, has been a force in your domestic situation for the past two to three years. Thus you have been – and continue to be – experimental and perhaps over-idealistic about your home, family members and relationships. You have been searching – for many years now – for a dream home, dream family and dream support network – in short, for the domestic ideal.

You have tried many different methods of attaining this. At times you tried to pretend that your current family relationships resembled your ideal. But your own perceptiveness wouldn't let you get away with this for too long. You saw that your family members are only human and at different stages of personal growth. To idealize or romanticize them is simply to ignore reality. Many of you tried to make them over in your own image – by force or through subtle psychological coercion. This too had its drawbacks as it produced periodic explosions of pent-up energy. Your family sensed the coercion and the explosions – though they themselves couldn't explain them – were their response to it.

Your search for the perfect home life will continue for quite a few years, leading you to ultimately discover your true spiritual family. This family will be connected to you by ties much stronger and more enduring than mere blood.

Happily, this year your domestic situation is vastly improved. It is happier, more harmonious and less restricting. This suggests a move to larger quarters and/or the departure of some family member who was causing disharmony and depression – the planetary symbolism suggests a sibling or in-law. After two to three years of a Saturn transit you seem better able to express your emotions in a positive and less destructive way. Over the past few years you have been forced to regulate your emotions. Now that family tensions are easing you have less negative energy to repress and regulate. Saturn's move out of your domestic situation suggests that a great and depressing burden or duty is being lifted from your shoulders.

There is a tendency for you to move house often. Your search for a dream house is not a one-off achievement but a series of steps leading up to your desired goal.

You are searching for the ideal community as well as the ideal home. Many of you may be experimenting with art colonies or spiritually-led communities.

Love and Social Life

Though there is nothing obstructing your love life this year, you seem more concerned with other issues than with love, romance and marriage. Of course you will certainly have your share of romance this year – especially when the aspects to Venus are prominent – but you prefer to work on getting on with yourself more. You discover that a lack of self-love and self-acceptance are major obstacles to finding love with others. If you don't love yourself, you will have trouble loving others and receiving love from others – no matter how hard they try to give you love.

The ability (perhaps we should call it a gift) to love the self is perhaps more difficult for Scorpio than for any other sign.

Why? Because Scorpios are the deepest people in the zodiac and the most intense. They see more profoundly into others and into themselves. Naturally, because of this it is more difficult for them to love. It's easy to love the outside – the good stuff that people show on the surface – but not so easy when you see all the flaws and imperfections. Learning to love both the dark and the light side of a person's character is Scorpio's greatest challenge.

Scorpios have the gift of transforming, exorcising and eliminating so that they can love. 'The only way I can love myself is to re-invent myself,' they think. This is Scorpio's road to self-love. And this re-invention of the self – of one's image and personality – has been going on for some years now. This year, you see the positive results of your work. Finally – at long last – you attain self-love, self-worth, self-acceptance. Once you have this you don't need to worry much about your relationships. Love will find you easily, effortlessly, harmoniously. It was always there.

In short, improve your love life this year by improving your sense of self-love and self-acceptance. When you encounter things about yourself that you can't love – either change them or eliminate them. And try to enjoy the process of change, because while it goes on it will give you the opportunity to exercise your genius. Your love – and not your rejection – will be the transforming agent.

Affairs of the heart – and torrid ones at that – are most prominent in your horoscope from 1st April to 4th July and 7th September to 9th December. This latter period promises to be particularly happy both for love and finances. It will also demonstrate to you the power of true self-love and self-acceptance.

Career and Finance

This year your career – your public and professional esteem – blossoms almost without any effort on your part. In fact this area of your life is not a priority right now. You expand careerwise because you are progressing personally. You get more respect, more honour, more recognition – and more money – because you recognize your own talents and worth.

So, expect rises, promotions, greater prestige and status this year. But what really interests you – much more than the glory and honours, nice though they are – is personal earnings. If it comes down to a choice between glory and money, you will take money. This is not always so for you, Scorpio – but this year it is true.

Part of the new image you are inventing for yourself has to do with wealth. You are seeing that to be wealthy you must project an image of wealth. In the beginning you find assuming the image of wealth quite uncomfortable. Being such a blunt and honest person, a part of you feels that you are 'posing' – faking it – putting on airs. These feelings are natural, yet you must continue to dress, carry yourself and otherwise act the part of a man (or woman) of substance. Why? Because reality tends to manifest according to our imagery. If you continue, the day will come – in 1994 – when you will feel quite comfortable with your new image. You will adjust to it. You will also become the wealthy person you envisioned. Great planetary forces are helping you make the transition.

The proper image is an important factor in increased earnings. Your unusual vitality gives you the ability to work and increase earnings in this way. Your naturally keen perceptions are very much enhanced this year and so your financial judgement, your investment ability and your power to distinguish the profitable from the unprofitable will increase. Because there is so much power in your own sign of Scorpio this year you can trust your natural instincts and inclinations in financial affairs. Feel free to earn money in whatever way you find most interesting.

Self-improvement

The major area for self-improvement this year is your personal image and appearance, as already discussed. This improvement will occur quite easily this year, as Saturn and most of the other long-term planets are co-operating with the process.

There is another area that could benefit from some self-improvement: your creative life. Those of you involved in the arts, professionally or as hobbyists, must now discipline yourselves creatively. You must focus more on the craft aspects of your work rather than the inspirational ones. With Neptune (universal lord of inspiration) so stimulated for many years now, you have no lack of inspiration and creative ideas. What's needed now is to put these ideas in the right form. This is your challenge – and it won't be easy – for the next few years.

Month-by-month Forecasts

January

Best Days Overall: 6th, 7th, 15th, 16th, 25th, 26th

Most Stressful Days Overall: 1st, 12th, 13th, 14th, 20th, 21st, 27th, 28th

Best Days for Love: 2nd, 3rd, 10th, 20th, 21st, 22nd, 23rd, 31st

Best Days for Money: 6th, 7th, 8th, 9th, 15th, 16th, 25th, 26th

Intellectual arguments are going to make you see the wisdom of pursuing mental interests this month, Scorpio. Any deficiency in your knowledge or ability to communicate is clear now and easier for you to correct. How to proceed – whether to go back to full-time education or to take independent courses in a given area – will be revealed to you by the new Moon of the 11th. The pursuit of these interests will have the added benefits of creating earnings opportunities and important contacts.

Relationships within the family – especially siblings and in-laws – are delicate and volatile. Nevertheless, nothing can dim your basic optimism and no person or group of people can lower your self-esteem. You know your self-worth.

There is an unusual line-up of planets in the sign of Capricorn this month. This is wreaking havoc with corporate and governmental hierarchies and with many people around you. But you personally seem untouched by it all. Your health and vitality are excellent – especially until the 20th.

If the truth be told, there is something about the stoic virtues of Capricorn that appeals to you. You can 'out-stoic' any Capricorn. You are in tune with the energy of the times.

On a career level you will do well, as the full Moon of the 26th will show. Your finances are going to be increasing all year – this month, especially until the 20th. After the 20th, domestic issues and family responsibilities put a dent into some of your added earnings. Extra expenses come up. But this is short term.

Though your 7th House of Love and Romance is not particularly active this month, your love planet (Venus) is. So, your social agenda is happy and active. Since Venus is in your 3rd House of Communication for the best part of the month, romantic opportunities come from within your neighbourhood, with or through the help of neighbours or within an educational setting. Courses given by your corporation are socially fulfilling.

February

> Best Days Overall: 2nd, 3rd, 11th, 12th, 21st, 22nd

SCORPIO

Most Stressful Days Overall: 9th, 10th, 16th, 17th, 23rd, 24th

Best Days for Love: 1st, 9th, 10th, 11th, 12th, 16th, 17th, 21st, 22nd

Best Days for Money: 2nd, 3rd, 11th, 12th, 21st, 22nd

In spite of your attempts to keep things harmonious, conflicts within your family are arousing intense passions this month, Scorpio. There are various reasons for this but the main one is change. Your new acceptance of yourself, your greater ability to get your own way, your sense of power and authority and your joy and expansiveness are creating changes in the family aura (energy field). Family members sense these changes subconsciously and feel uncomfortable with the new status quo. Once the new is accepted these passions die down. In the meantime, they can be unpleasant. Family members can feel – though it probably isn't so – that you're exerting too much authority over them. Talk to a counsellor or friend about your feelings or write them down. Don't hold them inside.

This is the month – especially until the 18th – for those DIY projects you've been wanting to do. Get your home – your domestic base – shipshape. Entertaining from home – though it sets you back a bit financially – seems pleasurable and profitable in the long term. Family gatherings are bittersweet now – with much love as well as a few barbs being tossed about.

Singles find love opportunities with old flames – even those from childhood. Those who want to win the heart of a Scorpio this month can do so by nurturing and providing him or her with emotional support.

Your finances are temporarily bogged down until the 18th, but after that they improve dramatically. Your self-esteem is an unusually vital factor in your earnings this year.

Your health is delicate until the 18th as well. The cool,

light-hearted energy of Aquarius makes you uncomfortable both psychologically and physically. You like focus and intensity. Abstract ideas and superficial talk bore you. People consider you too intense this month. After the 18th your vitality zooms back to its normal abundant levels.

Mercury's retrograde (backward motion) on the 11th shows a need for special care when communicating with insurance companies or stockbrokers. Don't give them excuses to misunderstand you.

March

Best Days Overall: 1st, 2nd, 10th, 11th, 12th, 20th, 21st, 22nd, 29th, 30th

Most Stressful Days Overall: 8th, 9th, 15th, 16th, 17th, 23rd, 24th

Best Days for Love: 1st, 2nd, 13th, 14th, 15th, 16th, 17th, 23rd, 24th, 31st

Best Days for Money: 1st, 2nd, 4th, 5th, 10th, 11th, 12th, 20th, 21st, 22nd, 29th, 30th, 31st

This is a happy month for you, Scorpio, for many reasons. The strong power in Pisces and the Water Element, which for others is uncomfortable and even depressing, is for you a joy. Your normally acute perception is deepened even further. The world and the people around you seem awash in a sea of emotion, but you're swimming quite comfortably. Your health and self-esteem are good and your vitality and energy are superabundant. In addition, your earnings are increased and your personal and social charisma are strengthened.

The planetary power for the better part of the month is in your 5th solar House of Fun, Creativity, Entertainment and Love Affairs. This is a time, therefore, for fun and games. By all means go to the theatre, to parties and sporting events. Let your hair down and enjoy yourself. Don't take life too seriously now.

Curiously enough, these leisure activities – this temporary break from the serious things in life – increase your earnings and social life. Speculations are favourable – alas, they would be even more so if Jupiter were moving direct. Luck is with you but payment could be delayed. This delay affects your overall financial life as well, yet it doesn't discourage you unduly – nor should it. The power behind you is so strong that these financial delays will only make the resulting outcome even more beneficial.

Earnings are always related to self-esteem to a degree, but this year – for complex astrological reasons – the connection is even more dramatic. When your self-esteem is high, earnings skyrocket. When it dips, so do your earnings. Your ego can – unfortunately – tend to be tied up with earnings. You feel that you are more when you have more – when you have less you feel that you are in some way diminished. Happily, this month and this year your self-esteem is essentially strong.

Your love and social life is happy during this period. Venus, your love planet works powerfully on your behalf in the sign of Pisces. Romantic opportunities are abundant. You feel more romantic and loving and others take notice. Love is altruistic and idyllic until the 8th. After that you want service from your lover; feelings are not enough. A current love relationship becomes more exciting and active – and perhaps unstable. Enjoy these rapid and stimulating changes.

April

>Best Days Overall: 7th, 8th, 17th, 18th, 25th, 26th

>Most Stressful Days Overall: 4th, 5th, 12th, 13th, 19th, 20th

Best Days for Love: 2nd, 3rd, 12th, 13th,
21st, 22nd

Best Days for Money: 7th, 8th, 17th, 18th,
25th, 26th, 27th, 28th

Most of the planetary power is concentrated in the western
half of your solar horoscope right now. With two important
planets going retrograde in your 1st House of Personal
Interest there is a strong signal from the cosmos that you need
to focus on the needs of others for a while. You must deal
with existing conditions – ease them – before you can start
to create your own new conditions. This is just temporary.
Later on the year you are going to have a lot of freedom to
create your own circumstances.

Work and issues at the workplace are highly emphasized
all month. The workplace is hectic. You're working hard.
Power struggles between co-workers are going on and you're
involved. There is a militancy and martial quality here. You
and your co-workers have a temporary need to fight for your
rights or to correct some injustice. In addition, your tendency
to put work goals over family duties creates some friction
within your family. Keep a balance between these two areas
of your life.

Your health is excellent until the 20th, after which you
should rest and relax more. Physical exercise is an especially
important key to maintaining good health during this period.

Your social life is also wonderful, active and happy all
month. Venus, your love planet operates on your behalf from
the sign of Taurus – her natural home. Venus is powerful
there. Your social charisma is strong. Serious love is in your
life – and you might be finding it a bit frightening. You are
not sure how much of your self-interest you need to give up
in the interests of love. Secondly, your love relationship
seems to affect your finances unduly. The cosmos is telling
you to play down your personal interests temporarily and
put your relationship first. Balance will come later on.

Have patience in financial matters right now. Payments and projects seem delayed or slowed down, but this is only temporary. The overall picture is good indeed. Aside from overspending on a current courtship, other expenses incurred through socializing – going to parties and maintaining your social contacts – also seem troublesome. Do your best to reduce your costs without offending anyone.

May

> Best Days Overall: 4th, 5th, 14th, 15th, 23rd, 24th, 31st
>
> Most Stressful Days Overall: 1st, 2nd, 3rd, 9th, 10th, 16th, 17th, 29th, 30th
>
> Best Days for Love: 1st, 2nd, 3rd, 9th, 10th, 11th, 12th, 13th, 23rd, 24th, 31st
>
> Best Days for Money: 4th, 5th, 14th, 15th, 23rd, 24th, 25th, 26th, 31st

It is best to rest and relax more until the 21st. On the overall level your health is wonderful but you are in a temporary energy low.

The solar eclipse of the 10th is powerful and important for you, Scorpio. It not only produces major changes in the world at large but in your life as well. All Scorpios will be affected to some degree; those of you with birthdays after November 15th will feel it most keenly and dramatically.

Be sure to avoid strenuous, taxing activities from the 9th to the 11th. Take a reduced, relaxed schedule. Long-term changes are taking place in a current marriage or love affair and in your self-image and self-esteem. Any short-term upheavals will benefit you in the end as they will highlight failings in a present affair. Your self-esteem is definitely going to increase as a result of this eclipse.

This eclipse also affects your career and professional status.

A positive career change – perhaps a new job – is in the offing. A shake-up within the corporate hierarchy creates opportunities for you.

The lunar eclipse of the 25th seems much less serious for you. It brings a sudden expense or financial upheaval – a prized possession might need repair. This is inconvenient but not devastating. This eclipse also serves to highlight some financial weakness that needs to be corrected.

Your health and vitality start to improve after the 21st, but you really come back to yourself next month.

Love is stormy, passionate and unstable most of the month. Basically your personal interests and those of your partner are at loggerheads. You want different things. If a middle way can be found, all is well and good. If not, a break-up is likely. Both you and your partner are unusually assertive and uncompromising right now. Your partner (governed by Venus) speaks boastfully and bombastically and is spending too much time travelling about without you, which makes you uncomfortable.

June

Best Days Overall: 1st, 10th, 11th, 19th, 20th, 28th, 29th

Most Stressful Days Overall: 5th, 6th, 7th, 13th, 14th, 25th, 26th

Best Days for Love: 1st, 5th, 6th, 7th, 10th, 11th, 21st, 22nd, 30th

Best Days for Money: 1st, 10th, 11th, 19th, 20th, 21st, 22nd, 28th, 29th

As you are naturally more subjectively-orientated, Scorpio, the unusual amount of planets going retrograde right now doesn't affect you as much as it does other signs. You can swing into the inner world more easily than other types and thus you can handle these energies to your greatest advantage.

What is called for now is review, re-assessment, correction and improvement in most of the departments of life. All of this begins within. When the planets start going forward again you will be in an excellent position – fully prepared – to go forward with them.

With life at such a standstill now it might be a good idea to take that foreign trip and enjoy yourself for a while – from the 9th to the 25th is a good time to do this. Take a leisurely approach to travel and be patient with the various delays. Enjoy the delays as much as the trip. Make the most of them.

Career issues are emphasized this month – and they will be important next month as well. Your love and career are inter-connected. Singles meet romantic prospects at the workplace and through those involved in their professional life. Your partner is unusually career-orientated and thus supports your urges for professional success. You socialize with your bosses and superiors and get to know them on a more personal level than before. Bosses enjoy playing Cupid during this period.

A romance at work has a strong element of conflict. Both of you are too caught up in your personal interests; there isn't room to focus on the relationship as a whole. Unless one of you can rise above personal interest this romance is in danger. Someone who is teasing you at work – perhaps even harassing you – has only true romance in mind.

The urge for professional success is further enhanced because you feel that your public and professional status will bring you love – will attract the person of your dreams. This is a big illusion but a useful one for now. Anything that helps you get that pay rise or promotion is useful.

Your health and self-esteem are good all month.

July

Best Days Overall: 7th, 8th, 9th, 16th,
17th, 25th, 26th

Most Stressful Days Overall: 2nd, 3rd, 4th,
10th, 11th, 23rd, 24th, 30th, 31st

Best Days for Love: 1st, 2nd, 3rd, 4th,
10th, 11th, 12th, 21st, 22nd, 30th, 31st

Best Days for Money: 7th, 8th, 9th, 16th,
17th, 19th, 20th, 25th, 26th

The current concentration of planetary power in the Water signs, though difficult for others is very comfortable for you, Scorpio. You are in one of the happiest and most productive intervals of your year. If only more of the planets were going direct you would see even more outward progress. Not to worry: you will see more of the obvious effects of your actions later on.

Your ability to navigate through all the moods, emotions and sensitivities of others enriches you and enhances your popularity. You are a light for others to follow. You know whom you can approach for what at any time. You know who needs to be avoided. You know how far you can push in certain areas. This is all automatic and instinctive to you.

Your self-esteem, self-worth and self-confidence are strong. Your earnings are high. Your sex appeal is unusually strong and love prospers.

Until the 11th love is just fun and games. Afterwards it gets more serious. You and your partner analyse – and perhaps criticize – your relationship. This criticism isn't malicious but just an attempt to purify your love – to cleanse it of alien motives. Giving practical service to your beloved in the spirit of friendly co-operation fosters your relationship.

Your partner's income is very much improved and his or her financial confidence is strong. Foreign developments help restore this confidence. Your personal earning power is also much stronger, as Jupiter starts going forward after a few months of backward motion. Speculations are favourable, for your psychic senses are even more uncanny than normal right now. You can smell the difference between a winner and a loser. Your personal appearance and image play important roles in your finances at this time. Your creative ability – and the knack for deriving profits from it – is enhanced.

Your career gets a major boost after the 23rd. You need to make a choice between professional prestige and earnings, between honour and the bottom line. Your solar horoscope suggests that you take the middle road; both are equally valid.

August

> Best Days Overall: 4th, 5th, 13th, 14th, 21st, 22nd, 23rd, 31st
>
> Most Stressful Days Overall: 6th, 7th, 19th, 20th, 26th, 27th
>
> Best Days for Love: 11th, 12th, 19th, 20th, 26th, 27th, 29th, 30th
>
> Best Days for Money: 4th, 5th, 13th, 14th, 15th, 16th, 21st, 22nd, 23rd, 31st

Though the Sun makes some stressful aspects to you until the 23rd, most of the planetary power is harmonious. The general introversion and subjectivity of the month are very comfortable for you, Scorpio. Moreover, the planetary power is shifting now to the eastern half of your solar horoscope, giving you ever more power to create conditions as you desire them.

Being able to create conditions is a great gift. Everyone has this power to some degree; some people more than others. At different times of life we have more or less of this power.

When you create conditions you create Karma. When you have to deal with existing conditions you are repaying karmic debts. Thus, before you create you must think through your project to be sure that the Karma you create is positive.

The Sun moves across the uppermost part – the Midheaven – of your solar horoscope this month. This is going to bring great career progress and opportunity. Your ability to administrate, organize and exert power over others is enhanced. Your leadership ability is strengthened. You are experiencing one of the career high-points of the year.

The career progress you make now involves some sacrifice of personal pleasure, but it's worth it. Moreover, it will lead – after the 23rd – to the manifestation of your fondest hopes and wishes and to a new circle of friends and acquaintances.

This career progress may also involve some financial sacrifice, but again, it is worth it. This financial sacrifice is only short term, while your career progress will be long term. Still, don't sacrifice your earnings completely for the sake of glory. Keep a balance.

Your finances get much better after the 23rd as your new status brings with it new earning opportunities and rises in pay. You make back what you lost earlier.

Singles find love opportunities within this new circle of friends. An acquaintance wants to be more than that. In love you prefer friendship over passion – and purity in love is unusually important to you right now.

September

Best Days Overall: 1st, 9th, 10th, 18th, 19th, 28th, 29th

Most Stressful Days Overall: 3rd, 4th, 15th, 16th, 22nd, 23rd, 24th, 30th

Best Days for Love: 8th, 9th, 18th, 19th, 22nd, 23rd, 24th, 28th, 29th

SCORPIO

Best Days for Money: 1st, 9th, 10th, 11th,
12th, 18th, 19th, 28th, 29th

The planetary power has now shifted from the western half
of your solar horoscope to the eastern half. This is good news
as you are now in a perfect position to create new conditions
and circumstances. You have greater independence now and
you will assert it. You have unusual power – and this will
carry on for a few months – for re-inventing yourself as you
will.

But this is only part of the good news. Pluto, your ruling
planet moves forward in your own sign, increasing and
enhancing your personal power and charisma. Your life
moves forward. Jupiter and Venus are also in your own sign
– bringing major personal pleasures, increases in income,
passionate and happy love and the fulfilment of your fondest
fantasies.

Your health is excellent all month, but you can enhance
your vitality even further by taking special care of your thighs
and stomach. Massage them regularly – especially if they
feel sore. A foreign trip is likely during this period and makes
you feel better physically. Over-eating and over-indulgence
in personal pleasures are perhaps the major health threats.

Resolving religious or philosophical conflicts will also help
your health. These aspects of life are usually overlooked in
the quest for good health. Many people know that physical
problems originate in the psyche, but few know that
psychic – or emotional – problems originate on the
philosophical, conceptual level.

There is both big money and enormous love in your life this
month (and this trend will get even stronger next month).
Your new self-image is one of wealth, beauty and glamour –
you cut an almost jet-set figure. You dress opulently and
elegantly, in only the finest fabrics and accessories. You
attract similarly stylish people. You are a magnet for both
money and love right now.

Many of you will cling to this new image – as it does have

255

its good points. Others will just play with it for a while and then move on to more serious things.

October

> Best Days Overall: 6th, 7th, 15th, 16th, 25th, 26th
>
> Most Stressful Days Overall: 1st, 13th, 14th, 20th, 21st, 27th, 28th
>
> Best Days for Love: 6th, 7th, 15th, 16th, 20th, 21st, 25th, 26th
>
> Best Days for Money: 6th, 7th, 8th, 9th, 15th, 16th, 25th, 26th

There is a major line-up of planets in your own sign all month, making this a high-point of the year and perhaps of your life.

Your spiritual and dream life is very active until the 23rd. You are charitable and generous – and you can well afford to be. Your self-esteem, self-confidence and personal charisma are at lifetime peaks right now. You get your way in most things, so be sure you know what you want.

Your self-image – the way that you dress and present yourself – continues to be one of understated elegance – covert wealth. Others perceive you this way as well. Your normally acute perceptions are further enhanced this month. You see auras, know the past and the future and have uncanny financial judgement.

There is both money and love in your life. On the love front, let a current relationship evolve and develop a bit. Don't schedule a marriage or make any serious commitment while Venus is retrograde – from the 13th onwards. You need some time to review and revise your love goals.

The universe is fulfilling all of your personal pleasure fantasies this month – and probably throwing in a few things that you never dreamed of! Gourmet meals, exquisite massages and new clothes and personal accessories are coming your way. Fantasies involving physical intimacy are also being fulfilled. This is not a month for dieting – though you should. The abundance of your favourite foods is probably too strong a temptation.

But the month is not all fun and games. You are working hard to achieve career goals and are probably involved in some power struggle at the office. Happily this works out in your favour. You seem well able to take on all comers.

November

> Best Days Overall: 3rd, 4th, 11th, 12th, 21st, 22nd, 30th

> Most Stressful Days Overall: 9th, 10th, 16th, 17th, 24th, 25th

> Best Days for Love: 3rd, 4th, 11th, 12th, 16th, 17th, 21st, 22nd, 30th

> Best Days for Money: 3rd, 4th, 5th, 6th, 11th, 12th, 21st, 22nd, 30th

There is so much power behind you and your efforts – your progress is so rapid – that it is inevitable that some retrenchment and correction must take place. It is rare that people improve themselves voluntarily – especially when they are developing and prospering. But the two eclipses this month will create the conditions – and provide the necessary spur – for improvement. They will flush out your past mistakes and current weaknesses so that you can correct them.

Definitely take a reduced and relaxed schedule around the 3rd and 18th. Those of you with birthdays in October will feel the solar eclipse of the 3rd most powerfully. Those of you with birthdays in mid-November will feel the lunar eclipse of the 18th more. If you avoid strenuous, taxing activities and view things philosophically, all of you will come through stronger and richer than before.

Your health is good all month, though, as indicated, the eclipses might flush out some old health problem and force its correction. Nevertheless, your vitality and self-esteem are basically excellent.

A relationship with a current love gets severely tested this month. Singles should welcome this, as it's better to see any flaws and weaknesses now than later on when it's too late to do anything about them. The mood in love is cautious.

Both eclipses affect your marital status. They herald long-term changes in this area of your life. Thus singles are likely to settle down in the next few months and those within committed relationships may split up. If the relationship is strong, however, the eclipse may signal that one of you will get involved in a business partnership of some sort.

Another important effect of these eclipses is that resistance and opposition to your further expansion and progress are being removed – dramatically and perhaps forcibly.

December

> Best Days Overall: 1st, 8th, 9th, 10th, 19th, 20th, 28th
>
> Most Stressful Days Overall: 6th, 7th, 13th, 14th, 15th, 21st, 22nd
>
> Best Days for Love: 1st, 8th, 9th, 10th, 13th, 14th, 15th, 19th, 20th, 28th, 29th
>
> Best Days for Money: 1st, 2nd, 3rd, 11th, 12th, 21st, 22nd, 29th, 30th

You are entering a month – and a new year – in which you turn your personal charm, good looks, magnetism and charisma into bottom-line profit. You will see that you needed to spend the past two years or so building your self-esteem in order to be ready for the huge increases in earnings that are about to take place. If you did not feel worthy of all this abundance you would not have been able to hold on to it.

Your personal glamour and charisma are still very strong all month. You get your way this month through charm and social grace. People enjoy giving in to you, giving you what you want and pleasing you. You project just the right blend of elegance, glamour and mystery – it is all there but you downplay it. Others find you irresistible.

Love is very much with you. A current love, indeed, seems to be with you all the time – in a live-in or 'quasi-live-in' situation. But you are getting ready to shift your attention over to earnings and possessions.

Sales, marketing, advertising, teaching, local travel and community activities are prominent in your horoscope after the 22nd. All are favourable, happy and very stimulating. All further your career and professional status.

A power struggle involving career issues seems resolved in your favour and you are ready to embark on pursuits that money and status can't really buy – intellectual interests, platonic friends, the development of scientific and technical ability and the realization of your fondest hopes and wishes.

Those of you in creative fields are undergoing a conflict between your artistic and commercial values. This is a tough conflict that has raged for thousands of years. You will have to work out your own compromise. Neither side can be totally ignored.

Your health is excellent all month.

Sagittarius

THE ARCHER

Birthdays from
23rd November
to 20th December

Personality Profile

SAGITTARIUS AT A GLANCE

Element – Fire

Ruling planet – Jupiter
   Career planet – Mercury
   Love planet – Mercury
   Planet of wealth and good fortune – Jupiter

Colours – blue, dark blue

Colours that promote love, romance and social harmony – yellow, yellow-orange

Colours that promote earning power – black, indigo

Gems – carbuncle, turquoise

SAGITTARIUS

Metal – tin

Scents – carnation, jasmine, myrrh

Quality – mutable (= flexibility)

Qualities most needed for balance – attention to detail, administration and organization

Strongest virtues – generosity, honesty, broad-mindedness, tremendous vision

Deepest need – to expand mentally

Characteristics to avoid – over-optimism, exaggeration, being too generous with other people's money

Signs of greatest overall compatibility – Aries, Leo

Signs of greatest overall incompatibility – Gemini, Virgo, Pisces

Sign most helpful to career – Virgo

Sign most helpful for emotional support – Pisces

Sign most helpful financially – Capricorn

Sign best for marriage and/or partnerships – Gemini

Sign most helpful for creative projects – Aries

Best sign to have fun with – Aries

Signs most helpful in spiritual matters – Leo, Scorpio

Best day of the week – Thursday

Understanding the Sagittarius Personality

If you look at the symbol of the archer you will gain a good, intuitive understanding of the people born under this astrological sign. The development of archery was humanity's first refinement of the power to hunt and wage war. The ability to shoot an arrow far beyond the ordinary range of a spear extended human horizons, wealth, personal will and power.

Today, instead of using bows and arrows we project our power with fuels and mighty engines, but the essential reason for using these new powers remains the same. These powers represent our ability to extend our personal sphere of influence – and this is what Sagittarius is all about. Sagittarians are always seeking to expand their horizons, to cover more territory and increase their range and scope. This applies to all aspects of their lives: economic, social and intellectual.

Sagittarians are noted for the development of the mind – the higher intellect – which understands philosophical, metaphysical and spiritual concepts. This mind represents the higher part of the psychic nature and is motivated not by self-centred considerations but by the light and grace of a higher power. Thus, Sagittarians love higher education of all kinds. They might be bored with formal schooling but they love to study on their own and in their own way. A love of foreign travel and interest in places far away from home are also noteworthy characteristics of the Sagittarian type.

If you give some thought to all these Sagittarian attributes you will see that they spring from the inner Sagittarian desire to develop. To travel more is to know more, to know more is to be more, to cultivate the higher mind is to expand and reach more. All these traits tend to broaden the intellectual – and indirectly, the economic and material – horizons of the Sagittarian.

The generosity of the Sagittarian is legendary. There are many reasons for this. One is that Sagittarians seem to have an inborn consciousness of wealth. They feel that they are rich, that they are lucky, that they can attain any financial goal – and so they feel that they can afford to be generous. Sagittarians don't carry the burdens of lack and limitation – which stop most other people from giving generously. Another reason for their generosity is their religious and philosophical idealism, derived from the higher mind. This higher mind is by nature generous because it is unaffected by material circumstances. Still another reason is that the act of giving tends to enhance their emotional nature. Every act of giving seems to be enriching and this is reward enough for the Sagittarian.

Finance

Sagittarians generally entice wealth. They either attract it or create it. They have the ideas, a vision of their paradise on Earth and they have the energy and talent to make it real. However, mere wealth is not enough. Sagittarians want luxury – earning a comfortable living seems small and insignificant to them.

In order for Sagittarians to attain their true earning potential they must develop better managerial and organizational skills. They must learn to set limits, to arrive at their goals through a series of attainable sub-goals or objectives. It is very rare that a person goes from rags to riches overnight. But a long, drawn-out process is difficult for Sagittarians. Like Leos, they want to achieve wealth and success quickly and impressively. Be aware, however, that this over-optimism can lead to unrealistic financial ventures and disappointing losses. Of course, no zodiac sign can bounce back as quickly as Sagittarius, but only needless heartache will be caused by this attitude. Sagittarians need to maintain their vision – never letting go of it – but also working towards it in practical and efficient ways.

Career and Public Image

Sagittarians are big thinkers. They want it all: money, name, fame, glamour, prestige, public acclaim and a place in history. They often go after all these goals. Some attain them, some don't – much depends on the individual's personal horoscope. But if Sagittarians want to attain public and professional status they must understand that these things are not conferred to enhance one's ego but in reward for the amount of service that one has performed for the whole of humanity. If and when they figure out ways to serve more, Sagittarians can rise to the top.

The ego of the Sagittarians is gigantic – and perhaps rightly so. They have much to be proud of. If they want public acclaim, however, they will have to learn to tone the ego down a bit, to become more humble and self-effacing, without falling into the trap of self-denial and self-abasement. They must also learn to master the details of life, which can sometimes elude them.

At their jobs Sagittarians are hard workers who like to please their bosses and co-workers. They are dependable, trustworthy and enjoy challenging work assignments and situations. Sagittarians are friendly to work with and helpful to their colleagues. They usually contribute intelligent new ideas or new methods that improve the work environment for everyone. Sagittarians always look for challenging positions and careers that develop their intellect, even if they have to work very hard in order to succeed. They also work well under the supervision of others, although by nature they would rather be the supervisors and increase their sphere of influence. Sagittarians excel at professions that allow them to be in contact with many different people and to travel to many new and exciting locations.

Love and Relationships

Sagittarians love freedom for themselves and will readily grant it to their partner. They like their relationships to be fluid, loose and ever-changing. Sagittarians tend to be fickle in love and to change their minds about their partners quite often.

Sagittarians feel threatened by a clearly defined, well-structured relationship, as it tends to limit their freedom. The Sagittarian tends to marry more than once in his or her life.

Sagittarians in love are passionate, generous, open, benevolent and very active. They demonstrate their affections very openly. However, just like the Aries they tend to be egocentric in the way they relate to their partners. Sagittarians should develop the ability to see another's point of view, not just their own. They need to develop some objectivity and cool intellectual clarity in their relationships so that they can develop better two-way communications with their partners. Sagittarians tend to be overly idealistic about their partners and about love in general. A cool and rational attitude will help them perceive reality more clearly and help them avoid disappointment.

Home and Domestic Life

Sagittarians tend to grant a lot of freedom to their family. They like big homes and many children and are one of the most fertile signs of the zodiac. However, when it comes to their children Sagittarians generally err on the side of allowing them too much freedom. Sometimes their children get the idea that there are no limits. However, allowing freedom in the home is basically a positive quality – so long as some measure of balance is maintained – for it enables all family members to develop as they should.

Horoscope for 1994

Major Trends

1993 was a year of communication, intellectual and scientific attainment and the fulfilment – to a degree – of your fondest hopes and wishes.

Where 1993 was a social year, 1994 is spiritual – a year of your partial 'withdrawal' from society; a year of communion with the deepest sources of wisdom and inspiration; a year of getting closer to whatever divinity you worship. The emphasis this year is on self-knowledge – of your own past and the ancient, collective past of the human race. It is a spiritual quest in the deepest sense of the word. And, though you are not too fond of introversion – you like to be out there mingling with people and exploring all the outer dimensions of life – this year some introversion is called for and is advised.

Part of the reason for this compelling spiritual need is that last year you were successful in fulfilling many of your fondest hopes and wishes. Theoretically you should be sated; you should be happy. But the cosmos has revealed to you – through all the stressful aspects to your 11th House of Fondest Wishes – that realizing some of your dreams did not make you as happy as you'd thought. In order to form new and better wishes, a temporary period of introspection – and some sacrifice – is called for. Understand that the things you are asked to sacrifice this year are not essentials. You sacrifice lesser things – some aspects of your social life, for example – in order to attain greater things – a state of inner grace.

You will be involved in charitable and philanthropic works this year. You shall derive great inner joy from helping the needy and the less fortunate. You will spend more time in prayer and meditation. You shall develop your ability to contact your own inner wisdom and inspiration – directly, personally and without intermediaries. You will become more interested in psychic activity and phenomena. You will develop a better understanding of your dream life. Perhaps most important, you will strengthen your intuitive powers and learn to follow their lead.

This year will see you discover secret enemies and learn how to defeat them. You will also discover secret support – secret friends and helpers – that you never knew you had before. Your inner life is more infinite, more exciting, more adventurous than your outer life. But don't worry about leading an eternally monastic lifestyle. By year's end you will have accomplished what was needed and be back in the world again – stronger, more attuned and better equipped to cope.

Health

Though your health does not seem to be a major concern this year – your 6th House of Health is not overly active – still there are things you should know. On 29th January, Saturn – the great cosmic tester – moves into a stressful aspect to you. This is a long-term trend that will affect you for the next two to three years.

Of course, one planet by itself is not enough to cause any serious health problem – especially when so many of the other long-term planets are making harmonious aspects to you. But your vitality will not be what you are accustomed to. Your physical limits – and endurance – will be tested. Sagittarians are noted for their superabundant energy and you like to always be on the go. Being the visionary that you are, you are unaware of limits – whether they be financial, intellectual or physical. To a Sagittarius, everything is possible. But for the next two years, you will see that your physical body has got its limits. And though these limits can be greatly expanded, they exist nevertheless.

Basically, Saturn is calling on you to set realistic physical perimeters for yourself. It wants to make sure that you get enough sleep, enough of the right kind of foods and enough overall relaxation. It is saying to you, 'yes, I will provide you with vitality for what you really need to do, but not for what is unnecessary.' Focus on priorities. Focus on essentials. Do more with less energy. Don't waste energy on things that don't concern you. Mind your own business and handle your true responsibilities – let the false ones go.

Your periods of greatest vitality this year will be from 20th March to 20th April, 23rd July to 23rd August and 22nd November to 21st December.

Your periods of lowest vitality will be from 18th February to 19th March, 20th May to 21st June and 24th August to 22nd September. These are the periods to watch out for, as other planets – in addition to Saturn – will make stressful aspects to you at these times. Be sure to rest and relax more during these periods. Listen to your body and its needs.

Home and Domestic Life

As with Scorpio and Libra, your domestic situation has been affected and made more turbulent and unstable because of Uranus and Neptune's rare conjunctions.(When two or more planets occupy the same place in the zodiac (within 10 to 15 degrees of one another) they are said to be conjunct, or conjoined. The results of this blending of influences depend very much on the nature of the planets involved. For example, if Venus is your ruling planet and is conjunct to Jupiter either in your birth chart or by transit (the daily movements of the planets), then Jupiter, the planet of good luck and expansion, influences your ruler in a very positive way.) Like these other signs, you have been searching for your dream house, dream family and ideal emotional support system. Like them, you have been experimenting in your domestic life. You have moved house many times. There have been some family 'disturbances' and realignments of family relations. You have tended to idealize your family members to the point where you no longer see them as people. All of this was – and still is – part of the celestial plan for your life.

You are being led to your ideal domestic situation. As long as you understand that this situation will come about as an evolutionary process – a gradual, continuing improvement – you will handle and even enjoy all the domestic turbulence going on. Don't be impatient for quick solutions – you will only increase the amount of instability in your emotional and family life.

Your domestic scene is further activated this year by Saturn's move into your 4th solar House of Home and Family. For men this means there are challenges and perhaps some disappointments to be faced with regard to their mother (or the mother figures in their lives). For women, it is their father (or father figures) who will seem over-controlling in the home and in family politics. They support you, but there are uncomfortable and restrictive conditions attached. Your solar chart indicates that they enforce the idea that your duty to your family should come before your own personal interests. They place responsibilities on you that are unenjoyable – but which are unavoidable. Where you would like more freedom and more experimentation, they push for traditional solutions and greater structure. Their call of duty is hard to ignore.

Your solar chart shows that you feel cramped in your everyday domestic scene. This could manifest as sheer lack of space: someone older moves in with you and there is less room for your normal activities. But it could also prove to indicate a lack of emotional space: you cannot express your feelings in your normal way. Cramped quarters often lead to depression. There is a coolness between you and your family. You relate to each other through duty rather than love and good feeling. Sibling rivalry deepens into sibling warfare. You will need to practise the art of forgiveness this year. You must try to bring love and good-will to your family and domestic situation.

This is your major challenge this year. Remember that the

decision to love is not dependent on others but on you. You needn't *like* everyone but you must *love* everyone. As long as you love you can safely avoid any family members – who are not part of your immediate household – who are difficult to get along with. This will minimize the disharmony. Remember, too, to love yourself as well.

This is a good year for redecorating at home. It's a good time for rearranging the furniture, switching the bedrooms round and adopting a new look for your home. There is not that great a need to add anything new – all you need do is make better use of the space you already have. Get as close as you can to your ideal home within your existing circumstances. The correct placement of objects and furniture – considered a great art form by many Eastern religions – can improve the psychic energy in your home dramatically. On a monetary note, your domestic costs should be reduced this year.

Love and Social Life

Spiritual and domestic interests take priority over your love life this year. This doesn't mean that you won't have a social life – of course you will – only that it is less important to you.

Basically your love life is not causing you any major problems, so you needn't focus on it too much. The cosmos doesn't impel you in any particular direction. You have a free hand to shape your social life as you will.

Mercury – a fleet and often erratic planet – is the lord of your love life. Its movements, positions, velocity and aspects are keys to how you will experience love this year. When Mercury moves forward at its normal high speed you tend to have great social confidence. You tend to get your way in love. When Mercury slows down, you become more cautious in love matters. When Mercury goes retrograde (backwards) you feel that you too are 'moving in reverse' in your relationships. Love issues which you thought were resolved come up again for review at these times.

Furthermore, because Mercury moves through the different signs and houses of your horoscope so quickly, your attitudes and needs in love also change very quickly. One month you want one thing, the next month something else. This social fickleness is normal for you – especially this year. All these short-term trends are covered in more detail in the month-by-month forecasts – so be sure to read them.

Though your love life is less dynamic overall this year, there will be periods when – because of the short-term planets – it will be quite active. These periods are from 26th April to 21st June and 4th July to 17th August. For singles the former period holds a passionate and very confusing affair – a real roller-coaster ride.

Career and Finance

This area of your life has been prominent in your solar horoscope for some years now. This trend continues in 1994. The way you earn your living and your attitudes to money and possessions are undergoing radical and revolutionary changes. Basically you are being led to economic and financial freedom. For most of you this quest for economic freedom has been a matter of trial and error. You try one thing and then another until you hit on the right investment, the right budget, financial plan, etc. You have been quick to try every scheme or approach that promises wealth and financial freedom. Now you are realizing that there is no universal system that works for everyone.

Uranus and Neptune are teaming up to upset the best-laid plans of mice and men. In order to succeed, you must understand that every soul comes into this world completely supplied with their own means to prosperity. Your supply is essentially spiritual – but it translates, via wonderful and miraculous processes, into 'cold cash'. Your way of earning a livelihood was preordained long before you were born. Your task is merely to discover it. This is the challenge and lesson of your Uranus-Neptune transit.

Self-improvement

Saturn moving through your 4th solar House of Home and Family Life shows that you are forced to manage and control your emotions more. You cannot afford to express negative emotion right now as this would only make your family situation even worse. Many times you are forced to bite your tongue and seethe inwardly. Managing your moods and emotions in this way is basically a good thing and, if you have not learned how to do so by now, this is a good year to start.

Be aware that managing your emotions is not the same thing as repressing them. The former is healthy and positive; the latter can destroy your well-being. When you are caught in a negative state don't just unload your feelings on innocent and unwilling victims who happen to be in your path. Talk to a friend, counsellor or professional therapist. If none of these is available, release your pent-up feelings by writing them out on a piece of paper – then throw the paper away. Then, try to direct your moods in a positive direction.

Month-by-month Forecasts

January

Best Days Overall: 1st, 8th, 9th, 17th, 18th, 19th, 27th, 28th

Most Stressful Days Overall: 2nd, 3rd, 15th, 16th, 22nd, 23rd, 29th, 30th

Best Days for Love: 2nd, 3rd, 10th, 11th, 22nd, 23rd, 31st

Best Days for Money: 4th, 5th, 6th, 7th, 10th, 11th, 12th, 13th, 14th, 15th, 16th, 22nd, 23rd, 25th, 26th

SAGITTARIUS

Though as a Fire sign you don't feel particularly comfortable with the massive concentration of planets in Capricorn (an Earth sign) right now, there are many redeeming features to this state of play – most notably for your financial life. With 60 to 70 per cent of the planets in your 2nd House of Money for the better part of the month, substantial improvements to your net worth are taking place. You are earning more and spending more. This is the month to acquire those prized items you've been coveting for so long. You are an uncannily smart shopper with a nose for a good deal. Your business sense is unusually sharp right now as well.

With all of this financial activity going on it is understandable that you are a little confused. But this confusion – happily – does not come from want but from abundance. One piece of advice might be offered: you may want to wait for the new Moon of the 11th before making long-term investments of extra capital. This new Moon will, as the month unfolds, clarify any dark financial places. From your solar horoscope it looks as if you're buying a home.

Although you do feel some psychological discomfort with the dominant Earth Energy of the period, your physical vitality and constitution remain strong. Your health is good all month. You also seem well able to exploit the current mood to aid your business life. People are yearning for safety, security, order and tradition. They feel cautious and prudent and are loath to try out new – especially untested – things. You, Sagittarius, are not naturally of this temperament at all – but it works for you on a business level.

With all this money rolling in, you are – for the early part of the month – unusually charitable and generous. This is fine until the 20th, but after then try to keep this unregulated giving in check. Give, of course, but in proportion to what you can comfortably afford.

Your love planet, Mercury is highly stimulated this month, but love matters are subordinate to your financial life. For you, love means financial support right now. Singles find themselves attracted to those much wealthier than themselves.

273

February

Best Days Overall: 4th, 5th, 14th, 15th, 23rd, 24th

Most Stressful Days Overall: 11th, 12th, 18th, 19th, 20th, 25th, 26th

Best Days for Love: 1st, 2nd, 3rd, 9th, 10th, 11th, 12th, 18th, 19th, 20th, 21st, 22nd, 27th, 28th

Best Days for Money: 2nd, 3rd, 7th, 8th, 11th, 12th, 21st, 22nd

You are going to be involved with your intellectual and communication interests this month, Sagittarius, and for the most part these activities are happy and successful. Courses, seminars, lectures and the like are very much the order of the day right now. Your intellectual capacities – always strong – are enhanced further. Only remember that Mercury, the lord of communication goes retrograde on the 11th and stays that way for the rest of the month. Try to schedule your marketing, mailing and sales activities for before this date. You will be successful regardless, but if you schedule important business for before the retrograde you will avoid unnecessary headaches and will succeed with less effort.

Mercury's retrograde also affects your love and social life. A current relationship needs more thought. Weddings or long-term commitments should not be embarked upon during this period. Have patience with your beloved. Singles can use this period to review and revise their social agenda. What do you really want in a lover or partner? This is the time to think things through. It is also a good time to analyse and improve your social skills.

Mercury is also your career planet, so during its retrograde motion try to avoid major career moves. Wait until next month.

When there is so much power in the sign of Aquarius – as

exists until the 18th – people generally tend to be cool, mental and detached. Sometimes they are completely divorced from their passions and enthusiasms. Everything has to be logical and scientific. Thus your hot, fiery, uplifting temperament is much appreciated by others this month. You heat them up – motivate them – without putting out your own fire. Your health and self-esteem, therefore, are especially good until the 18th. After that try to rest and relax more.

Earnings are steady (at a good level) for the better part of the month. But after the 18th, they get even stronger. Again, your solar horoscope shows that you are spending money on – and perhaps saving other money for – a home. You are spending on your family and they reciprocate by providing you with financial opportunities. Property deals are favourable. A family business venture promises greater earnings.

March

> Best Days Overall: 4th, 5th, 13th, 14th,
> 23rd, 24th, 31st
>
> Most Stressful Days Overall: 10th, 11th,
> 12th, 18th, 19th, 25th, 26th
>
> Best Days for Love: 1st, 2nd, 8th, 9th,
> 13th, 14th, 18th, 19th, 20th, 21st, 23rd,
> 24th, 29th, 30th, 31st
>
> Best Days for Money: 1st, 2nd, 6th, 7th,
> 10th, 11th, 12th, 20th, 21st, 22nd, 29th,
> 30th

The overwhelming power in your solar horoscope is in the lower – or subjective – half of your solar chart. Thus you are much more interested in issues such as personal happiness, family and emotional harmony than in outside, public or career concerns. This is unusual for you, Sagittarius. Right now you would rather be in emotional harmony than successful – and this is all to the good. There are times in life when we need to get these things in order. The power in Pisces – a Water, emotional and introverted sign – is making you more aware of family values, of the importance of a strong support system, of being a better parent and the like.

You are analysing your emotions and moods this month. You are making great psychological progress which will lead – in the future – to a stronger career and public image. The higher you go, the deeper must be your foundation.

The duties to your family and the chores of everyday living weigh heavily on you this month. Rest and relax more. Handle tasks in order of priority and let lesser things go. Though you are the optimist *par excellence* of the zodiac even you feel the pull of the whirlpool of negative emotion at times. Consider this self-knowledge. You are looking at feelings that were always there beneath the surface. The fact that they've come out – through doing trivial chores and perhaps because of some conflicts within the family – lets you resolve them forever.

This is a subjective, introverted month. Even socially you want to be a hermit, staying at home with your beloved. You want nurturing in love. Your social charisma will improve as Mercury starts to go forward on the 5th. But still you don't seem to stray far from home in the pursuit of romance.

Your energy, vitality and zest for life come back as the Sun moves into hot Aries on the 20th. Spring is always a happy period for you, but this year it is even happier and more welcome. Most – though not all – of the drudgery of life is off you and you feel like going out, partying and seeing the world again. You become more like your usual extroverted self.

April

Best Days Overall: 1st, 9th, 10th, 19th, 20th, 27th, 28th

SAGITTARIUS

Most Stressful Days Overall: 7th, 8th, 14th, 15th, 21st, 22nd

Best Days for Love: 2nd, 3rd, 7th, 8th, 9th, 10th, 12th, 13th, 14th, 15th, 19th, 20th, 21st, 22nd, 30th

Best Days for Money: 2nd, 3rd, 7th, 8th, 17th, 18th, 25th, 26th

The situation with your family seems a bit 'militant' this month. You display a tendency to get things done by force rather than diplomacy. Do your best to keep your passions in check, but don't repress negative emotion. Express it in a way that damages no one – with a counsellor or friend. Get negative feelings behind you as soon as possible and direct your moods positively. The expression of the anger you feel will dispel any tendency to depression – and more importantly, will prevent things from getting too hot to handle.

There seems to be lot of work going on around the house – repairs, redecorating and/or renovating. This too, perhaps, contributes to family tensions.

Aside from the above this is a happy month. You are definitely having more fun, going out more, playing more. Love is hot and passionate. You tend to jump into things without forethought – only to be sorry later on. But nothing will deter you now. Spring fever is upon you and you are quite willing to take a few lumps in return for pleasures gained.

You are not at all interested in the serious side of love right now. You want to play with your partner – to have some fun. Those involved with a Sagittarius should take note. Entertain him or her and he or she is yours. Mercury's speedy and direct motion again shows great social confidence and the tendency to be fickle in love. It's not really fickleness, just that your needs and tastes in love are changing rapidly.

Financial issues are volatile most of the month. Big

financial surprises – unexpected earnings and unexpected expenses – come your way. Your earnings stabilize after the 20th and by the end of the month you should have a net increase in personal wealth.

Your health is excellent all month but especially before the 20th. Keep your throat and the neck loose and relaxed – pay special attention to this region and your health will be even better than it has been of late.

May

> Best Days Overall: 6th, 7th, 8th, 16th, 17th, 25th, 26th

> Most Stressful Days Overall: 4th, 5th, 11th, 12th, 13th, 19th, 20th, 31st

> Best Days for Love: 1st, 2nd, 3rd, 11th, 12th, 13th, 21st, 22nd, 23rd, 24th, 31st

> Best Days for Money: 4th, 5th, 14th, 15th, 23rd, 24th, 27th, 28th, 31st

Until the 21st you are trying to reconcile your work goals – the demands of your job – with your urges for fun and pleasure. This is at best a difficult balancing act. The demands of the workplace seem to win – but not completely.

In a way it is well that you are focusing on your job. Major shake-ups and upheavals are about to happen and you don't want to give 'the powers that be' any excuse for involving you in their negative plans. The solar eclipse of the 10th is going to trigger these things off. The solar horoscope shows a radical change in work and work philosophy – this could mean a revamping of management and management style.

A minor health issue will come up for resolution this month – though it is nothing serious. The demands of the workplace also conflict with your spiritual and philanthropic activities. Remember the old maxim, 'Render unto Caesar that which is Caesar's and render unto God that which is God's.' Your partner's spiritual life gets shaken up as well. Listen attentively and non-judgmentally to your partner's dreams and ESP experiences. He or she just needs to talk to someone.

The more important eclipse as far as you're concerned is the lunar eclipse of the 25th that occurs in your own sign. Those of you with November birthdays will feel it more keenly – though all of you will be affected to some degree. Rest and relax more from the 24th to the 26th. Don't invite trouble by entering into risky, adventurous pursuits just then. Take a reduced, relaxed schedule. Break records another day.

Your social agenda is most interesting during this period. A lover or would-be lover goes to unbelievable lengths to win your heart. He or she seems willing to stop at nothing. You have a taste for the unusual in love as both Mercury and Venus are 'out of bounds' for the better part of the month. Romance is exciting and opportunities plentiful. Good communication and the pursuit of common intellectual interests help foster romance.

June

Best Days Overall: 3rd, 4th, 13th, 14th, 21st, 22nd, 30th

Most Stressful Days Overall: 1st, 8th, 9th, 15th, 16th, 28th, 29th

Best Days for Love: 1st, 8th, 9th, 10th, 11th, 19th, 20th, 21st, 22nd, 28th, 29th, 30th

Best Days for Money: 1st, 10th, 11th, 19th, 20th, 23rd, 24th, 28th, 29th

The subjectivity – the inward-orientation – of the current period doesn't sit well with you, Sagittarius – not physically and not psychologically. It's just not your style. You want to be out there doing things, achieving, conquering the world – and inter-galactic space as well! Your feelings of frustration are understandable. As difficult as this must be, the wild horses of your soul need to be reined in right now. Rest and relax more. The universe has not stopped but only paused temporarily. It is taking an in-breath; presently it shall breathe out – causing renewed activity.

Your love and social life is active at this time, though you should not schedule a marriage after the 12th. Caution in love is definitely indicated. Someone who is a teacher (or desires to be a teacher) or spiritual guide is now romantically involved with you. Let the relationship grow and develop. You want passion and he or she wants to teach. The new Moon of the 9th is going to clarify your love life as the month progresses. Whether your problem is too much love (which seems likely now) or not enough, the necessary knowledge for how to proceed will be given you. Clarity is the greatest gift we can ask of the celestial powers, because with clarity the next step is easily seen.

This is a good period to review your career goals and objectives. The clearer you become on these issues, the better able you will be to take advantage of the opportunities awaiting you in the next few months.

With your love and financial planets all moving backwards now avoid making major purchases or long-term financial (or love) commitments. Take whatever constructive steps you can in these areas and then let go. Things are out of your hands right now. Other people have to make decisions and they need time to review and re-assess things. Cumbersome bureaucracy seems involved here. Meanwhile, learn the virtue of patience.

SAGITTARIUS

July

Best Days Overall: 1st, 10th, 11th, 19th, 20th, 27th, 28th, 29th

Most Stressful Days Overall: 5th, 6th, 12th, 13th, 25th, 26th

Best Days for Love: 1st, 5th, 6th, 7th, 8th, 9th, 10th, 11th, 12th, 16th, 17th, 21st, 22nd, 25th, 26th, 30th, 31st

Best Days for Money: 7th, 8th, 9th, 16th, 17th, 21st, 22nd, 25th, 26th

All of the energy in Water signs, though it does not affect your health, does make you feel that your fire is being put out. Even you – with your superabundant optimism – have a tough time staying enthusiastic right now. However, there are some redeeming elements to the coming month.

With your ruling planet Jupiter finally going forward again after some months of backward motion you feel that your life is progressing again. Mercury, your love planet, also starts going forward this month, improving your social charisma and increasing romantic opportunities. So, regardless of what you might feel, the objective reality is quite good.

Financial issues are still a bit frustrating as plans, deals and investments are delayed. To compensate, however, your partner's income is sharply on the rise. Your ability to make money for others and to attract investors to your pet projects is also strong. People from your distant past – perhaps childhood friends – reappear during this period as either potential lovers or investors. Debts will be paid this month as well. In financial matters, mood is paramount. Avoid making important financial decisions when you are tired or depressed. Investors will tune in to what you really feel about a project rather than to what you say.

Travel opportunities increase as the month progresses. A

trip by water – though slower – is better than air or ground travel now.

In love you are aggressive and courageous – but a bit fickle and moody as well. You see something you like and chase it. When you get it your mood changes and you want something else. Meanwhile, lovers want to be nurtured and to indulge in a bit of nostalgia. Give in to their need for talking out their feelings – though these could at times be negative or traumatic. You can be of real service to your beloved if you just listen without judgement.

Career progress is made after the 11th, as women in your work life promote your goals. But this is just a prelude to more important developments that will happen next month.

August

Best Days Overall: 6th, 7th, 15th, 16th, 24th, 25th

Most Stressful Days Overall: 1st, 2nd, 3rd, 8th, 9th, 21st, 22nd, 23rd, 29th, 30th

Best Days for Love: 1st, 2nd, 3rd, 6th, 7th, 11th, 12th, 15th, 16th, 18th, 19th, 20th, 26th, 27th, 29th, 30th

Best Days for Money: 4th, 5th, 13th, 14th, 17th, 18th, 21st, 22nd, 23rd, 31st

You are making great strides psychologically and spiritually now. If you have been using the energies properly you will now have deeper insights into other people and why they feel as they do. During this period there is more fun in your life. Some of the general sluggishness and moodiness is lifted.

There is some conflict now between your inner spiritual experiences and organized religion, but this conflict is only on the surface. On some quite deep level the two teachings converge – they are actually harmonious. Look for that deep level.

SAGITTARIUS

Your health is excellent until the 23rd, after which you should rest and relax more and deal only with priorities. With the demands of your career so strong then, you will need to think long and hard as to what your true priorities are. It is very important for your health that you maintain a loving heart and harmonious love and social relationships right now. Praise and enjoy everyone. If there is someone in your life whom you cannot praise, let that person move out of your life. You cannot afford – energywise – to be around that kind of person.

The health of your kidneys is particularly vital to your overall health during this period. A good reflexologist or kinesiologist can stimulate and strengthen these organs in a drugless, preventive way. Green is a good colour to wear after the 23rd.

Personal earnings are not what they should be this month, but your ability to work with other people's money is very much enhanced. Investors are interested in speculating on a pet project of yours. You will choose glory and prestige over money at this time and this is a wise choice. Earnings will follow in due course. Great career progress is made after the 23rd and the charitable works you are doing are aiding this along.

Love is fun-filled and passionate most of the month. Mercury's speedy forward motion shows that your social charisma and confidence are strong. Singles are dating many different people. Your affections and needs change rapidly. A love you meet after the 18th will do much for your career.

September

Best Days Overall: 3rd, 4th, 11th, 12th, 20th, 21st, 30th

Most Stressful Days Overall: 5th, 6th, 18th, 19th, 25th, 26th

283

Best Days for Love: 7th, 8th, 9th, 15th, 16th, 18th, 19th, 25th, 26th, 27th, 28th, 29th

Best Days for Money: 1st, 9th, 10th, 13th, 14th, 18th, 19th, 28th, 29th

With most of the planets moving forward now and congregating in the top and eastern halves of your chart, you are entering a strong period of achievement. You are independent. You create conditions and circumstances that the world must accept. You don't need to adapt to the world; the world needs to adapt to you. Build wisely. The thrust now is to outer, objective success – the career heights. You are concerned with your place in society and within your profession. Emotional harmony and personal happiness can wait as far as you are concerned. You can't be bothered with unpleasant family burdens right now – you've got mountains to climb.

Great career progress is being made. Your circle of friends and acquaintances is enlarging. Career moves are being guided by the hands of a higher power, as the new Moon of the 5th will show. Friends and partners are pushing your career success. But a conflict is brewing over finances. Keep the mood calm and compromise on money.

Healthwise, rest and relax more until the 23rd. By all means do what is necessary to aid your career, but avoid the unnecessary. Your kidneys may need special care – a good reflexologist, masseur, chiropractor, acupuncturist or kinesiologist will know how to stimulate them in a drugless, natural way. Harmony in love – and this might be difficult right now – and balanced (neither too much nor too little) sexual activity is also important healthwise. Your vitality improves dramatically after the 23rd.

But your major joy right now comes from spiritual matters. Always a generous person, this month you are even more so. Whatever is happening outside, inside you know you are rich and can afford to give. The joy that you get from this is payment enough. Great and happy spiritual revelations are coming to you. You have a chance to solve some of the great mysteries of life – mysteries that the greatest minds of all ages have grappled with. For you these mysteries may now be solved.

October

> Best Days Overall: 1st, 8th, 9th, 17th, 18th, 19th, 27th, 28th

> Most Stressful Days Overall: 2nd, 3rd, 15th, 16th, 22nd, 23rd, 24th, 30th, 31st

> Best Days for Love: 6th, 7th, 13th, 14th, 15th, 16th, 22nd, 23rd, 24th, 25th, 26th

> Best Days for Money: 6th, 7th, 10th, 11th, 15th, 16th, 25th, 26th

Charity, altruism, spirituality and utopian causes are dominant this month, Sagittarius. Always altruistic, this month you are even more so. You are acutely aware of the changes that need to take place to make the world a better place and you are ready to do your bit. Charitable, philanthropic and ministerial activities are fascinating. They offer you a way of being of service to *all*, to the world at large. Political causes also interest you, but ministerial interests outweigh them as the month progresses.

You are working behind the scenes right now. You are content to do good works and to exercise power covertly. The idea of anonymous power delights you as it makes you less a target for the opposition. Covert struggles result in your favour. You never had any inkling as to the depth of your secret support. Your status in a spiritual organization goes up. Prayer and meditation bring illuminating spiritual experiences.

Your love life is also 'behind the scenes' and perhaps should be kept that way for a while. A current relationship is not yet ready for the public eye. Enjoy it in secret. With Mercury going retrograde from the 9th to the 30th avoid making major career or romantic changes. Give yourself time to analyse the situation more thoroughly. When in doubt do nothing – though this is difficult advice for you to follow.

Your health and self-esteem are excellent all month. Your personal image is changing drastically. You are re-inventing yourself along spiritual lines. You dress and present yourself with understated elegance. You project an aura of mysterious glamour. People can't quite make out what you're about and you like that.

Finances are improving dramatically. Stalled projects get the go-ahead now as both Uranus and Neptune start moving forward in your 2nd House of Money. The retrograde of Venus from the 13th onwards suggests that you should be more prudent and cautious at work and with friends. Mistakes at work will only have to be rectified – to your cost and aggravation. Best to do it right the first time.

November

Best Days Overall: 5th, 6th, 14th, 15th, 24th, 25th

Most Stressful Days Overall: 11th, 12th, 19th, 20th, 26th, 27th

Best Days for Love: 1st, 2nd, 3rd, 4th, 9th, 10th, 11th, 12th, 19th, 20th, 21st, 22nd, 30th

Best Days for Money: 3rd, 4th, 7th, 8th, 11th, 12th, 21st, 22nd, 30th

This is a mixed and volatile month – both personally and for the world at large. Whenever there is as much power in the sign of Scorpio as there is this month you can expect people to be explosive and intense. When there is power in Scorpio people become more uncompromising and extreme in their positions. If their positions are just, great progress can be made. If they are unjust – look out.

So, the psychological atmosphere right now is a bit too intense for your liking. You are optimistic, happy and fiery. Intense emotions threaten to smother your fire. The two eclipses this month will trigger this fervent Scorpio energy into dynamic activity. Take a reduced schedule around the 3rd and the 18th.

The good news this month is that you are more independent, more able to shape your life according to your own tastes. You are much less dependent on others for your progress. Also, the uncomfortable psychological atmosphere – tense, edgy, volatile – doesn't affect your health or general vitality. Nor does it affect your finances – which are stronger than they've been in months. In fact, you can expect the two eclipses to enhance your income, for the shake-ups they produce in the world at large and in those around you provide financial opportunities for you. Your net worth increases by month's end.

The two eclipses are removing obstructions to your spiritual and psychological progress – two important areas of late. Your spiritual progress gets severely tested. Secret, covert enemies and obstacles (many of which lurk in your own mind) get flushed out and can now be dealt with. Secret friends and supporters are also unmasked. Your status in a spiritual or charitable organization undergoes radical change. Watch what happens within this organization over the next six months. A shake-up at work ultimately benefits you.

Your love life is improving day by day. Singles find love in spiritual organizations. Those looking for love will profit from meditating on their love ideal rather than running around seeking it in all the wrong places. Keep love affairs secret this month. Flaunting a current affair will only draw negative vibrations to you.

December

Best Days Overall: 2nd, 3rd, 11th, 12th, 21st, 22nd, 30th

Most Stressful Days Overall: 8th, 9th, 10th, 16th, 17th, 23rd, 24th

Best Days for Love: 1st, 2nd, 3rd, 8th, 9th, 10th, 11th, 12th, 16th, 17th, 19th, 20th, 23rd, 24th, 28th, 29th

Best Days for Money: 1st, 4th, 5th, 8th, 9th, 10th, 11th, 12th, 19th, 20th, 21st, 22nd, 28th, 30th

With 80 to 90 per cent of the planets still in the eastern half of your solar chart, this month you are more independent than you've been in a long time. Your destiny is truly in your own hands. You can create heaven or hell at your pleasure. Learn to create heaven.

This heralds a very happy 1995. Jupiter, your ruling planet and the planet of wealth and good fortune, is moving into your own sign on the 9th and will stay there for the next year. This is a further indication of your ability to create. You are not at the mercy of other people now and can pursue and fulfil your personal desires. Moreover, your social life doesn't seem to suffer – as it usually does – as you pursue your own interests. On the contrary, it seems to prosper. Partners and friends are happy to please you. Others admire – and perhaps even envy – your self-assertion and independence.

Love is very much in your life right now. A live-in or 'quasi-live-in' relationship is on the cards. Your partner goes to amazing lengths – way beyond the norm or beyond what you yourself would expect – in order to please you. There is such unity between you and your beloved that there is almost no feeling of 'You' and 'Me'. You two are one.

Life is straightening out and it is good. Your health and vitality are superabundant, your self-esteem and self-worth are at all-time highs. Earnings increase – and rather easily at that. The financial blockages of earlier in the year are now forgotten. Stalled projects and ideas are in full swing.

If there is a financial problem it is not in earnings *per se*, but in the fact that you don't particularly enjoy some of the things that you have to do in order to make money. Your ego feels deflated. This is a conflict that many of us go through at different times of our lives. Don't ignore your personal joy. Look for ways to incorporate it into your working life – at first gradually and eventually totally.

Your spiritual and philanthropic life is still quite strong this month, but over the long term you are coming out of your spiritual hibernation. You are about to enter a period where you apply what you've learned to your personal life.

Capricorn

ỳ

THE GOAT
Birthdays from
21st December
to 19th January

Personality Profile

CAPRICORN AT A GLANCE

Element – Earth

Ruling planet – Saturn
  Love planet – Moon
  Money planet – Uranus
  Planet of health and work – Mercury
  Planet of home and family life – Mars

Colours – black, indigo

Colours that promote love, romance and social harmony – puce, silver

Colour that promotes earning power – ultramarine blue

Gem – black onyx

CAPRICORN

Metal – lead

Scents – magnolia, pine, sweet pea, wintergreen

Quality – cardinal (= activity)

Qualities most needed for balance – warmth, spontaneity, a sense of fun

Strongest virtues – sense of duty, organization, perseverance, patience, ability to take the long-term view

Deepest needs – to manage, take charge and administrate

Characteristics to avoid – pessimism, depression, undue materialism and undue conservatism

Signs of greatest overall compatibility – Taurus, Virgo

Signs of greatest overall incompatibility – Aries, Cancer, Libra

Sign most helpful to career – Libra

Sign most helpful for emotional support – Aries

Sign most helpful financially – Aquarius

Sign best for marriage and/or partnerships – Cancer

Sign most helpful for creative projects – Taurus

Best sign to have fun with – Taurus

Signs most helpful in spiritual matters – Virgo, Sagittarius

Best day of the week – Saturday

Understanding the Capricorn Personality

The virtues of Capricorns are such that there will always be those for or against them. Many admire them, many dislike them. Why? It seems that it is because of Capricorn's power urges. A well-developed Capricorn has his or her eyes set on the heights of power, prestige and authority. In the sign of Capricorn ambition is not a fatal flaw but rather the highest virtue.

Capricorns are not frightened by the resentment their authority may sometimes cause. In Capricorn's cool, calculated, organized mind all the dangers are already factored into the equation – the unpopularity, the animosity, the misunderstandings, even the outright slander – and a plan is always in place for dealing with these things in the most efficient way. To the Capricorn, situations that would terrify an ordinary mind are merely problems to be managed, bumps on the road to ever-growing power, effectiveness and prestige.

Some people attribute pessimism to the Capricorn sign, but this is a bit deceptive. It is true that Capricorns like to take into account the negative side of things. It is also true that they love to imagine the worst possible scenario in every undertaking. Other people might find such analyses depressing, but Capricorns only do these things so that they can formulate a way out – an escape route or 'golden parachute'.

Capricorns will argue with success. They will show you that you are not doing as well as you think you are. Capricorns do this to themselves as well as to others. They do not mean to discourage you but rather to root out any impediments to your greater success. A Capricorn boss or supervisor feels that no matter how good the performance there is always room for improvement. This explains why Capricorn supervisors are difficult to handle and even infuriating at times. Their actions are, however, quite often effective – they can get their subordinates to improve and become better at their jobs.

CAPRICORN

Capricorn is a born manager and administrator. Leo is better at being king or queen, but Capricorn is better at being prime minister – the person who administrates the monarchy, government or corporation, the person actually wielding power.

Capricorn is interested in the virtues that last, in the things that will stand the test of time and trials of circumstance. Temporary fads and fashions mean little to a Capricorn – except as things to be used for profit or power. Capricorns apply this attitude to business, love, to their thinking and even to their philosophy and religion.

Finance

Capricorns generally attain wealth and they usually earn it. They are willing to work long and hard for what they want. They are quite amenable to forgoing a short-term gain in favour of a long-term benefit. Financially, they come into their own later on in life.

However, if Capricorns are to attain their financial goals they must shed some of their strong conservatism. Perhaps this is the least desirable trait of the Capricorn. They can resist anything new merely because it *is* new and untried. They are afraid of experimentation. Capricorns need to be willing to take a few risks. They should be more eager to market new products or explore different management techniques. Otherwise, progress will leave them behind. If necessary, Capricorns must be ready to change with the times, to discard old methods that don't work in modern conditions.

Very often this experimentation will mean that Capricorns have to break with existing authority. They might even consider changing their present position or starting their own ventures. If so, they should be willing to accept all risks and just get on with it. Only then will a Capricorn be on the road to highest financial gain.

Career and Public Image

A Capricorn's ambitiousness and quest for power are evident. It is perhaps the most ambitious sign of the zodiac – and usually the most successful in a worldly sense. However, there are lessons Capricorns need to learn in order to fulfil their highest aspirations.

Intelligence, hard work, cool efficiency and organization will take them a certain distance but won't carry them to the very top. Capricorns need to cultivate the social graces, to develop a social style along with charm and an ability to get along with people. They need to bring beauty into their lives as well as efficiency and to cultivate the right social contacts. They must learn to wield power and have people love them for it – a very delicate art. They also need to learn how to bring people together in order to fulfil certain objectives. In short, Capricorns require some of the gifts – the social graces – of the Libra to get to the top.

Once they've learned this, Capricorns will be successful in their careers. They are ambitious, hard workers who are not afraid of putting in the required time and effort. Capricorns take their time in getting the job done – in order to do it well – and they like, slowly but surely, moving up the corporate ladder. Being so driven by success, Capricorns are generally liked by their bosses, who respect and trust them.

Love and Relationships

Like Scorpio and Pisces, Capricorn is a difficult sign to get to know. They are deep, introverted and like to keep their own counsel. Capricorns don't like to reveal their innermost thoughts. If you are in love with a Capricorn be patient and take your time. Little by little you will get to understand him or her.

Capricorns have a deep romantic nature, but they don't show it straight away. They are cool, matter of fact and not especially emotional. They will often show their love in practical ways.

CAPRICORN

It takes time for a Capricorn – male or female – to fall in love. They are not the love-at-first-sight type. If a Capricorn is involved with a Leo or Aries, these fire types will be totally mystified – to them the Capricorn will seem cold, unfeeling, unaffectionate and unspontaneous. Of course none of this is true, it's just that Capricorn likes to take things slow. They like to be sure of their ground before making any demonstrations of love or commitment.

Even in love affairs Capricorns are deliberate. They need more time to make decisions than is true of the other signs of the zodiac, but given this time they get just as passionate. Capricorns like a relationship to be structured, committed, well regulated, well defined, predictable and even routine. They prefer partners who are nurturers and they in turn like to nurture their partners. This is their basic psychology. Whether such a relationship is good for them is another issue altogether. Capricorns have enough routine in their lives as it is. They might be better off in relationships that are a bit more stimulating, changeable and fluctuating.

Home and Domestic Life

The home of a Capricorn – as with a Virgo – is going to be neat, orderly and well-organized. Capricorns tend to manage their families in the same way they manage their businesses. Capricorns are often so career-driven that they find little time for the home and family. Capricorns should try to get more actively involved in their family and domestic life. Capricorns do, however, take their children very seriously and are very proud parents, particularly should their children grow up to become respected members of society.

Horoscope for 1994

Major Trends

Where 1993 was a serious work, career and financial year, 1994 shapes up to be a more social year; a year in which you develop 'intangible assets' – the intellect, friendships and the ability to communicate and to relate with others as equals.

The focus on your personal image, the way you dress and the way you want others to perceive you, continues this year. This has been and will continue to be a long-term trend.

Perhaps more than any other sign you, Capricorn, understand that life here on Earth is a school. Every year – and every lifetime for that matter – we are given opportunities to develop different aspects of our character. This character-building may sound abstract but it has intensely practical implications. Our destiny arises from our character.

Where for the past two to three years your character had developed through your pursuit of financial and career goals – just as valid a path to growth as any other – this year you develop through your friendships. As a rule you know very well how to relate to others on a hierarchical level (how to relate to bosses and underlings). But do you know how to relate to equals? This is the agenda for this year's character building.

Health

Your health is unquestionably better in 1994 than it has been for many years. Saturn, your ruling planet, receives happy aspects this year, while Jupiter moves from the stressful aspect it occupied in 1993 to a harmonious one this year.

Your 6th House of Health is not particularly active this year, showing that you don't need to pay too much attention to health matters.

CAPRICORN

However, as in 1993, you are receiving an unusual influx of spiritual energy – Uranus and Neptune are still closely conjoined in your own sign. This 'downpour' tends to purify and purge one of anything undesirable – long-held toxins, germs, etc. Sometimes these purgings are abrupt and precipitous. They should not be considered evidence of disease but of growing health.

You have been undergoing – for some years now – an intellectual, emotional and physical cleansing. Uncomfortable though this may be while it is going on, the end result – a new and regenerated body – is worth it. In addition, this year these 'cleansings' are milder and you have more vitality with which to handle them. They don't make you feel as uncomfortable as they have sometimes done in the past.

Uranus and Neptune are in your 1st House of the Body and Personal Image. This shows that you are projecting a unique, original – and very unconventional – kind of glamour. You like the newest, most avant-garde fashions. The more shocking, provocative and anti-establishment, the better. This is fun and, if it gives you pleasure, carry on. But Uranus and Neptune are also making you test your physical limits. You find yourself wanting to know how many so-called physical limitations are real and how many stem merely from past conditioning? The only way to find out is to test them – but do be careful.

Your best periods healthwise will be from 1st to 20th January, 20th April to 20th May, 23rd August to 22nd September and 21st to 31st December.

Your most stressful health periods – overall – will be from 20th March to 19th April, 21st June to 22nd July and 23rd September to 23rd October. Be sure to rest and relax more at these times.

Home and Domestic Life

Your 4th solar House of Home and Family is not a particularly prominent one this year, Capricorn. You are not unduly concerned with family and domestic issues. Consider this a fortunate sign. It means there is nothing amiss – nothing too serious, anyway – and no need to divert a lot of your attention here. The cosmos does not impel you in any particular direction. You are given a free hand.

Mars is the planet that rules your domestic interests, Capricorn. Its movements, positions, velocity and aspects are keys to the way you experience this area of life. The short-term trends it dictates are discussed in the month-by-month forecasts.

One major point to mention, however, is that Mars moves speedily for the first five months of the year – until 24th May. You have more zest, energy and confidence in family and home issues during this time. You get things done around the house quickly and speedily and you tend to get your way with family members. From 4th July to 4th October, however, Mars moves slowly. Over this time you show greater prudence and cautiousness in the home and with your family. You take more time over decisions and are less likely to assert your will over your family.

Because your 4th House will get activated by the short-term, fast-moving planets at certain times this year, there will be periods when familial demands are stronger than usual. This period will be from 8th March to 24th May. On 8th March, Venus activates your domestic sphere, bringing you opportunities to create harmony with other family members and to generate pleasure from home entertainments. The Sun then activates your 4th House on 20th March, giving you more zest and energy for the simple pleasures of home and hearth and illuminating psychological issues and family relationships. This is a good time to work on building a stable home base. On 14th April, Mars (your home and family life planet) activates its own sphere in your solar horoscope. This will create a 'take charge' attitude in the home. Home repairs and construction projects are well aspected then. It also makes you more 'combative' at home – so be careful.

Love and Social Life

Your romantic life is not prominent in this year's solar horoscope. Of course there will be romance in your life and, naturally, there will be periods when there is more and periods when there is less. This is due to the fluctuating nature of the short-term, fast-moving planets. But on an overall level romance takes a back seat to other issues this year. Consider this fortunate; you are being given a free hand to shape your love life as you see fit.

You are more concerned with intellectual, platonic friendships this year than with romance. You get more fulfilment and joy from these friendships than from more torrid, passionate ones. Because passion is not involved, these relationships tend to be less threatening – and are less likely to be hurtful. Thus you are free to gain insights into aspects of other people's personalities, of their mental faculties, thought-processes, knowledge and perception. What you lose in passion you gain in knowledge.

This is also a year when you are working out your own personal identity issues and it's difficult to conduct a romance when you are not quite clear about who you are. Your self-concept is very much in a state of evolution. You are much better off working out these issues – and some of the answers you come up with will truly amaze you! – than promoting your love life. When these issues are clear you will be in a much better position to attract romance. The work you are doing on your self-concept is important and has a long-range impact on your happiness. As you change your romantic tastes will change. Besides, you want a partner who is going to love the real you and who is in harmony with the image you want to manifest. Those of you who are involved with Capricorns romantically please take note.

Singles will find that they tend to attract others who are similarly unclear about who they are. As is to be expected, this may needlessly complicate romance.

Those of you who are within a committed love relationship will find that the personal changes you undergo change the relationship. If your partner can flow with the change, all well and good. If not, the partnership may seem shaky at times.

Your most active romantic periods this year are from 21st May to 15th June, 21st June to 22nd July and 17th August to 4th October.

Since the Moon is the planet that controls your love life, Capricorn, you are generally very moody when it comes to love. Your ardour and enthusiasms wax and wane with the Moon. When the Moon waxes you have more social charisma and are more aggressive in love matters. When the Moon wanes you feel less socially confident and you tend to get rid of people in your life. Since the Moon moves around your chart more rapidly than any other planet – every 28 days or so – you experience dramatic monthly highs and lows in love (you can read more about these in the month-by-month forecasts). As a general statement for 1994, however, love blooms best when the Moon is in Cancer or Scorpio – about four to five days each month.

Career and Finance

1993 was a very powerful career year. You made great progress in your professional standing and public esteem. You received promotions and rises at work – and you worked hard to earn them.

This year you seem sated with these things. You are where you want to be in your profession – at least for now. This year you begin your search for financial freedom.

The effect of Uranus and Neptune on your health and self-image has already been mentioned. But this dynamic duo is at work on your financial life as well, for Uranus is your money planet.

You are searching for a kind of 'idealized' financial state. You may be reluctant to admit this, as your dream seems so far beyond the realm of possibility. But if you keep in mind that many great achievements began as dreams you will not heap scorn on your hopes. You will mull them over in your heart and nurture them in secret.

These grandiose dreams spur you to unusual experimentation in financial matters. You are willing to try any new-fangled financial system, fad or technique that promises easy wealth. Although your innate work ethic makes the idea of 'easy money' anathema to you, you are open to new ideas. And this is a good start. You've had – and will continue to have – some failures and some successes. This is the nature of trial and error. As you continue to explore unconventional and non-traditional earning practices you will hit upon the method that works for you.

You are tired of the old. Tired of tradition. Yet, don't go too far overboard. Business and financial traditions are not all bad. There are elements of good in them. Keep the good things and apply them to your new ventures. Perhaps you will explore the metaphysical, spiritual aspects of finance, or get involved in fledgling industries that the establishment has ignored. Or maybe you will invent or be involved financially – either as a worker, investor or promoter – of a new technological breakthrough.

Self-improvement

You will see a big improvement in your friendships of the mind. You will expand your circle of this type of friend this year. This area of yours brings you great happiness and fulfilment. You can enhance this expansion by being open to it.

There is also another area that you might like to work on this year: your ability to make new friends. You need to work on your communication skills, to learn to express yourself intellectually. This is a year to take courses, pursue intellectual interests and study the art of communication. Developing your interests will give you things to talk about when you meet potential new friends. You will feel that you are not only the recipient of their knowledge but that you, in turn, also have knowledge to contribute. You will be highly esteemed this year because of this.

This is also a good year to get involved in improving your neighbourhood and community. You don't need to look for far-off charities – stick close to home.

Month-by-month Forecasts

January

> Best Days Overall: 2nd, 3rd, 10th, 11th, 20th, 21st, 28th, 30th

> Most Stressful Days Overall: 8th, 9th, 15th, 16th, 22nd, 23rd

> Best Days for Love: 2nd, 3rd, 10th, 11th, 22nd, 23rd, 25th, 26th, 31st

> Best Days for Money: 2nd, 3rd, 6th, 7th, 10th, 11th, 12th, 13th, 14th, 15th, 16th, 20th, 21st, 25th, 26th, 29th, 30th

This will be one of your best and happiest periods of the year, Capricorn. Enjoy.

Seldom have you experienced so much power in your own sign at one time. For the better part of the month 60 to 70 per cent of the total planetary power is focused in Capricorn. You can expect superabundant vitality. You get your own way in most things as you assert your will with unusual force – and the celestial powers back you up. You may not even realize how much strength you are projecting. You make what seems a harmless and light-hearted remark and others are devastated by it. Every little request you make is taken as a command. This is not your fault, it's just that so much energy comes through you. You need to modulate your tone: speak more softly and slowly.

Don't waste the awesome power behind you right now. You can achieve any goal you set your sights on. This is the time to push for your ambitions. Aside from the fact that there is so much of your own Capricorn energy around, every planet is moving forward this month – a highly unusual turn of events – indicating that this is the time for achievement.

With your self-esteem so high, love goes well indeed. You have unusual personal charisma. You project both strength and charm – power and glamour. Others are sure to take notice. Love is physical and sensual this month. You are loved for your personality, true – but more for your body!

Personal pleasures of all kinds are offered to you in abundance. You may be tempted to overindulge over the short term (and who can blame you?), but take care over the long term.

Financial issues are highly activated all month and are successful. After the 20th, though, you have to work a little harder than you have been.

February

> Best Days Overall: 7th, 8th, 16th, 17th, 25th, 26th
>
> Most Stressful Days Overall: 1st, 14th, 15th, 21st, 22nd, 27th, 28th
>
> Best Days for Love: 1st, 9th, 10th, 11th, 12th, 21st, 22nd
>
> Best Days for Money: 2nd, 3rd, 7th, 8th, 9th, 10th, 11th, 12th, 16th, 17th, 21st, 22nd, 25th, 26th

Though February is unquestionably a period of personal and financial achievement, you can make things even better by taking a few precautions.

Mercury's retrograde on the 11th happens in your 2nd and 3rd solar Houses – the Houses that deal with Money and Communication respectively. Thus, take extra care about communicating in general and especially when it comes to money matters. When dealing with banks, brokers or merchants make sure that everything is spelled out in detail. Check all purchases, when received, for defects or missing parts. Make sure that you and all other parties are clear on all details before you undertake any major purchases or long-term financial commitments.

With so much planetary power in your Money House this month you are not going to be able to avoid financial dealings altogether, but you can make them easier.

As you know from reading the Career and Finance section of your general horoscope for this year (see page 300), intellectual interests will be prominent in your life for the next few years. They are particularly so after the 18th, although Mercury's retrograde can create some annoying glitches. Remember, again, to take nothing for granted when communicating.

The cool Aquarian energy that dominates for the better part of this month is very comfortable for you. Your levels of self-esteem and self-confidence are high. Your health will be excellent all month as well.

You have so much going for you financially right now that even Mercury's retrograde will not affect things unduly – it might cause you some annoyance but won't hinder your earnings. Elders, superiors and women are co-operating with your financial goals. Family members are working actively and aggressively on your behalf as well. You can't lose.

Conflicts over finances still seem to be an issue with some of your friends, but any alienation is short term. By the 18th these issues should be resolved. You have to understand that some of the people you are friendly with believe that money is everything. Financial conflicts are serious matters to them.

Love and social interests are very much subordinate to finance this month. Nevertheless, the waxing Moon going through your 7th House of Love on the 21st and 22nd shows that you will not completely neglect this area of your life. Your social charisma is strong and love awaits you as soon as you show some interest.

March

> Best Days Overall: 6th, 7th, 15th, 16th, 17th, 25th, 26th

> Most Stressful Days Overall: 13th, 14th, 20th, 21st, 22nd, 27th, 28th

> Best Days for Love: 1st, 2nd, 10th, 11th, 12th, 13th, 14th, 20th, 21st, 22nd, 23rd, 24th, 31st

> Best Days for Money: 1st, 2nd, 8th, 9th, 10th, 11th, 12th, 16th, 17th, 20th, 21st, 22nd, 25th, 26th, 29th, 30th

Most of the power in this month's solar horoscope is concentrated in the lower, subjective half of your chart. Career ambitions and outward success take a back seat to subjective, emotional issues. You want personal happiness and a stable home base. Your career, though important, can wait.

Always ambitious, Capricorn, there is a method to your madness. You are marshalling important emotional support – getting your own household in order – in order to achieve your public goals. A cherished wish is temporarily delayed so that when it does manifest it will be more exquisite than you envisioned.

Education is important this month; educational opportunities are increased. You attend lectures and the like but you are also learning intuitively and through your dreams.

Sales and marketing activities are unusually favourable after the 5th as Mercury starts to go forward again. What you know is more important than whom you know as far as financial success is concerned. Your career also benefits from your increased knowledge and ability to communicate.

Your health is excellent until the 20th. You enjoy the subjective, introverted kind of energy that is in the cosmos during this time. After the 20th rest and relax more, as your domestic situation promises to be volatile and exciting. A move – probably local – seems on the cards. A new beginning is made in the home.

There's little you can do about a disappointing relationship with a platonic friend. Place your attention on your education and home life and let the relationship go. Only time can resolve this.

Earnings are stronger and more enjoyable before the 20th than afterwards. After the 20th you need to work much harder to maintain your standard of living. Expenses on the home go up after the 20th, although the long-term picture for your finances is positive.

Your love life seems relatively unimportant this month as the 7th House of Love is not active. Of course you will socialize, but you won't pay undue attention to this part of your life. The Moon waxes as it moves through your House of Love, showing that you have strong social charisma. On or near the time of the full Moon of the 27th your lover is going to boost your career.

April

> Best Days Overall: 2nd, 3rd, 12th, 13th, 21st, 22nd

> Most Stressful Days Overall: 9th, 10th, 17th, 18th, 23rd, 24th

CAPRICORN

Best Days for Love: 1st, 2nd, 3rd, 9th, 10th, 11th, 12th, 13th, 17th, 18th, 20th, 21st, 22nd, 30th

Best Days for Money: 2nd, 3rd, 4th, 5th, 7th, 8th, 12th, 13th, 17th, 18th, 21st, 22nd, 25th, 26th

Rest and relax more until the 20th and do your best to resolve emotional issues. With 70 to 80 per cent of the planets in the lower half of your solar horoscope right now you long for personal happiness and a happy home life. Emotional harmony still comes before objective, professional success.

The situation at home and with members of your household dominate this month. Circumstances get increasingly martial and militant as the month progresses. The good part is that old angers and grievances come to the surface and are resolved.

There is a lot of work going on in the home – repairs, redecorating, renovating and the like. Your tendency is to rush into home improvement without adequate forethought. This contributes in part to the unrest in the home. But all of this is temporary. By next month all these issues are resolved. The new Moon of the 11th is bringing with it important information on how to unravel these problems – which are both physical and emotional.

Domestic expenses put a strain on your wallet until the 20th. After that, though, earnings soar. Speculations become very favourable as well. Increased earnings come from creative projects, property, farming and the cosmetics industry. Money is earned pleasurably and easily.

Your health improves dramatically after the 20th, though you still need to be careful about emotional upheavals and temper tantrums. Your self-esteem increases dramatically after the 20th as well, as you enjoy the down-to-earth energy of Taurus. The pace of life slows down a bit and that suits you just fine. Mercury's speedy forward motion shows that your health needs will vary greatly as the month progresses. Until the 9th you need to take more care of your feet – massage them and don't wear shoes that cramp them. After the 9th take better care of your head (massage it regularly) and also of your emotional life. After the 25th take better care of your throat and neck.

Your love life improves after the 20th as well, though you are more interested in the fun side of romance than in getting serious.

May

> Best Days Overall: 9th, 10th, 19th, 20th, 27th, 28th
>
> Most Stressful Days Overall: 6th, 7th, 8th, 14th, 15th, 21st, 22nd
>
> Best Days for Love: 1st, 2nd, 3rd, 9th, 10th, 11th, 12th, 13th, 14th, 15th, 19th, 20th, 21st, 23rd, 24th, 29th, 30th, 31st
>
> Best Days for Money: 1st, 2nd, 3rd, 4th, 5th, 9th, 10th, 14th, 15th, 19th, 20th, 23rd, 24th, 27th, 28th, 29th, 30th, 31st

This is a happy and harmonious month for you, Capricorn. This month you understand the Biblical quotation, 'A thousand shall fall at thy side and ten thousand at thy right hand but it shall not come nigh unto thee.'

The two major eclipses this month create upheavals and long-term changes in the world at large and in many of the people around you, but you emerge from all this turmoil unscathed and happy. Your health and vitality are excellent all month. Opportunities for fun and pleasure abound. Your creativity is enhanced and many playful types of romance come to you.

The solar eclipse of the 10th creates long-term changes in a creative project by pointing out some of the project's shortcomings, which can then be corrected. Your relationship with your children is improving, but it needs to get worse before it can get better. You will be shown clearly what corrections need to be made as the month progresses.

Your mother's income (or the income of a mother figure) seems in a state of turmoil, but this is only temporarily. Income from a domestic – a work-at-home kind of project – is not what you expected but will improve with time. The value of your home seems temporarily lowered, but this is all on paper. Personal earnings are strong all month, especially until the 21st.

The lunar eclipse of the 25th also leaves you relatively unscathed. Your dream life is over-active at this time. Nightmares are likely but they present you with a good opportunity to learn how to deal with any fears they bring up. Write down any unresolved terrors from the past, as well as your feelings about them. Look at the pictures they evoke calmly and rationally.

Your charitable and philanthropic interests are changing over the long term, as are your attitudes towards a spiritual organization to which you belong.

Your partner's health is not what it should be, but you can be a positive force here. His or her poor health could be contributing to your relationship's current instability. Chances are that his or her upset has nothing to do with you. When people don't feel well they say and do all kinds of things. It's not them talking but their dis-ease.

A friend's income takes a sharp drop – temporarily, due to a sudden expense – and you might be called upon to help.

June

> Best Days Overall: 5th, 6th, 7th, 15th, 16th, 23rd, 24th

> Most Stressful Days Overall: 3rd, 4th, 10th, 11th, 17th, 18th, 30th

Best Days for Love: 1st, 8th, 9th, 10th, 11th, 17th, 18th, 21st, 22nd, 28th, 29th, 30th

Best Days for Money: 1st, 5th, 6th, 7th, 10th, 11th, 15th, 16th, 19th, 20th, 23rd, 24th, 25th, 26th, 28th, 29th

Although many planets are retrograde right now this has little effect on you. You are used to handling delays and foul-ups. No one needs to teach you patience or tell you to look at the big picture and the long-term view. These things are ingrained in your character. So, while other people are biting their nails in tension and frustration you are calm and collected. You get on with the practical things that need to be done and wait for the oppressive atmosphere to clear up.

Perhaps your biggest challenge right now is communicating your insights to others so that you can help them get through this frustrating time. If you can manage this you are truly an inspired guide. True leadership is only apparent when times are tough. When things are going well practically anyone can lead.

Until the 21st you are involved with work issues and achieving your work goals. Your normally prodigious work ethic is magnified now. After the 12th be extra careful about how you communicate to co-workers or employees. With Mercury retrograde they are apt to misunderstand you. This same advice applies to your current love, because Mercury, the lord of your work affairs, retrogrades in your 7th House of Love. Don't be afraid to ask questions and nail down apparently trifling details. This can save you a lot of heartache later on. Better to let people think you are a bit 'thick' than go away from a meeting only half-certain or in doubt as to what was decided. Getting things clear is not a sign of being thick, but a sign of intelligence.

Your social life becomes very active after the 21st, but romance is turbulent and unstable. Rebuffs and sudden break-ups can arise out of misunderstandings. There is conflict between you and your lover on personal interests – that is, your personal interests seem to conflict. Each of you needs to see the other's viewpoint more clearly. Yet, in spite of this the chemistry between you remains strong. Making up is as passionate and pleasurable as breaking up is painful.

Rest and relax more after the 21st.

July

> Best Days Overall: 2nd, 3rd, 4th, 12th, 13th, 21st, 22nd, 30th, 31st

> Most Stressful Days Overall: 1st, 7th, 8th, 9th, 14th, 15th, 27th, 28th, 29th

> Best Days for Love: 1st, 7th, 8th, 9th, 10th, 11th, 12th, 16th, 17th, 21st, 22nd, 27th, 28th, 29th, 30th, 31st

> Best Days for Money: 2nd, 3rd, 7th, 8th, 9th, 12th, 13th, 16th, 17th, 21st, 23rd, 24th, 25th, 26th, 30th, 31st

Leave financial issues aside right now and focus on your work goals. Work for love of it, not for money. Focus on providing the best possible service or product – for, though payment will not come to you straight away, it will come eventually, with interest.

Your wealth is accruing on subjective, inner levels now where you cannot see it. You will see that this growth is just as important as the more obvious kind.

Mercury, your health planet, starts to go forward and Mars enters your 6th House of Health on the same day – the 3rd July. This indicates that exercise and mood-control play unusually important roles in keeping you healthy right now. Your health is not what it should be until the 23rd, but by maintaining emotional harmony and getting adequate exercise you will help yourself pull through. A nourishing diet and psychological therapies are also called for. After the 23rd your health improves dramatically.

Your love life is unusually active all month. Love is moody, fickle and unpredictable. You are kept guessing as to what will happen next, but for you this only adds to the excitement. If you can discern your lover's mood you will better understand the situation. Singles have a tendency to retreat to the past in their quest for romance. Old flames have a new allure. A current love affair can be strengthened by recalling past experiences that were pleasurable – such as your first date, first kiss and the like. Nostalgia can definitely enhance romance.

Though your personal earnings are sluggish you don't want for anything this month. You can amass future treasure by helping others make money now. Your partner's income increases – along with his or her generosity – after the 23rd. Investors come into your life after the 23rd as well. Earnings seem dependent on circumstances beyond your control – primarily the financial position of other people.

Your interest in intellectual pursuits seems to have spurred the same interest in your parents and other members of your household.

August

Best Days Overall: 8th, 9th, 17th, 18th, 26th, 27th

Most Stressful Days Overall: 4th, 5th, 11th, 12th, 24th, 25th, 31st

Best Days for Love: 4th, 5th, 6th, 7th, 11th, 12th, 15th, 16th, 19th, 20th, 26th, 27th, 29th, 30th, 31st

Best Days for Money: 4th, 5th, 8th, 9th, 13th, 14th, 17th, 18th, 19th, 20th, 21st, 22nd, 23rd, 26th, 27th, 31st

CAPRICORN

YOUR PERSONAL HOROSCOPE 1994

The planets are getting ready to shift over to the eastern hemisphere of your solar horoscope, Capricorn, but they're not quite there yet. For just a little while longer you have to adapt to – and deal with – situations as you find them. You are reaping the effects of Karma you created in the past. Dealing with these circumstances will help you grow as a human being and will clear the decks for future creativity – coming your way very soon.

The usual conflict between three facets of your life – personal desires/inclinations, career and social duties – is very much highlighted during this period. You are forced to juggle these three different claims on your attention. Remember the middle way. And don't leave your physical needs out of the picture.

Your health is excellent all month – but especially after the 23rd. But in spite of your superabundant energy and glamorous appearance you can't speed up your receipt of earnings. They seem to creep along at their own pace. The reason for this is that this area is not in your power right now. Others have to decide on things. You must be patient.

Your love life is active in spite of your lack of enthusiasm. Social demands seem to cramp your style now. Family members – especially your parents – are urging you (perhaps in a pushy way) to go out and date more. They enjoy playing Cupid right now. The man or woman who nurtures and serves you now will win your heart.

Though earnings are not what they should be or will be, there is definite improvement after the 23rd. Earnings increase and partners are more generous with you. Definitely consider the foreign trip proposed by your partner after the 23rd. It seems profitable and enjoyable as well.

Your career proceeds favourably all month. What you lack in earnings is made up for in prestige and honours granted you. Your public popularity is enhanced. Women are recommending you for promotion and otherwise boosting your status. Until the 23rd focus on paying off debts and otherwise strengthening your financial position for the future. You might find it useful to apply for one big loan to pay off all the smaller ones. This is also a good time to approach investors about a business or pet project.

September

> Best Days Overall: 5th, 6th, 13th, 14th, 22nd, 23rd, 24th
>
> Most Stressful Days Overall: 1st, 7th, 8th, 20th, 21st, 28th, 29th
>
> Best Days for Love: 1st, 5th, 6th, 8th, 9th, 13th, 14th, 18th, 19th, 24th, 25th, 26th, 28th, 29th
>
> Best Days for Money: 1st, 5th, 6th, 9th, 10th, 13th, 14th, 15th, 16th, 18th, 19th, 22nd, 23rd, 24th, 28th, 29th

Always ambitious, this month you are even more so, Capricorn. Career-driven might be a better description. There are various reasons for this.

First off, 60 to 70 per cent of the planets are congregated at the top of your solar chart. This power at the top of your chart makes you extol outward, objective success over personal happiness and family harmony. You'd rather have glory than the dubious honour of tending to your family any day of the week. Not all people feel this way and there have been many times in your life when even you haven't felt this way. This is just the way it is now.

This overwhelming urge to career success – and you will make real progress – heightens tensions with your family and lover. They feel you are not there for them – and they are probably right. Chances are that you will be travelling more and getting more involved with work-related groups.

After the 23rd, 80 to 90 per cent of the planets will be in the eastern half of your chart. This indicates great independence and self-assertion. You have unusual power for creating conditions and circumstances and the world must accept them. Others need to adapt to you rather than vice versa.

Your health is excellent until the 23rd, after which you should rest and relax more. Mind your knees, colon and lungs. Have a health practitioner stimulate and strengthen these areas in a drugless, natural way. Prevention is better than a cure.

Socially you are both aggressive and nurturing, as is your partner. Your greatest social bliss right now seems to come from new – and platonic – friends. You appreciate the uncomplicated purity of platonic, mental friendships this month. You are mixing with the high and mighty, the rich and powerful, the beautiful and glamorous right now. They conspire to foster true love and career success for you. They can offer you solutions to relationship or career problems – as many of them have been through these conflicts themselves. Keep your eyes and ears open.

October

Best Days Overall: 2nd, 3rd, 10th, 11th, 20th, 21st, 30th, 31st

Most Stressful Days Overall: 4th, 5th, 17th, 18th, 19th, 25th, 26th

Best Days for Love: 4th, 5th, 6th, 7th, 13th, 14th, 15th, 16th, 24th, 25th, 26th

Best Days for Money: 2nd, 3rd, 6th, 7th, 10th, 11th, 12th, 13th, 14th, 15th, 16th, 20th, 21st, 25th, 26th, 30th, 31st

With 80 to 90 per cent of the planets concentrated in the eastern and top-most part of your solar horoscope chart, Capricorn, you are busy bringing about career conditions that are exactly as you want them. Seldom have you enjoyed such freedom and independence in career matters. Outward success has always been important to you and this month it becomes even more so.

Your career *carte blanche* brings with it responsibility and a need to think things through more clearly. For you – and society at large – will have to live with whatever you create. The retrograde of Venus will be a refreshing career pause that gives you time for this re-thinking and re-evaluating.

Pay rises, promotions, honours and recognition continue to come to you this month. Your professional standing increases. Men are especially helpful. The only 'fly in the ointment' is the retrograde of Mercury in your 10th House of Career from the 9th to the 30th October. This creates a tendency for miscommunication with those involved in your career. It also complicates any dealings you may have with the government and your superiors. Take more care in the way you communicate; make sure that others understand your true message.

Your social circle continues to expand all month. A group or social organization that you belong to dissolves and you join a new one. Rich and powerful friends are helping you in love and with your career. Your fondest fantasies are coming to pass.

Personal earnings still take a back seat to professional prestige, but they are improving nevertheless. Stalled projects move forward again as Uranus, your money planet, starts going direct after many months of retrograde motion. Whom you know is as important financially as who you are and what you do.

Your romantic life is not especially active this month. Romance will wax and wane with the Moon. You seem more interested in passion than in romance. From the 1st to the 5th and from the 19th to the 30th you have little enthusiasm for love interests. However, affairs of the heart proceed more smoothly from the 5th to the 19th.

November

Best Days Overall: 7th, 8th, 16th, 17th, 26th, 27th

Most Stressful Days Overall: 1st, 2nd, 14th, 15th, 21st, 22nd, 28th, 29th

Best Days for Love: 3rd, 4th, 11th, 12th, 21st, 22nd, 24th, 25th, 30th

Best Days for Money: 3rd, 4th, 7th, 8th, 9th, 10th, 11th, 12th, 16th, 17th, 21st, 22nd, 26th, 27th, 30th

The universe is starting to move forward again. The wheels of progress are turning. By month's end *all* the planets will be in direct motion. Look for long-term and fundamental change. The two eclipses this month are a further signal of this. Any opposition to your progress is being removed – in dramatic and perhaps surprising ways.

Blockages to a creative project are being removed by both eclipses. An upheaval with friends and in a socially- or scientifically-orientated group to which you belong ultimately benefits you. False friends are leaving the picture and new ones are entering it.

With so many planets in the eastern sector of your chart you are more independent and creative than you've been in a long time. You are in the unique position of being able to shape your life in exactly the way you want. True friends are going to help you do it. Your fondest hopes and wishes are coming to pass now. All the preparations you have made these past few months when things seemed stalled have now put you in a position to take advantage of the opportunities being offered. For this, according to many sages, is what good luck is – when opportunity meets preparation.

What you thought was the true, objective condition of things is being radically changed by the eclipses – which explode the prison walls of your perception. The barriers to your Promised Land are there no more. Enter now with confidence.

Your health is excellent all month, though you should take a reduced schedule around the 3rd and the 18th – the days of the eclipses. This is not so much for your own sake but because others tend not to be up to par. Avoid activities that call for you to depend on others or for which others need to give 100 per cent. Schedule these activities for another time.

The lunar eclipse of the 18th tests a current love relationship. Is it just fun and games or something more serious? Is it friendship or real love? The eclipse will reveal the truth.

December

Best Days Overall: 4th, 5th, 13th, 14th, 15th, 23rd, 24th

Most Stressful Days Overall: 11th, 12th, 19th, 20th, 25th, 26th

Best Days for Love: 1st, 2nd, 3rd, 8th, 9th, 10th, 11th, 12th, 19th, 20th, 23rd, 24th, 28th, 29th

Best Days for Money: 1st, 4th, 5th, 6th, 7th, 11th, 12th, 13th, 14th, 15th, 21st, 22nd, 23rd, 24th, 30th

With all the planets moving forward this month and with the overwhelming majority of them in the eastern sector of your chart you've taken matters into your own hands – seized the forces of destiny – and are charting your own independent course. This is one of those times when you live life on your own terms. You seem beholden to no one. But – and there is always a but – are you creating what is right? Are you too personal in your desires? Some introspection this month will help ensure that you create what your really want to create, what is best for you and for all.

CAPRICORN

A great spiritual expansion is taking place this month – and in the coming year. You feel a need to contact the source of life within you directly and without intermediaries. A wonderful spiritual guide is coming into your life who will help you do this. He – for it seems to be a man – will give you the secret support and guidance that are indispensable in these undertakings. This spiritual expansion is going to require some personal sacrifice on your part. Give up lesser, temporary interests in favour of more permanent ones. The new Moon of the 2nd is going to show you how to do this and will bring you other spiritual knowledge as well. It also initiates a new social cycle – more altruistic and more committed. You are being given the knowledge to shape your love life and your relationships as you desire them.

Your charitable and volunteer work is important to you for the better part of the month. You are unusually generous in your giving.

Earnings are unusually good. Your financial intuition is lofty yet practical. Though you have not yet attained the financial heights, you can certainly see them – and this is real progress.

The cosmos is supporting your intellectual pursuits this month. There is good news from an educational setting and from neighbours. Sales, marketing and communication activities all go unusually well and build your self-esteem.

Your health is wonderful all month but especially after the 22nd when the Sun energizes your own sign. The period after the 22nd is exceptionally good for earnings as well.

Aquarius

≋

THE WATER-BEARER
Birthdays from
20th January
to 18th February

Personality Profile

AQUARIUS AT A GLANCE

Element – Air

Ruling planet – Uranus
  Love planet – Venus
  Money planet – Neptune
  Planet of home and family – Venus

Colours – electric blue, grey, ultramarine
blue

*Colours that promote love, romance and social
harmony* – gold, orange

Colour that promotes earning power – aqua

Gems – black pearl, obsidian, opal,
sapphire

320 ·

AQUARIUS

Metal – lead

Scents – azalea, gardenia

Quality – fixed (= stability)

Qualities most needed for balance – warmth, feeling and emotion

Strongest virtues – great intellectual power, the ability to communicate and to form and understand abstract concepts, love for the new and the avant-garde.

Deepest needs – to know and to bring in the new

Characteristics to avoid – coldness, rebelliousness for its own sake, fixed ideas

Signs of greatest overall compatibility – Gemini, Libra

Signs of greatest overall incompatibility – Taurus, Leo, Scorpio

Sign most helpful to career – Scorpio

Sign most helpful for emotional support – Taurus

Sign most helpful financially – Pisces

Sign best for marriage and/or partnerships – Leo

Sign most helpful for creative projects – Gemini

Best sign to have fun with – Gemini

Signs most helpful in spiritual matters – Libra, Capricorn

Best day of the week – Saturday

Understanding the Aquarius Personality

In the Aquarius-born, the intellectual faculties are perhaps the most highly developed of any sign in the zodiac. Aquarians are clear, scientific thinkers. They have the ability to think abstractly and to formulate laws, theories and clear concepts from masses of observed facts. Geminis might be very good at gathering information, but Aquarians take this a step further, excelling at interpreting the information gathered.

Practical people – men and women of the world – mistakenly consider abstract thinking as impractical. It is true that the realm of abstract thought takes us out of the physical world, but the discoveries made in this realm generally end up having tremendous practical consequences. All real scientific inventions and breakthroughs come from this abstract realm.

Aquarians, more so than most, are ideally suited to explore these abstract dimensions. Those who have explored these regions know that there is little feeling or emotion there. In fact, emotions are a hindrance to functioning there; thus Aquarians seem – at times – cold and emotionless to others. It's not that Aquarians haven't got feelings and deep emotions, it's just that too much feeling clouds their ability to think and invent – and this cannot be tolerated or even understood by some of the other signs. This Aquarian objectivity is ideal for science, communication and friendship.

Aquarians are very friendly people, but they don't make a big show about it. They do the right thing by their friends, even if sometimes they do it without passion or excitement.

Aquarians have a deep passion for clear thinking. Second in importance, but related, is their passion for breaking with the establishment and traditional authority. Aquarians delight in this, because for them rebellion is like a great game or challenge. Very often they will rebel strictly for the fun of rebelling, regardless of whether the authority that they defy is right or wrong. Right or wrong has little to do with the rebellious actions of an Aquarian because to a true Aquarian authority and power must be challenged as a matter of principle.

Where Capricorn or Taurus will err on the side of tradition and the status quo, an Aquarian will err on the side of the new. Without this virtue it is doubtful whether any progress would be made in the world. The conservative-minded would obstruct progress. Originality and invention imply an ability to break barriers; every new discovery represents the toppling of an impediment to thought. Aquarians are very interested in breaking barriers and making walls tumble – scientifically, socially and politically. Other zodiac signs, such as Capricorn, also have scientific talents. But Aquarians are particularly excellent in the social sciences or humanities.

Finance

In financial matters Aquarians tend to be idealistic and humanitarian – to the point of self-sacrifice. They are usually generous contributors to social and political causes. When they contribute, it is different than when a Capricorn or Taurus contributes. A Capricorn or Taurus may expect some favour or return for their gift; an Aquarian contributes selflessly.

Aquarians tend to be as cool and rational about money as they are about most things in life. Money is something they need and they set about scientifically to acquire it. No need for fuss; they get on with it in the most rational and scientific ways available.

Money to the Aquarian is especially nice for what it can do, not for the status it may bring (as is the case for other signs). Aquarians are neither big spenders nor penny-pinchers and use their finances in practical ways, for example to facilitate progress for themselves, their families or even strangers.

However, if Aquarians want to reach their fullest financial potential they will have to explore their intuitive nature. If they follow only their financial theories – or what they believe to be theoretically correct – they may suffer some losses and disappointments. Instead, Aquarians should call on their intuition – which knows without thinking. For Aquarians, intuition is the short-cut to financial success.

Career and Public Image

Aquarians like to be perceived not only as the breakers of barriers but also as the transformers of society and the world. They long to be seen in this light and to play this role. They also look up to and respect other people in this position and even expect their superiors to act this way.

Aquarians prefer jobs that have a bit of idealism attached to them – careers with a philosophical basis. Aquarians need to be creative at work, to have access to new techniques and methods. They like to keep busy and enjoy getting down to business straight away, without wasting any time. They are often the quickest workers and usually have suggestions for improvements that will benefit their employers. Aquarians are also very helpful with their co-workers and welcome responsibility, preferring this to having to take orders from others.

If Aquarians want to reach their highest career goals they have to develop more emotional sensitivity, depth of feeling and passion. They need to learn to narrow their focus on the essentials and concentrate more on their job. Aquarians need 'a fire in the belly' – a consuming passion and desire – in order to rise to the very top. Once this passion exists they will succeed easily in whatever they attempt.

Love and Relationships

Aquarians are good at friendships, but a bit weak when it comes to love. Of course they fall in love, but their beloved always gets the impression that they are more a best friend than a lover.

Like the Capricorn they are cool customers. They are not prone to display passion nor to demonstrate their affections outwardly. In fact, they feel uncomfortable when their mate hugs and touches them too much. This doesn't mean that they don't love their partners. They do, only they show it in other ways. Curiously enough, in relationships they tend to attract the very things that they feel uncomfortable with. They seem to attract hot, passionate, romantic, demonstrative types of people. Perhaps they know instinctively that these are qualities they lack and so seek them in a partner. In any event, these relationships do seem to work, the Aquarian's coolness calming his or her more passionate partner while the fires of passion warm the cold-blooded Aquarian.

The qualities Aquarians need to develop in their love life are warmth, generosity, passion and fun. Aquarians love relationships of the mind. Here they excel. If the intellectual factor is missing in a relationship, an Aquarian will soon become bored or feel unfulfilled.

Home and Domestic Life

In family and domestic matters Aquarians can have a tendency to be too nonconformist, changeable and unstable. They are as willing to break the barriers of family constraints as they are those of other areas of life.

Even so, Aquarians are very sociable people. They like to have a nice home where they can entertain family and friends. Their house is usually decorated modernly and full of state-of-the-art appliances and gadgets – an environment Aquarians find absolutely necessary.

If their home life is to be healthy and fulfilling Aquarians need to inject it with a quality of stability – yes, even some conservatism. They need at least one area of life to be enduring and steady; this area is usually their home and family life.

Venus, the planet of love, rules the Aquarian's 4th solar House of Home and Family as well, which means that when it comes to the family and child-rearing, theories, cool thinking and intellect are not always enough. Aquarians need to bring love into the equation in order have a great domestic life.

Horoscope for 1994

Major Trends

If you have learned the lessons of the past two to three years, Aquarius, you have a lot of good things – a lot of satisfaction – to look forward to in 1994. A real reversal of fortune occurs. All the glory and recognition seemingly denied you these past few years is now yours – with interest. It's as if your merits – all the good that you did, the extra work and the long hours – were stored in some invisible, 'cosmic' bank account collecting interest to be paid to you at the appropriate time. Jupiter is making the payment. He moves from your 9th House of Religion and Philosophy into your 2nd House of Career. That is where restitution will be made (but more on this later).

Your health is going to improve dramatically in 1994 as Saturn moves away from your sign and into another. The negative spell of gloom and doom, of restriction and coldness moves off you. You are in a new era and you can feel it. A new sense of freedom – always so important to you, Aquarius – comes into your life. Your natural tendency, of course, is to go wild with it – to overuse or misuse your freedom. Though this is understandable, it is not advisable. Too much – unstructured – liberty can lead to as many problems as too little.

Your inner spiritual development continues to be important this year and proceeds much more easily than last year. Real inner progress is made.

Where 1993 was an educational year, 1994 is a year when you apply what you have learned to the practicalities of life. This is a financial and career year.

Health

For the past two to three years Saturn has been sitting on your Natal Sun, restricting your physical energy, making you aware of your physical limits and causing you to restructure your lifestyle. There were many positive results of this. Maybe you slimmed down and became more diet conscious. You reduced physical activities to a realistic level – a level that you could handle. Every minor bodily shortcoming was revealed to you. It was as if an invisible gang of conspirators were criticizing every organ, every feature, every gesture – every little mole and birthmark – you had. This kind of thing is not usually very good for one's self-esteem, but it had some positive effects. The things that were in your power to change were changed. The things that you couldn't change were accepted and loved. All of this is good.

But now Saturn is moving off you and you will feel an immediate sense of lightness, buoyancy and optimism – as if great weights were being lifted from you. Your vitality will increase naturally. The strength you have gained over the past few years will further magnify your sense of well-being. You have greater and deeper confidence in your body and in what it can do. Better still, you avoid getting yourself embroiled in physical impossibilities. You are strong within your established limits.

Jupiter has this year moved into a stressful aspect to you. Healthwise, this can create problems of overindulgence. Be careful not to go overboard or you may gain back all the weight you've lost over the past two to three years. Are you strong enough to resist all the alluring temptations put before you this year? If so, you are in a perfect position, from the standpoint of health, to pursue and achieve tremendous career goals.

327

Your best health periods this year will be from 20th January to 18th February, 20th May to 21st June and 22nd September to 23rd October.

Your most stressful health periods will be from 20th April to 19th May, 23rd July to 23rd August and 24th October to 22nd November. Rest and relax more during these periods.

Home and Domestic Life

Home and family issues are not major priorities this year, Aquarius. You seem willing to sacrifice the pleasures of home and hearth in order to further your career. Career comes first; your family and home can wait. Of course, this attitude can create some short-term problems with family members, but these seem easily smoothed over. With Jupiter and Pluto occupying the most elevated points of your solar horoscope your family seems very well aware – on an inner level – that you are spiritually called to your career right now. They desire to co-operate with this. In seven years or so adjustments will have to be made, but for now, they seem co-operative. Bigger issues are at stake than their personal comforts. Moreover, they probably know (and if not, be sure to explain to them) that the attaining cherished professional goals now means greater domestic happiness further on down the road.

This quiescence on the home-front should be considered fortunate. Nothing major is amiss and so no extra attention need be given it.

Of course you will not be able to avoid home issues and family demands *completely*. There will be times during the year when these issues will take priority – and you will have to do a juggling act between family and career. Your most active and demanding domestic period will be from 1st April to 4th July.

AQUARIUS

Love and Social Life

The last major activation of your 7th House of Love and Marriage took place in 1991. You have already achieved most of your major social priorities and this area of life is now stable and reposed. The cosmos neither helps nor hinders unduly in these matters. Consider this fortunate as it shows that you have a free hand to shape your love life as you will.

Your social life seems centred around platonic friendships rather than torrid romances. This is a long-term – at least two years in length – trend. Positive changes in your professional status propel you into another social stratum. Thus you 'disappear' in a sense to old acquaintances and meet a set of new ones. You mix with the 'high and mighty', the rich and the powerful. You meet people well able to fulfil your career aspirations and who seem kindly disposed towards you. For those of you who are married or involved in a serious commitment this adds another dimension to your social life. Singles will enjoy this status quo more in future, as the contacts you make over the next two years could very well lead to more serious romance later on. Thus, seemingly casual contacts are a lot deeper than at first meets the eye.

In 1993, elders and authorities seemed to hound you, harass you, restrict and control you. Now the high and the mighty consider you their friend. They support you.

Be sensitive to the feelings of old, long-established acquaintances. They tend to feel neglected – left behind. Many of them cannot follow you to the exalted heights that you attain. Let them know that you still care about them. Resist the temptation to be brusque, to exact vengeance for old wrongs or to otherwise make them feel rejected. Remember, the same people you pass on the way up you will meet again on the way back down. Life is cyclical.

There are two really passionate romantic periods this year for you, Aquarius: 15th June to 23rd August and 4th October to 12th December. This latter period promises to be the most exciting and happy. Singles will most likely find that special someone then – probably from within the ranks of your new acquaintances. Existing relationships are likely to ripen into serious commitments. Married people will have great joy and satisfaction within their relationship. It is a time when both love and career prosper.

Career and Finance

Your finances have been a priority for many years now. This period has been one of searching, discarding, trials and errors, successful and not-so-successful experiments – a long-term probe into the unknown. You are searching for the ideal financial state – a state of absolute financial freedom. At times you can see your dream quite vividly. At other times it seems a million miles away. Detractors call you unrealistic for having such high aspirations. Sometimes you feel that way yourself – so much does this fantasizing contradict your experience and common sense.

You have probably, over the past few years, tried every 'get-rich-quick' scheme in the book. Yet in spite of all these trials and travails there is something in you that knows intuitively that you will succeed. You have been to the mountain-top and have seen the promised land – no amount of negative testimony or hurtful experience can erase this inner knowledge. Yes, financial freedom *does* exist and you can achieve it!

Keep the faith, Aquarius. All new and untried things tend to run contrary to 'common sense'. What you need in your financial life is a little *uncommon* sense. Believe in and follow your intuitive leads. Your vision is basically true, but you need patience (especially for the next two years or so).

True, you are earning more this year, but you seem to be spending more as well. Extra financial burdens are laid on you. Your challenge in 1994 is to manage what you have more effectively. Cut unnecessary costs. Learn the art of budgeting. Be a smarter shopper. Sell off possessions that you no longer need or use. Become financially leaner and meaner.

Aside from this, your solar chart shows that you are quite willing to sacrifice short-term earnings for long-term career growth. Your professional standing among your peers is more important to you than mere money-making. Glory comes before gold.

Indeed, your urge for status is understandable. The new career heights that are being revealed to you this year will produce greater earnings in the future. Investing in your career is definitely better than investing in a money market fund or the stock-market. And while your material possessions won't increase this year, the people you socialize with and your bosses are not going to let you suffer any lack. They are unusually favourable towards you.

Jupiter conjoined with Pluto in your 10th House of Career is generally interpreted by astrologers as a signal for great, mass success. You impress the public in a deep and formidable way. How this will translate into earnings will manifest later on.

Self-improvement

This year you will be forced to manage your earnings better. Learning to budget is not really in your nature, so this is going to be difficult. You can make things easier on yourself if you understand the art of budgeting and what it entails. First off, recognize that a good budget is not to be followed slavishly; it is meant as a *guide* to spending. It is normal to go a little over or under at different times. As a guide, it should be viewed not as a restriction but as a liberation. You are liberated from financial fear and want. You know what you can safely spend. You don't go chasing after things that are beyond you. This also saves you time, worry and attention. Your mind is free to find more cost-conscious alternatives.

A good budget should include everything that you really need – in proportion. If it deprives you of anything truly needful it is not a well-constructed budget. Creating a budget is useful in that it forces you to set priorities – orders of importance. It is a form of meditation, for you become mentally clear as a result. The richer you become the greater will be your need to budget – for the richer you are, the greater your need to control your spending.

Month-by-month Forecasts

January

Best Days Overall: 4th, 5th, 12th, 13th, 14th, 22nd, 23rd, 31st

Most Stressful Days Overall: 1st, 6th, 7th, 20th, 21st, 27th, 28th

Best Days for Love: 1st, 2nd, 3rd, 10th, 11th, 22nd, 23rd, 27th, 28th, 31st

Best Days for Money: 2nd, 3rd, 6th, 7th, 10th, 11th, 15th, 16th, 20th, 21st, 25th, 26th, 29th, 30th

This is a highly spiritual month in a highly spiritual year for you, Aquarius. There is a lot going on in your inner world, your dream life and your spiritual life. These are unquestionably the dominant interests for the better part of this month.

After a few years of a Uranus-Neptune transit through your 12th solar House of Spiritual Wisdom and Charity you have been spiritually awakened. By now you are all well aware that your inner world is larger, richer and probably more interesting than your outer world – the mundane world of everyday life. You see clearly now that the world of the five senses is only a part of something infinitely larger. This month you get even more verification of this.

AQUARIUS

This is a month of miracles, when the so-called laws of the physical world are nullified for you. Your spiritual powers are increased and strengthened. You see into the past and future. You have the gift of prophecy. Telepathy becomes a living reality for you. You are able to contact great and noble beings from outside our space-time frame. You understand the mysteries of life. The true, unwritten history of the species is revealed to you. Anything you need to know this month will come to you in exactly the form that satisfies your needs best. You may learn a vital truth from a book, or a friend may utter some chance phrase, or you may hear a still small voice while sleeping. Don't be frightened by these things, they are typical – and quite natural – 12th-House phenomena.

Your intuition is so sharp – so trustworthy – right now that money comes to you with little effort – and often in miraculous ways. You are seeing the true source of your financial supply.

With all this going on it is only natural that you may want to seclude yourself and explore further. You know that you haven't even begun to plumb the depths or scaled the heights of this miraculous world. A little seclusion is surely called for. However, with your career going so well and with so many planets moving into your own sign of Aquarius during the latter part of the month you won't be able to seclude yourself as much as you would like. Give to each aspect of life its proper due.

Some of you are going to join spiritual organizations. Some of you are seriously considering joining a monastery or nunnery; others will either begin to study for the ministry or join ministerial organizations. Don't rush into anything. Delay any long-term moves until the latter part of the month – see how you feel about things when the planetary power activates your 1st House of Body and Personal Image.

February

Best Days Overall: 1st, 9th, 10th, 19th, 20th, 27th, 28th

Most Stressful Days Overall: 2nd, 3rd, 16th, 17th, 23rd, 24th

Best Days for Love: 1st, 9th, 10th, 11th, 12th, 21st, 22nd, 23rd, 24th

Best Days for Money: 2nd, 3rd, 7th, 8th, 11th, 12th, 16th, 17th, 21st, 22nd, 25th, 26th

With so many of the short-term planets moving through your own sign of Aquarius this month you are feeling quite good indeed. Your vitality is superabundant and your self-esteem is high. Your personal charisma is strong and you are getting your way in most things. Venus in your sign is making you more glamorous and charming. You have to 'fight' others off – so clamorous are their advances. You can't help it if you are irresistible right now. Enjoy the positives and try to overlook the negatives of this situation.

There are more opportunities for personal pleasure right now – gourmet dinners, massages, romantic delights and the like are being offered in abundance. Indulge yourself, by all mean, but don't get lost in ecstasy. Remember your career goals.

Finances are particularly good this month. Your enhanced feelings of self-worth make you more valuable and increase your earnings. Your subtle form of aggressiveness enables you to go after what you want without antagonizing anyone. In fact, others find your aggressiveness quite charming.

Your financial intuition and judgement continue to be superhuman – uncanny – especially after the 18th. Original, innovative ideas are certainly well worth testing right now. Your intuition will supply you with ideas, but you must supply a structure, form and organization for them.

This is a month of important financial breakthroughs. The retrograde of Mercury from the 11th onwards suggests caution when it comes to speculations. Be especially careful about how you communicate to children during this time, as they are likely to misunderstand you. The full Moon of the 26th increases your partner's income and his or her generosity towards you – but because Mercury is retrograde there could be a delayed reaction in he or she actually giving you any money or gifts. Be patient and these things will come to you.

In love you are self-assertive at present. Partners and lovers seek to please you and are sensitive to your whims. You seem to hold all the cards in a current relationship. Singles have no need to run after love. Love pursues you – almost unavoidably.

March

Best Days Overall: 8th, 9th, 18th, 19th, 27th, 28th

Most Stressful Days Overall: 1st, 2nd, 15th, 16th, 17th, 23rd, 24th, 29th, 30th

Best Days for Love: 1st, 2nd, 10th, 11th, 12th, 13th, 14th, 23rd, 24th, 31st

Best Days for Money: 1st, 2nd, 6th, 7th, 10th, 11th, 12th, 15th, 16th, 17th, 20th, 21st, 22nd, 25th, 26th, 30th

Though you are not overly comfortable with all the emotional mush around you – everyone seems awash in feelings and no one seems capable of thinking or reasoning any more – this intuitive energy is nevertheless enriching you and strengthening your financial acumen.

Your financial judgements are uncannily sound and prophetic right now. What's most interesting is that, though you follow your intuition, you have both feet quite firmly on the ground. This is a truly winning combination.

Money, profitable ideas and earning opportunities come to you from many sources at this time. With 70 to 80 per cent of the planets operating on your behalf it's as if you have legions of financial helpers. Some of these profitable sources are dreams, intuitions, religious and charitable institutions, lovers, family, neighbours, psychics and astrologers. Money seems to come from all over. Nor is there any doubt that you are ready to spend it in all kinds of directions – to enter into all kinds of ventures. Let the new Moon of the 12th clarify any financial confusion.

Though you are psychologically uncomfortable with all this Water energy right now, your health is excellent. You are not affected physically. The psychological atmosphere will change dramatically on the 20th when the Sun moves into Aries. More optimism, activity and energy become apparent in those around you. All of your extra earnings now make it possible for you to study and pursue intellectual interests.

Your social life is quite active this month – and though you are romantic and unusually emotional in love – romance takes a back seat to money matters. You want generous support from your lover. You find common ground with each other in financial interests and buying new things. Singles find romantic opportunities in the normal pursuit of financial goals and at shopping precincts.

You have finally put it all together – a happy love life, ample earnings and good health. Enjoy.

April

> Best Days Overall: 4th, 5th, 14th, 15th, 23rd, 24th
>
> Most Stressful Days Overall: 12th, 13th, 19th, 20th, 25th, 26th
>
> Best Days for Love: 1st, 2nd, 3rd, 9th,

AQUARIUS

10th, 11th, 12th, 13th, 19th, 20th, 21st, 22nd, 30th

Best Days for Money: 2nd, 3rd, 7th, 8th, 12th, 13th, 17th, 18th, 21st, 22nd, 25th, 26th

The celestial powers are activating your financial life, intellectual interests and domestic situation this month, Aquarius. Your spiritual development – so important to you of late – is being tested. You should welcome this, as you can only really know how far you've come when you meet with opposition and/or resistance.

Your intuition, visions, dreams and evolving psychic powers are being attacked, criticized, doubted and otherwise undermined. The way out is to realize that no one can argue against success. Others can scream and shout but your success speaks for itself. The same is true of the numerous charitable works you are doing. Though others question and even attack your motives, your rewards are the good feelings and satisfaction these works bring you. When you are attacked for doing what you know to be good and true, rejoice. Your future remuneration will be even greater and your critics will have to eat their words.

Your financial confidence is still powerful until the 14th. Your capacity for hard work, persistence and courageous action is emphasized now. People see you as financially fearless, a risk-taker. Little do they know that there is a method to your madness. You know that your are taking no risks but following your infallible intuition.

Healthwise you are stronger than you were last month. The hot and passionate energies of Aries stimulate and warm you. Your mental agility is also enhanced. Sales and marketing activities go well, as you really believe in what you sell and your enthusiasm sways others. This is a good month to take lessons in a sport. After the 20th try to rest and relax more. The slight lessening of your vitality will not last long.

Next month you will feel 100 per cent better.

Your love life is fiery, passionate and intense. Your partner is especially ardent. Spring fever has struck him or her. A passionate Aries comes into your life this month – someone from your neighbourhood. Let the new Moon of the 11th clarify this encounter and show you where to go next. Definitely don't rush into anything yet.

May

> Best Days Overall: 1st, 2nd, 3rd, 11th, 12th, 13th, 21st, 22nd, 29th, 30th
>
> Most Stressful Days Overall: 9th, 10th, 16th, 17th, 23rd, 24th
>
> Best Days for Love: 1st, 2nd, 3rd, 9th, 10th, 11th, 12th, 17th, 19th, 20th, 21st, 23rd, 24th, 29th, 30th, 31st
>
> Best Days for Money: 4th, 5th, 9th, 10th, 14th, 15th, 19th, 20th, 23rd, 24th, 27th, 28th, 31st

Rest and relax more until the 21st, Aquarius, as emotional issues seem unusually intense right now. Who would think that nebulous emotions could drain a person so? Just one tense family encounter leaves you feeling like you've laboured on a chain-gang for 12 hours.

The solar eclipse of the 10th signals a long-term and profound change in your domestic sphere. This could mean a move or major repair job. Inadequacies in the home – which you have perhaps ignored or swept under the carpet – are highlighted so that correcting them becomes easier. The same is true of old family tensions and resentments. They have to be confronted, dealt with and resolved one way or another. Your relationship with your parents seems tense. Both you and they should take a reduced, relaxed schedule from the 9th to the 11th. Don't invite problems by scheduling gruelling, demanding tasks during this period. Keep things light. Pray, meditate, plan, rest and let go of your problems for now.

The way you earn money is changing over the long term. The income of brothers, sisters and in-laws changes dramatically at this time. Short-term upheavals lead to long-term positive gains.

Life lightens up considerably after the 21st. Opportunities of personal pleasures are abundant and you take advantage of them. You are going out more, entertaining more and being more creative. Your health improves as well.

The lunar eclipse of the 25th brings changes in your friendships and in the workplace. New technology changes the way you work and the nature of your job.

Once some resentments get cleared with your partner – a short-term row brought on by the eclipse of the 10th – your love life proceeds harmoniously. The row helps clear of the air. It leads to having more fun and joy in the relationship. This is what you need right now, anyway.

June

Best Days Overall: 8th, 9th, 17th, 18th, 25th, 26th

Most Stressful Days Overall: 5th, 6th, 7th, 13th, 14th, 19th, 20th

Best Days for Love: 1st, 8th, 9th, 10th, 11th, 13th, 14th, 17th, 18th, 21st, 22nd, 28th, 29th, 30th

Best Days for Money: 1st, 5th, 6th, 7th, 10th, 11th, 15th, 16th, 19th, 20th, 23rd, 24th, 28th, 29th

With 60 per cent of the planetary power retrograde this

month it seems to you that the universe has stopped, that everything you've been working towards is in limbo. This is not strictly true, but it does seem that way to you. In reality great progress is being made behind the scenes, on the invisible levels of existence. When the astrological aspects become right again, you will see the outward signs of this progress. Happily, the cosmos has been training you for the past few years in subjective, inner functioning, so you will handle this retrograde period with great ease.

Utilize this 'cosmically-ordained' holiday to have some fun. Leave career and money issues for a while. Go out to the theatre. Take a diverting holiday – and leave your work at home. Go to concerts and art galleries. Throw and attend parties. Hone your creative writing skills and work on your hobbies – the things you do just for fun. There is plenty of time for work after the 21st.

Your health is excellent all month but especially before the 21st.

Domestic demands (such as the need to attend to some home repairs) conflict with career demands. Give the domestic area priority right now. Career issues can't be speeded up anyway, whereas you have a real opportunity to get domestic issues out of the way. A conflict with your parents (or parental figures) will be resolved next month. This problem is not anything essential or basic, just a question of moods. When the mood is right for fighting, fighting occurs. When the mood changes all rancour is forgotten.

Your love life is the one area that goes forward this month. It is the bright spot in a temporarily dismal landscape. With love all things are possible. You feel that you can live on love this month. Love is exciting, tender and nurturing. You and your partner go to unusual lengths to nurture each other. You also socialize in strange and unusual locales – way out of your normal orbit. Singles find love opportunities through their family and family connections. An old flame is back in your life.

July

Best Days Overall: 5th, 6th, 14th, 15th,
23rd, 24th

Most Stressful Days Overall: 2nd, 3rd, 4th,
10th, 11th, 16th, 17th, 30th, 31st

Best Days for Love: 1st, 7th, 8th, 9th,
10th, 11th, 12th, 16th, 17th, 21st, 22nd,
27th, 28th, 29th, 30th, 31st

Best Days for Money: 2nd, 3rd, 4th, 7th,
8th, 9th, 12th, 13th, 16th, 17th, 21st,
22nd, 25th, 26th

The extreme emotionalism, moodiness and general introversion in the air right now doesn't make you feel very comfortable, Aquarius. Science, logic and reason – your fortes – are not especially prized right now. You will have more success in communications if you appeal to people's emotions rather than their minds. This is a style of communication that you are not used to.

Your health and vitality – as well as your self-esteem – are not what they should be. Rest and relax more. Creative hobbies such as making music, painting and creative writing can help you maintain your health. These pursuits allow you to express your feelings in a constructive way. Harmony with your beloved is also an important factor in your health right now.

You feel the need to counteract the general sluggishness of the day with sports, dancing and other physical activity. But you are likely to be doing these things alone. People in general are not in the mood for physical exertion right now – although after the 23rd these pursuits will be back in style again.

Nowhere is this moodiness more apparent than in your current relationship. Your partner seems especially high-strung; the state of your love life depends on what kind of mood he or she is in. You feel nostalgic about 'the way you were'. Your mind – and that of your lover – travels back to the beginnings of the relationship. You also think of old flames fondly and old loves come back into your life.

Singles find love opportunities at each workplace or in the doctor's surgery. Romance comes from those involved in your work or health. Love is expressed through nurturing for most of the month. After the 23rd love is expressed more extrovertly. There are parties and entertainment events. Your partner is in the mood for fun and is also more stable in his or her affections.

In financial matters, be patient. Much progress is being made behind the scenes.

August

Best Days Overall: 1st, 2nd, 3rd, 11th, 12th, 19th, 20th, 29th, 30th

Most Stressful Days Overall: 6th, 7th, 13th, 14th, 26th, 27th

Best Days for Love: 6th, 7th, 11th, 12th, 15th, 16th, 19th, 20th, 26th, 27th, 29th, 30th

Best Days for Money: 4th, 5th, 8th, 9th, 13th, 14th, 17th, 18th, 21st, 22nd, 23rd, 26th, 27th, 31st

With 70 to 80 per cent of the planets focused in the western half of your solar horoscope you are involved in situations and conditions that you did not create – or so you think. You are all tied up with the needs of others now and everything you want to do seems dependent on others. Don't let this frustrate you. You are learning lessons in social grace and clearing the decks for future creativity. Having control is nice, but relinquishing control can also be nice. Think of life as an adventure.

AQUARIUS

Your health and self-esteem are not what they should be for the better part of the month. Rest and relax more. Engage in some healthy – but not overly strenuous – exercise. Your social life – very active right now – is also important healthwise. Harmony with friends and in love has an unusual impact on your health. After the 18th, a pure, nutritious diet becomes an important health factor.

Singles have two prominent romantic interests at this time: someone from work or involved in your health – a doctor or nurse – and someone more prominent, someone athletic and creative. You find if difficult to choose between the two. One serves you while the other entertains you. Let the new Moon of the 7th clarify this situation.

You are attending more parties and functions – and going out more to seek entertainment.

Earnings are not what they should be, but after the 23rd they improve a great deal. There isn't much you can do to speed things up, as both earnings and opportunities for earnings depend on other people over whom you've no control. Your career and professional prestige, though, become very much enhanced after the 23rd.

September

Best Days Overall: 7th, 8th, 15th, 16th, 25th, 26th

Most Stressful Days Overall: 3rd, 4th, 9th, 10th, 22nd, 23rd, 24th, 30th

Best Days for Love: 3rd, 4th, 5th, 6th, 8th, 9th, 13th, 14th, 18th, 19th, 24th, 25th, 26th, 28th, 29th, 30th

Best Days for Money: 1st, 5th, 6th, 9th, 10th, 13th, 14th, 18th, 19th, 22nd, 23rd, 24th, 28th, 29th

You are now going to reap the rewards for all the spiritual, charitable and philanthropic work that you have done over the past few years. Your good deeds have put the universe in your debt and the celestial powers know how to reward you.

Big things are going on now in your finances and career, as 70 to 80 per cent of the planets are in the top part of your solar horoscope chart. You have been reclusive and inner-orientated long enough. Now is the time to translate what you have learned into objective success. Family and home issues can wait – in fact your family seems to support your career objectives and is quite willing to make sacrifices so that you can attain them.

Personal earnings still seem on hold but they are in fact still developing on a deeper level. Your partner's income is increased and he or she is more generous with you. The rich and powerful are favourably disposed to you now and will make up – through loans, investments, earning opportunities, advice and financial favours – whatever you may lack in personal earnings. You won't want for anything material this month. You pay off debts fearlessly and execute plans for business ventures confidently. If you focus on making profits for others, you yourself will benefit in due course.

Your social and professional status is probably at a lifetime peak now. Honours and awards come to you. You have the potential for mass popularity – if you can accept it. Pay rises (which may take effect later on) and promotions are coming your way. A corporate shake-up leaves you sitting pretty. You socialize with the high and mighty – the powerful and beautiful people.

Take that trip with confidence, as the money for it will come in due course.

Your health is excellent all month.

AQUARIUS

October

Best Days Overall: 4th, 5th, 13th, 14th, 22nd, 23rd, 24th

Most Stressful Days Overall: 1st, 6th, 7th, 20th, 21st, 27th, 28th

Best Days for Love: 1st, 4th, 5th, 6th, 7th, 13th, 14th, 15th, 16th, 24th, 25th, 26th, 27th, 28th

Best Days for Money: 2nd, 3rd, 6th, 7th, 10th, 11th, 15th, 16th, 20th, 21st, 25th, 26th, 30th, 31st

This is a month of great personal, financial and career progress. Most of the frustrations and obstacles to your desires are now being removed. Uranus, your ruling planet, moves forward this month after many months of retrograde motion. Neptune, your money planet, also goes direct. The overwhelming dominance of planetary power is still concentrated – even more than it was last month – at the top portion of your solar horoscope chart, increasing your ambition to a point where some call you 'career driven'. All of this is part of the great plan.

This is a good period in which to take advantage of whatever educational opportunities are offered you. You will need all the credentials you can get later on as you expand your career. Foreign travel is quite likely early in the month. Travel and education not only enhance your career, but your love life as well. In fact it may be love more than career that leads you to a university course, or to a church for Bible lessons.

You want and admire culture and education in a partner. Singles especially long for a partner they can look up to – someone more educated, someone 'above' them in status. Those in a relationship want – and will get – career and educational support from their partner.

After the 23rd you definitely must rest and relax more. Your trip to new career heights is draining, both physically and psychologically. Sometimes you wonder whether it is all worth it. But the view from the top convinces you that it is. Success can be as stressful as failure. Focus on priorities and listen to your body.

When it comes to your ambitions, your normally cool and rational Aquarian personality becomes more focused and intense, more like the typical Scorpio. Your intensity and concentration are amazing, even to you. Nothing stands in your way.

If you have been managing your money properly until now, the extra income that comes in this month can be put towards a heart's desire. Elders, parents, bosses and authority figures are helping you reach your financial goals. The rich and powerful look on you favourably. Earning opportunities come from the top rather than from the grass roots.

November

> Best Days Overall: 1st, 2nd, 9th, 10th, 19th, 20th, 28th, 29th
>
> Most Stressful Days Overall: 3rd, 4th, 16th, 17th, 24th, 25th, 30th
>
> Best Days for Love: 3rd, 4th, 11th, 12th, 21st, 22nd, 24th, 25th, 30th
>
> Best Days for Money: 3rd, 4th, 7th, 8th, 11th, 12th, 16th, 17th, 21st, 22nd, 26th, 27th, 30th

Nothing can stop your rise to the career heights, which seems quite dramatic now. Of course, there are those who will attempt to oppose you – but they will be exposed by the solar eclipse of the 3rd. Even they are useful to you as they will reveal weaknesses and flaws that need to be corrected. Your success is inexorable and inevitable.

This month's two eclipses will remove any obstructions to your progress – in your outward life (the solar eclipse of the 3rd) and home life (the lunar eclipse of the 18th). The forward motion of all the planets by month's end further signals your forward advancement.

Changes in career – and responsibilities at work – are creating changes at home. You can't devote as much time to the home as you usually do. But these family and domestic upheavals are short term and will be resolved quickly. A new and better domestic order will be made manifest.

Your career changes also affect your relationship with your lover. He or she feels neglected. This is the price of success. You need to learn to juggle the different claims on your attention.

The corporate hierarchy is being severely shaken up and restructured. This benefits you. Your position will be stronger than before.

Those of you with January birthdays will feel the solar eclipse quite strongly. Those of you with mid-February birthdays will be more affected by the lunar eclipse of the 18th more. Men will be more affected by the solar eclipse, women more by the lunar one. Take a reduced schedule on those days.

In general rest and relax more. Handle the most pressing priorities and let the less urgent ones go. The challenge for you is to decide what is and what is not a priority. You will have to live with your decision.

Don't be overly concerned about the irrationality, the intensity and extremism of the people around you. This is not your personal style and you find it uncomfortable, but it will pass. As mentioned, the unusual line-up of planets in the sign of Scorpio is the cause of all this emotionalism.

December

Best Days Overall: 6th, 7th, 16th, 17th, 25th, 26th

Most Stressful Days Overall: 1st, 13th, 14th, 15th, 21st, 22nd, 28th

Best Days for Love: 1st, 2nd, 3rd, 8th, 9th, 10th, 11th, 12th, 19th, 20th, 21st, 22nd, 23rd, 24th, 28th, 29th

Best Days for Money: 1st, 4th, 5th, 8th, 9th, 10th, 11th, 12th, 13th, 14th, 15th, 21st, 22nd, 23rd, 24th, 30th

With 40 to 60 per cent of the planets in Earth signs, fancy ideas and airy theories – no matter how brilliant – will not further your career or increase your earnings. You have to make things sound practical and cost-effective. You must demonstrate the workability of your proposals. People are results-orientated right now. With your money planet in an Earth sign and with practical Saturn in your 2nd House of Money, you should have no problem projecting a down-to-earth image.

Though you are not especially comfortable with all this Earth energy, your health and self-esteem are not affected. Your health is excellent all month. Moreover, with your 11th House of Friends and Group Activities super-active – both this month and in the coming year – you are doing what you want to do and what you do best: dealing with groups and socializing. These, your favourite activities, are also happy and profitable for you right now. You are learning more about science, technology and group dynamics.

Your love life is also just the way you like it. Friendly, cool – but not too cool – with plenty of intellectual conversation and real equality between you and your partner. Singles find love through group activities. Your circle of platonic friends is widened considerably. With a group behind you you feel there is nothing you can't accomplish.

You are still in a cycle of progress and creative independence. You are living life on your terms; you hold the reins of destiny in your own hands. Dare to create the conditions that you desire for yourself. Dare to step out on your own. Dare to demand what you will from life – and watch how the world conforms to your demands.

Your new career status has attracted richer, more powerful people into your social circle. They are in a position – and possess the resources – to make your fondest dreams come to pass. They may not necessarily drop a bundle of money on you, but they have the knowledge and connections to help you manifest these dreams for yourself.

Pisces

♓

THE FISH
Birthdays from
19th February
to 20th March

Personality Profile

PISCES AT A GLANCE

Element – Water

Ruling planet – Neptune
  Love planet – Mercury
  Planet of home and family life – Mercury

Colours – aqua, blue-green

Colours that promote love, romance and social harmony – earth tones, yellow, yellow-orange

Colours that promote earning power – red, scarlet

Gem – white diamond

PISCES

Metal – tin

Scent – lotus

Quality – mutable (= flexibility)

Qualities most needed for balance – structure and the ability to handle form

Strongest virtues – psychic power, sensitivity, self-sacrifice, altruism

Deepest needs – spiritual illumination, liberation

Characteristics to avoid – escapism, keeping bad company, negative moods

Signs of greatest overall compatibility – Cancer, Scorpio

Signs of greatest overall incompatibility – Gemini, Virgo, Sagittarius

Sign most helpful to career – Sagittarius

Sign most helpful for emotional support – Gemini

Sign most helpful financially – Aries

Sign best for marriage and/or partnerships – Virgo

Sign most helpful for creative projects – Cancer

Best sign to have fun with – Cancer

Signs most helpful in spiritual matters – Scorpio, Aquarius

Best day of the week – Thursday

Understanding the Pisces Personality

If Pisceans have one outstanding quality it's their belief in the invisible, spiritual and psychic side of things. This side of things is as real to them as the hard earth beneath their feet – so real, in fact, that they will often ignore the visible, tangible aspects of reality in order to focus on the invisible and so-called intangible ones.

Of all the signs of the zodiac, the intuitive and emotional faculties are the most highly developed in the Pisces. They are committed to living by their intuition and this can at times be infuriating to other people – especially those who are materially, scientifically or technically orientated. If you think that money or status or worldly success are the only goals in life, then you will never understand a Pisces.

Pisceans have intellect, but to them intellect is only a means by which they can rationalize what they know intuitively. To an Aquarius or a Gemini the intellect is a tool of knowing. To a well-developed Pisces it is only a tool by which to *express* knowing.

Pisceans feel like fish in an infinite ocean of thought and feeling. This ocean has many depths, currents and sub-currents. They long for purer waters where the denizens are good, true and beautiful, but they are sometimes pulled to the lower, murkier depths. Pisceans know that they don't generate thoughts but only tune in to thoughts that already exist; this is why they seek the purer waters. This ability to tune in to higher thoughts inspires them artistically and musically.

Since Pisces is so spiritually orientated – though many Pisceans in the corporate world may hide this fact – we will deal with this aspect in greater detail, for otherwise it is difficult to understand the true Pisces personality.

There are four basic attitudes of the spirit. One is outright scepticism – the attitude of secular humanists. The second is an intellectual or emotional belief, where one worships a far-distant God figure – the attitude of most modern church-going people. The third is not only belief but direct personal spiritual experience – this is the attitude of some 'born-again' religious people. The fourth is actually unity with the divinity, intermingling with the spiritual world – this is the attitude of yoga. This fourth attitude is the deepest urge of a Pisces and a Pisces is uniquely qualified to perform this work.

Consciously or unconsciously, Pisceans seek this union with the spiritual world. The belief in a greater reality makes Pisceans very tolerant and understanding of others – perhaps even too tolerant. There are instances in their lives when they should say 'enough is enough' and be ready to defend their position and put up a fight. However, because of their qualities it takes a good deal of doing to get them in that frame of mind.

Pisceans basically want and aspire to be 'saints'. They do so in their own way and according to their own rules. Others should not try to impose their concept of saintliness on a Pisces, because he or she always tries to find it for him- or herself.

Finance

Money is generally not that important to Pisces. Of course they need it as much as the next fellow and many of them attain great wealth. But money is not generally a primary objective. Doing good, feeling good about oneself, peace of mind, the relief of pain and suffering – these are the things that matter most to a Pisces.

Pisceans earn money intuitively and instinctively. They follow their hunches rather than their logic. They tend to be generous and perhaps overly charitable. Almost any kind of misfortune is enough to move a Pisces to give. Although this is one of their greatest virtues, Pisceans should be more careful with their finances. They should try to be more choosy about the people they lend money, so that they are not being taken advantage of. If they give money to charities they should follow it up to see that their contributions are put to good use. Even when Pisceans are not rich, they still like to spend money on helping others. In this case they should really be careful, however: they must learn to say no sometimes and help themselves first.

Perhaps the biggest financial stumbling block for the Pisces is general passivity – a *laissez faire* attitude. In general Pisceans like to go with the flow of events. When it comes to financial matters, especially, they need to be more aggressive. They need to make things happen, to create their own wealth. A passive attitude will only cause loss and missed opportunity. Worrying about financial security will not provide that security. Pisceans need to go after what they want tenaciously.

Career and Public Image

Pisceans like to be perceived by the public as people of spiritual or material wealth, of generosity and philanthropy. They look up to big-hearted, philanthropic types. They admire people engaged in large-scale undertakings and eventually would like to head up these big enterprises themselves. In short, they like to be connected with big organizations that are doing things in a big way.

If Pisceans are to realize their full career and professional potential they need to travel more, educate themselves more and learn more about the actual world. In other words, they need some of the unflagging optimism of the Sagittarius in order to reach the top.

Because of all their caring and generous characteristics, Pisceans often choose professions through which they can help and touch the lives of other people. That is why many Pisceans become doctors, nurses, social workers or educators. Sometimes it takes a while before Pisceans realize what they really want to do in their professional lives, but once they find a career that lets them manifest their interests and virtues they will excel at it.

Love and Relationships

It is not surprising that someone as 'other-worldly' as the Pisces would like a partner who is practical and down-to-earth. Pisceans prefer a partner who is on top of all the details of life, because they dislike details. Pisceans seek this quality in both their romantic and professional partners. More than anything else this gives Pisces a feeling of being grounded, of being down-to-earth him- or herself.

As expected, these kind of relationships – though necessary – are sure to have many ups and downs. Misunderstandings will take place because the two attitudes are poles apart. If you are in love with a Pisces you will experience these fluctuations and will need a lot of patience to see things stabilize. Pisceans are moody, intuitive, affectionate and difficult to get to know. Only time and the right attitude will yield Pisceans' deepest secrets. However, when in love with a Pisces you will find that riding the waves is worth it because they are good, sensitive people who need and like to give love and affection.

When in love, Pisceans like to fantasize. For them fantasy is 90 per cent of the fun of a relationship. They tend to idealize their partner, which can be good and bad at the same time. It is bad in that it's difficult for anyone in love with a Pisces to live up to the high ideals set.

Home and Domestic Life

In their family and domestic life Pisceans have to resist the tendency to relate only by feelings and moods. It is unrealistic to expect that your partner and other family members will be as intuitive as you are. There is a need for more verbal communication between a Pisces and his or her family. A cool, unemotional exchange of ideas and opinions will benefit everyone.

Some Pisceans tend to like mobility and moving around. For them too much stability feels like a restriction on their freedom. They hate to be locked in one location forever.

The Sign of Gemini sits on Pisces' 4th solar House (of Home and Family) cusp. This shows that the Pisces likes and needs a home environment that promotes intellectual and mental interests. They tend to treat their neighbours as family – or extended family. Some Pisceans can have a dual attitude towards the home and family – on the one hand they like the emotional support of the family, but on the other they dislike the obligations, restrictions and duties involved with it. For Pisces, finding a balance is the key to a happy family life.

Horoscope for 1994

Major Trends

In 1993 your concerns were mainly psychological and spiritual. You explored the deeper aspects within yourself. For the most part this was enjoyable, for no one likes to explore the spiritual depths more than you do, Pisces. You learned how to re-invent yourself, how to transform yourself more effectively. You also had to eliminate many unnecessary things from your life – sometimes quite forcibly. Where normally you rise above conditions quite intuitively, in 1992 and 1993 you had to create a system, an order, a methodology for transcendence.

In 1994, you are going to apply many of these lessons to your practical, everyday life. 1994 is a bittersweet year, Pisces. On the one hand, most of the major, long-term planets are quite kind to you – they make wonderful aspects to you. On the other hand, Saturn, the great tester, moves into your sign on 29th January. Although this is ultimately for your highest good, such a transit is rarely pleasant. Yet, because you have so much other help it will not be unduly unpleasant. You are well able to handle whatever is thrown at you.

Saturn is going to have a dual action on you. On the one hand it will test your physical limits and your normally abundant vitality will be less abundant. You will feel restricted, hemmed in by circumstances or other people. For most of the year, elders and authorities seem quite stern, demanding and judgmental. Yet in spite of all this Jupiter's magnanimous actions are expanding your horizons and enhancing your self-esteem. Somehow, no matter how hard they try, authorities cannot break your spirit.

For most of the year it is wise to shine silently and keep a low profile. Work steadily and persistently towards your goals and by the end of the year, the glory and recognition will come – with interest. For at that time you will see Saturn's secret benevolence. The strength it gave you, by helping you to streamline your life and affairs and master the weaker points of your character, are all enduring gifts that will stand you in good stead for the rest of your life.

Health

Your 6th House of Health is relatively inactive in 1994, showing that your health is basically good and that you are not overly concerned with it.

Under normal circumstances Saturn's transit could produce health problems as it tends to limit the overall vitality. However, you are receiving so many wonderful aspects from the other planets that much of Saturn's action is neutralized and you will receive only its positive benefits. This is an excellent year to diet, lose weight, exercise and otherwise get your body in shape. Saturn will not allow you to do these things in a slipshod way, either. You will need to embark upon an organized, structured and steady regime.

Saturn will force you to recognize your physical limitations. Obviously, you can't be everywhere, do everything and see everybody, as you would like to. You have to set priorities. You have to evaluate your physical energy realistically and decide what you are and are not capable of.

Don't take on tasks that require 12 hours a day when your body is only capable of working for ten. Saturn is going to force you to manage your physical resources more realistically.

Towards the end of the year Jupiter will move into your 10th House of Career, making a stressful aspect to you. This will be a further signal to rest and relax more and to handle only priorities. Your ambitions for career success will tempt you to overwork. But you will feel the effect of this more in 1995 than in 1994.

Your periods of greatest vitality for the coming year will be from 18th February to 20th March, 21st June to 22nd July and 23rd October to 22nd November.

Your periods of least vitality for the year ahead will be from 20th May to 20th June, 23rd August to 22nd September and 23rd November to 21st December. Schedule yourself accordingly.

Home and Domestic Life

Though your 4th House of Home and Family is relatively quiet this year, there will be periods – because of temporary activations by the fast-moving planets – when these issues become priorities. These are from 26th April to 21st June and from 4th July to 17th August. Dealings with family members are especially volatile during this last-mentioned period. Financial issues bring up potential conflicts. But these short-term spats pass very quickly. Basically, the cosmos is giving you a free hand to shape your domestic life as you see fit. It neither impels nor obstructs your desires.

Keep in mind that Mercury is the planet that controls your emotional and family situation. When Mercury moves speedily and receives helpful aspects, family matters go well and you tend to get your own way at home. When Mercury slows down, you become more cautious and almost hesitant in domestic matters – you take your time making decisions regarding the home. When Mercury goes retrograde (backwards) you tend to feel that you are going backwards as well – insofar as domestic issues are concerned. When the aspects to Mercury are stressful, your dealings with your family tend to get stressful as well. The month-by-month forecasts discuss these short-term trends more thoroughly.

Love and Social Life

The most recent major activation of your love life was in 1992. This was a banner social year. Many of you got married or involved in serious relationships that year. All of you made important new friends of the heart and otherwise expanded your social sphere. Whatever your social goals were, you probably attained them then.

1993 was a year for love affairs and creativity. It was a year when you explored the physical intimacy – the conjugal aspects – of your relationship.

This year your love life takes a back seat to many other things. You are more concerned with developing new mental friends – platonic friends – than with romantic opportunities. You value friends who can satisfy you intellectually over those who can only satisfy you romantically. You enjoy the cool, non-threatening mix of people over the torrid, one-pointed focus of a romance. Furthermore, you feel called upon to participate in utopian social causes of a collective, worldwide nature and group activities can satisfy this urge better than a one-on-one romance.

Of course you don't completely give up your romantic interests this year, but with Saturn on your Ascendant you seem to want to spend more time by yourself. You are working out issues of self-esteem and self-worth, which can only be done in solitude. Detractors who can't and won't understand you might call you 'anti-social'. This is not so. For when these issues are worked out, love will bloom and grow for you more strongly than ever.

Singles must be careful about projecting an image of coldness, sternness and separateness. You might not be doing this consciously, but others will let you know about it. Keep a smile on your face and warmth in your heart. Take care not to wallow in depression – about the state of the world, about how your friends treat you, about your personal limitations, etc. Depressed people have trouble attracting love – worse, when they do attract love it tends to be with another depressed person. So the negativity tends to get amplified.

Recognize your limitations and love yourself in spite of them. Love yourself with all your mortal shortcomings. In this process you will discover magically that what you – or others – consider to be shortcomings are merely manifestations of your genius incorrectly understood. Self-love and self-acceptance will pave the way for fulfilling romance. It is right for you to focus on personal concerns rather than relationships. For without a 'self' there can be no relating to others.

Your most active romantic periods will be from 11th July to 7th August, 18th August to 22nd September and 12th to 31st December.

Career and Finance

This area is prominent in your 1994 solar horoscope, Pisces. You are more concerned this year with gaining public and professional prestige than with mere money-making – and this is wise. You are involved in building your career, your life's work. Your long-term career achievements will live on long after you've gone.

Most of this year is really a preparation for the greater good that is to come. You are building the philosophical foundations of career success. Younger Pisceans are making educational choices that will affect their career later on. They are, in effect, deciding which career to pursue. More mature Pisceans are working out the philosophical and ethical issues of power and authority and how they should be handled. Many others are presented with higher educational opportunities that pertain directly to their career (their employers will foot the bill).

For most of the year you seem to be labouring in obscurity. Bosses are coercive and over-controlling. They want to make you over completely in their image. This is understandably trying and difficult. Hang on and keep the faith in yourself. Some of their criticisms are valid, some not. Look at the valid points and do your best to correct them. The other points can be safely ignored.

This 'persecution' is only temporary. The persecutors are going to leave, in a major corporate upheaval. The people who are your bosses at the beginning of the year may very well not be your bosses by year's end. Your new supervisors are much more favourably disposed towards you. By the end of the year you can expect a promotion and a rise in pay.

If you are self-employed you can expect to gain greater standing within your industry and among your peers. You will be called on to be an administrator or manager. This is when you will appreciate the discipline of the current Saturn transit. You will be better able to manage others because you have learned to manage yourself.

On the financial front, the only possible obstacle to earnings – aside from your general lack of interest – is the potential lack of self-esteem and self-worth. When your personal stock in yourself goes down, your earnings tend to go down. If you feel you are worthless, than you will be worthless. There is a difference between inflated ideas of self-worth and a healthy, realistic sense of self-esteem. Saturn will correct any over-inflation, but don't let this depress you – you are worth more than you think.

Self-improvement

By your nature you are mystically-orientated, Pisces. It is normal for you to pay more attention to the invisible, the abstract, the formless and the timeless. This is what makes you such an inspired and creative person – and what makes you such a mystery to friend and enemy alike.

For the past few years you have been even more mystically-orientated than usual. Time, form, structure and the nitty-gritty details of life have been ignored. They seemed meaningless compared to the beauties of the eternal. Many of you went too far overboard in the spiritual direction and ignored your duties on Earth. This year you need to correct the balance. Many of you are going to learn that though the Earth is finite it is just as spiritual in its essence as anything in the heavens. Misunderstanding this is to make a serious spiritual and philosophical error.

This year you must begin to look at the world with new eyes. You must handle your earthly duties as if they were spiritual ones. You must take charge now of your physical body, environment and true earthly duties with joy and reverence. This is not to say that you should spend all your time on materialism and accumulating earthly possessions. These should be handled with dispatch, in an organized and super-efficient way. True spirituality means mastering every level of existence – and this includes financial and domestic duties. If you master the 'Earth Plane' you will liberate yourself for higher studies. Plus, you will amass skills – in the mundane details of everyday life – that will stand your career in good stead later on.

Month-by-month Forecasts

January

Best Days Overall: 6th, 7th, 15th, 16th, 25th, 26th

Most Stressful Days Overall: 2nd, 3rd, 8th, 9th, 22nd, 23rd, 29th, 30th

PISCES

Best Days for Love: 2nd, 3rd, 10th, 11th, 22nd, 23rd, 29th, 30th, 31st

Best Days for Money: 2nd, 3rd, 6th, 7th, 10th, 11th, 15th, 16th, 17th, 18th, 19th, 20th, 21st, 25th, 26th, 31st

You don't especially care for the incredible line-up of planets in the sign of Capricorn (an Earth sign) this month, Pisces. It makes people too materialistic, too practical, too results-orientated for your taste. People seem overly focused on the material world and its needs. Your flowing, intuitive nature feels hemmed in by all this – it's almost like being in prison to you. Yet, there are redeeming features here.

First off, this energy strengthens your physical constitution. Your health will be excellent all month. Second, it makes you more grounded. You are less apt to fly off into wild, impractical fantasies right now. Third – and most importantly – you have a special ability at this time – and the world will help you in this – for making your dreams and fantasies practical and workable.

This month you realize that having good ideas is not enough. They need to be structured and made to work within the harsh realities of everyday life. Friends and associates are especially helpful when it comes to translating thought into action.

This is an unusually social month. You are making new platonic friends. You are active with groups and organizations. You are more politically involved than normally. Group actions can improve conditions in the world and you want to a be part of that. And, though you get involved in these groups for altruistic reasons, these activities have got romantic potential. Those of you who are in a committed relationship will find that if you both get involved in the same organization this will strengthen your relationship. Singles will meet romantic partners. A casual friendship will deepen into something more as time goes on.

Group activities have other benefits this month as well. They create financial opportunities and important business contacts. But these are mere side-effects of something that comes out of more sincere motives.

Group activities dominate the month. After the 20th, though, you might be less political and more involved with charitable and philanthropic causes.

February

Best Days Overall: 2nd, 3rd, 11th, 12th, 21st, 22nd

Most Stressful Days Overall: 9th, 10th, 16th, 17th, 23rd, 24th

Best Days for Love: 1st, 2nd, 3rd, 9th, 10th, 11th, 12th, 19th, 20th, 21st, 22nd, 25th, 26th, 27th, 28th

Best Days for Money: 1st, 2nd, 3rd, 9th, 10th, 11th, 12th, 14th, 15th, 19th, 20th, 21st, 22nd, 27th, 28th

Saturn, the cosmic tester, moved into your own sign of Pisces at the tail-end of last month. This generally heralds a 'buckling-down', serious kind of mood, but you won't feel the full brunt of it yet as so many positive short-term planets are moving into your sign this month.

Until the 18th your spiritual, charitable, philanthropic life is very much stimulated. Always a spiritual and charitable person, this month you are more so. You are positively saintly and altruistic, in fact, generous not only with your time and money but with yourself – with your physical energy.

You are seeing again – you have always known this – that the way out of any difficult situation is the way in – especially when it comes to financial difficulty. All your normally sharp ESP senses are further enhanced. You are being guided step by step and moment by moment to your personal Promised Land.

The new Moon of the 10th occurs in your 12th House of Spiritual Wisdom and Charity this month, promising to clarify and answer the problems and questions posed by all this inner activity.

The power in your 12th House further emphasizes your normally reclusive nature. But after the 18th the call of the body and the world asserts itself and you are ready to mingle again.

The Sun's entry into Pisces on the 18th spurs your work interests. You are an unusually hard and disciplined worker during this period. You don't mind taking a back seat at work for the good of all. This makes you even more productive. It is best to avoid office politics now. Bosses are stern with you, but they can be charmed.

Your health is excellent all month and you are more able to lose weight and keep to exercise regimes in spite of all temptation. Though much personal pleasure is offered to you, with stern Saturn on your Sun there is little likelihood that you will over-indulge.

Mercury's retrograde on the 11th suggests caution in love. A current love affair needs review and evaluation. Your social life feels like it's going backwards instead of forwards – but this is not the case. You should not be asserting yourself socially right now.

March

Best Days Overall: 1st, 2nd, 10th, 11th, 12th, 23rd, 24th, 29th, 30th

Most Stressful Days Overall: 4th, 5th, 18th, 19th, 25th, 26th, 31st

Best Days for Love: 1st, 2nd, 8th, 9th, 13th, 14th, 20th, 21st, 23rd, 24th, 25th, 26th, 29th, 30th, 31st

Best Days for Money: 1st, 2nd, 10th, 11th, 12th, 13th, 14th, 20th, 21st, 22nd, 29th, 30th

This is a powerful month in a powerful year, Pisces. First off, between 50 and 60 per cent of the planets are moving through your own sign, energizing and vitalizing you and giving you great personal charisma and magnetism. You achieve more with less effort and tend to get your way this month. The overwhelming dominance of the Water Element for most of this month is also very comfortable for you. Fish know how to navigate the waters of emotion.

Your normally strong intuition is even stronger this month. Moreover, you are appreciated for this quality now – whereas quite often you are castigated for it. People in general seem to understand you better now and they appreciate your ways. Your feelings of self-esteem and self-worth are strong.

Earnings will increase all month. After the 20th be careful about over-spending out of a misplaced optimism. Spend money on what you need and what gives you pleasure, but don't waste cash just because you feel you have money to burn. Until the 7th, profitable ideas come to you in meditation, prayer and dreams. After the 7th your physical appearance – unusually attractive and glamorous right now – brings financial opportunities. Friends are both supportive and a source of these opportunities.

A chance for foreign travel will materialize after a few delays. It is best to wait till after the 5th before you set out.

A current relationship which was going backwards straightens out after the 5th. Love is idyllic and altruistic all month. Singles meet old flames – or people who remind them of old flames. This month you are interested in love for the personal pleasures it brings – not just sexual pleasure, either. You especially enjoy the good meals, the touching and sweet talk. Your lover seems eager to boost your self-esteem –

though in truth, you are so strong right now you don't really need an extra boost!

Most of the planets are in the eastern half of your horoscope this month, Pisces, showing that you are more concerned with personal issues rather than relationships. Take care not to get too self-centred in love. This configuration also shows that you are in a period where you create circumstances rather than have to react to them. You have great control over your life right now.

April

Best Days Overall: 7th, 8th, 17th, 18th, 25th, 26th

Most Stressful Days Overall: 1st, 14th, 15th, 21st, 22nd, 27th, 28th

Best Days for Love: 2nd, 3rd, 7th, 8th, 9th, 10th, 12th, 13th, 19th, 20th, 21st, 22nd, 30th

Best Days for Money: 7th, 8th, 9th, 10th, 17th, 18th, 19th, 20th, 25th, 26th, 27th, 28th

Your levels of physical energy and vitality continue to be high and you assert yourself with unaccustomed force right now. True, you try valiantly to tone things down but you are involved in a constant struggle between expressing your personal desires frankly and suppressing them. The danger of too much suppression is that these desires will eventually explode at some future time.

This month there are also conflicts between spending and budgeting, self-assertion and timidity, action and inaction, friendship and money, self-indulgence and asceticism. Keep things in balance; don't go too far either way.

Both your love and financial life are quite active now – and both – for complex astrological reasons – are connected intimately. Your partner is financially supportive and provides practical earning opportunities. Love comes out of your normal pursuit of financial goals and through people associated with your financial life – employers, bankers, financial planners and the like. Both lovers and those involved in your financial life seem quite eager to please you right now. This is the time to apply for that loan, credit card or line of credit. This is the time – especially when the Moon waxes – to buy that luxury item you've coveted for so long.

You definitely get your way in financial matters now. There is a sense of financial fearlessness about you – a courage and aggressiveness that make you successful. The new Moon of the 11th occurs in your 2nd House of Money this month and is providing you with all the information you need to reach your financial goals. Proceed with confidence – but not with rashness.

You show great fearlessness in love matters as well. Others fall over themselves to please you. Your wishes are their commands. You are creating the conditions and circumstances of your health, love and financial life.

A spiritual adviser has withdrawn himself (he seems to be male, judging from your solar horoscope) from you for a while. Probably because you are so self-absorbed at the moment that you're not ready to hear what he has to say.

May

Best Days Overall: 4th, 5th, 14th, 15th, 23rd, 24th, 31st

Most Stressful Days Overall: 11th, 12th, 13th, 19th, 20th, 25th, 26th

Best Days for Love: 1st, 2nd, 3rd, 11th, 12th, 13th, 19th, 20th, 21st, 22nd, 23rd, 24th, 31st

Best Days for Money: 4th, 5th, 6th, 7th, 8th, 14th, 15th, 16th, 17th, 23rd, 24th, 27th, 28th, 31st

There are two eclipses this month which promise great change in the world in general and in the people around you. This is an exciting, turbulent and active month.

Of the two eclipses, the lunar one of the 25th seems the more serious for you personally. All Pisces will feel it to a degree; those of you with February birthdays will feel it most. Be sure to rest and relax more from the 24th to the 26th. In fact you should be taking a reduced schedule from the 21st onwards. Your energy and vitality are not what they should be until after the eclipse.

This lunar eclipse happens in your 10th House of Career, signalling long-term changes there. A dramatic shift in the corporate hierarchy is taking place. New positions open up and a new style of management takes over.

This change in your job situation is indicated by the solar eclipse of the 10th as well. This eclipse will affect many areas of your life. Creative projects create storms. Their short-comings are highlighted so that they can be improved. A new love affair will either end or get more serious now. Income derived from publishing or travel is reduced temporarily. There are deep-seated issues that need correcting here. Your parents are tense with you. Superiors are more demanding than usual.

The solar eclipse also seems to affect your communications. Answering machines, word processors, telephone and fax services seem affected. Modes of transport are unreliable. These foul-ups are particularly annoying in that you tend to rely heavily on these things this month. Interest income takes a temporary dive; you might perhaps consider a higher yielding investment. Yet in spite of all this your personal earnings increase. Your earning power is strong and nothing can dim your courage or optimism.

In love you need a little nurturing. Happily, your partner seems quite willing to give it. A home-cooked meal, the pleasures of hearth and home are more appealing to you now than wild flitting about. Your social charisma is strong and your partner goes to unusual – unbelievable – lengths to win your heart. Singles are looking for love in unusual places right now – probably from out of their very distant past.

June

> Best Days Overall: 1st, 10th, 11th, 19th, 20th, 28th, 29th
>
> Most Stressful Days Overall: 8th, 9th, 15th, 16th, 21st, 22nd
>
> Best Days for Love: 1st, 10th, 11th, 15th, 16th, 19th, 20th, 21st, 22nd, 28th, 29th, 30th
>
> Best Days for Money: 1st, 3rd, 4th, 5th, 6th, 7th, 10th, 11th, 15th, 16th, 19th, 20th, 23rd, 24th, 28th, 29th, 30th

Rest and relax until the 21st, Pisces, as your vitality is not what it should be until then. When the Sun moves into Cancer your enthusiasm picks up dramatically – almost miraculously. This is an unusually subjective month even for someone like you who is accustomed to – and even enjoys – subjective activities.

Great psychological progress and insight is made now. Unlike other, more extroverted people you long to penetrate the inner side of life. Your ability to break inner barriers – to penetrate into the emotional and spiritual depths – is very much enhanced this month. It's as if the entire cosmos supports this endeavour and you need not rely on your own personal efforts.

With 60 per cent of the planets in retrograde motion, many other people besides yourself are more introverted now. You are in a perfect position to demonstrate leadership and help people understand how to work from within – how to exercise their imagination constructively – how to rise above material conditions. Your virtues and gifts are well appreciated – especially after the 21st.

Love and career issues are on hold this month. If productive actions present themselves to you, take advantage of them; then let go. Don't try to resist the temporary slow-down. Take joy in the delays as much as in moving speedily forward. Enjoy the rests as much as you do the music.

In love, educated, cultured and nurturing types appeal to you. A teacher has a romantic interest in you. Old flames come back into your life. But no permanent decisions or commitments should be made just yet – especially not after the 12th when Mercury, your love planet, starts to go retrograde.

Career offers should be studied more carefully now. Nail down all details and don't rest until the whole picture is clear to you. Don't make major career moves after the 12th. Wait until next month when Mercury starts going forward again. This is a good time to begin acquiring the educational credentials you need to further your career. Seminars that deal with career-related subjects are favourable.

Finance is an area where you make progress this month. Here your boldness and aggressiveness pay off. Sales are profitable, but make them before the 12th.

July

Best Days Overall: 7th, 8th, 9th, 16th, 17th, 25th, 26th

Most Stressful Days Overall: 5th, 6th, 12th, 13th, 19th, 20th

Best Days for Love: 1st, 7th, 8th, 9th, 10th, 11th, 12th, 13th, 16th, 17th, 21st, 22nd, 25th, 26th, 30th, 31st

Best Days for Money: 1st, 4th, 5th, 7th, 8th, 9th, 14th, 15th, 16th, 17th, 23rd, 24th, 25th, 26th, 27th, 28th, 29th

There are a lot of advantages to being a 'fish', as you will learn this month. Fish do not drown in water as other signs do. They revel in it. With 50 per cent of the planets in Water signs you are in your element now and this enables you to display your virtuosity. Even though 40 per cent of the planets are in retrograde motion, this does not disturb you too much. Actually, this just fosters your natural introversion. Your psychic powers are enhanced and your sensitivities are even stronger than usual. Your health, self-esteem and self-worth are unusually strong. This will translate into a healthier bank account and greater professional prestige.

People in general are quite preoccupied with the past during this period. And while you tend to be more forward-looking, this trend does not concern you. By looking at the past, you can see the future much more clearly. Moreover, your insight into emotions – many of which originate in our ancient, collective past – is deepened by looking to the past. You make great psychological and spiritual progress this month.

Your earning ability continues to be strong, but this month you lavish money on your home and family. You are – as is true of most people – quite aware of your duties to the family. Family members are financially supportive and a source of earning opportunity. Your ability to circumvent logic and speak directly to people's feelings are important factors in your financial success this month.

Mercury, your love planet, begins to move forward after the 3rd – just so is your love moving forward. Problems in a current relationship are resolved. There is fun with a lover. And though your lover is moody, this just adds to the fun as far as you are concerned. Fun and nurturing are the qualities that bring happiness in love right now. Singles are thinking of having children now. The joys of having one's own family seem irresistible.

Your ability to enjoy yourself – to take a light-hearted approach to life – is a great key to maintaining good health at this time. Emotional harmony and understanding are also important. You are attending – or throwing – more parties. This is wonderful, just be mindful of your waistline!

August

> Best Days Overall: 4th, 5th, 13th, 14th, 21st, 22nd, 23rd, 31st
>
> Most Stressful Days Overall: 1st, 2nd, 3rd, 8th, 9th, 15th, 16th, 29th, 30th
>
> Best Days for Love: 6th, 7th, 8th, 9th, 11th, 12th, 15th, 16th, 18th, 19th, 20th, 26th, 27th, 29th, 30th
>
> Best Days for Money: 1st, 2nd, 3rd, 4th, 5th, 11th, 12th, 13th, 14th, 21st, 22nd, 23rd, 24th, 25th, 31st

Most of the planetary power is centred in the western half of your solar horoscope, Pisces. Thus the time of self-assertion is over. You must now depend on others if you are to attain cherished goals. You don't create conditions and circumstances right now but must adapt yourself to the conditions created by others. It's time to develop your social skills. The needs of others must come before your own personal needs right now. Curiously, if you handle this period well you will find that your own needs are quite well taken care of.

Until the 23rd you need to balance work and play harmoniously. Both the urge to personal pleasure and the demands of the workplace are strong in your chart. If you can make your work enjoyable – and this means you have to put joy into it – you will have solved the puzzle given you by the celestial powers.

Happily, your social life is fulfilling. Mercury's speedy direct motion brings you confidence and social charisma.

Your judgement of people and lovers is acute. For the better part of the month love means just a good time. But after the 18th you get more serious. Singles get proposals of marriage. Marrieds work to make their relationship a genuine partnership. With Venus in Libra from the 7th onwards most people are more romantic and relationship-orientated right now. Those of you already in love can pop the big question at this time.

After the 23rd try to rest and relax more. Take care of others by all means, but mind your own physical energy. If your energy goes 'down the tubes', you won't be any good to others. Your heart is your most vulnerable organ right now. Reduce stress in your life, let a reflexologist, masseur or acupuncturist stimulate your reflexes, especially those connected to the heart. Emotional harmony in love and with friends will also promote good health. Don't allow your self-esteem to get too low, either. This will be difficult since so much of what happens this month depends on how others evaluate you, thus there is a natural tendency to let others define who you are.

Finances are volatile this month. Creative projects will go through some gruelling alterations before you reap profits from them. Avoid speculations – especially after the 16th.

September

Best Days Overall: 1st, 9th, 10th, 18th, 19th, 28th, 29th

Most Stressful Days Overall: 5th, 6th, 11th, 12th, 25th, 26th

Best Days for Love: 5th, 6th, 7th, 8th, 9th, 15th, 16th, 18th, 19th, 26th, 27th, 28th, 29th

Best Days for Money: 1st, 9th, 10th, 18th, 19th, 20th, 21st, 28th, 29th

Most of the planets are concentrated in the western half of your solar horoscope this month, Pisces. You feel much more dependent on other people – and their good graces. You need to adapt to existing circumstances rather than create your own. This is not as bad as it may sound, for the conditions that have been created seem better than those you would have created on your own – better, in fact, than your most vivid fantasies.

Love, transformation, religion and travel are your dominant interests this month. Your need to concern yourself with the interests of others – to put their welfare above your own – makes you especially popular. Everyone wants to be your friend – some out of good motives and some out of selfish ones. You will weed out these false friends later on (after the 23rd of the month).

Singles have abundant romantic opportunities – a long-term commitment is in the offing. You are likely to meet potential lovers at parties, church socials and even religious services. Love becomes more passionate and intense after the 4th. Towards the end of the month there are romantic opportunities with rich, powerful and ultra-glamorous types of people. You meet them either at religious functions or in an educational setting.

Definitely make that foreign trip. It promises to be fantastic – something you'll remember for the rest of your life.

Though your social life is happy and your ability to earn profits for others is good, your path of greatest happiness and success this month lies in educational, religious and book publishing pursuits. If you are attending college or university there is great happiness and success involved within this calling. A scholarship or other important financial help is forthcoming. You are admitted to that prestigious university you've always wanted to attend. If you are a writer this is the month to submit your manuscript to a publisher, as those in the book publishing world look on you with great favour. Writers also receive inspiration for future books. Royalties come during this period. If you are a publisher or if you are involved in this industry, this is the time when the books you are producing become unusually successful.

Whatever you do for a living, definitely try to pursue religious interests – as the expansion of your personal philosophy of life brings great happiness.

Rest and relax more until the 23rd. After that your vitality will improve dramatically.

October

Best Days Overall: 6th, 7th, 15th, 16th, 25th, 26th

Most Stressful Days Overall: 2nd, 3rd, 8th, 9th, 22nd, 23rd, 24th, 30th, 31st

Best Days for Love: 2nd, 3rd, 6th, 7th, 13th, 14th, 15th, 16th, 22nd, 23rd, 24th, 25th, 26th, 30th, 31st

Best Days for Money: 6th, 7th, 8th, 9th, 15th, 16th, 17th, 18th, 19th, 25th, 26th, 27th, 28th

With so much power in Water signs this month – between 50 and 60 per cent of the planets – you swim comfortably in your native element. This will be one of the best months of your year. Your health, self-esteem, self-worth and self-confidence are unusually strong and are boosted further by Neptune's direct motion – after many months of going retrograde.

With most of the planets in the western half of your chart, you are still totally involved with other people and their needs – and have little time or inclination to pursue your own. What you lose in independence you make up for in social popularity. Your needs are taken care of by the largesse of others – and abundantly so. Have no fear of putting the universe in your debt, for the world is kindly disposed to you now.

Transformation and education are the two most important matters this month. Until the 23rd you need to weed out your social agenda – purify it of what is undesirable. Your work is appreciated and makes profit for others. After the 23rd higher education becomes even more important to you than it has been in the past. Take advantage of the educational and travel opportunities offered you. A voyage by sea is indicated.

All good things come to you this month, whatever field you pursue. Writers get their books published now. Students of religion receive spiritual illumination. Stockbrokers and bankers land that big account. Applications to universities are accepted. Your mental horizons expand. Wise and beneficent spiritual guides come into your consciousness and guide you to all things.

Personal earnings are improved this month, but through hard work. You do better by the generosity of partners than from your own personal earnings. Your partner's siblings provide substantial opportunities – and perhaps an expensive gift. The parent of a co-worker makes you an offer and bestows a gift. Your partner is active in the community and a side-effect of this is that it provides you with financial opportunities as well.

Your love life needs patience this month as Mercury goes retrograde. Give your partner space. What he or she lacks in romantic ardour is made up for in financial generosity. Singles should not schedule a wedding during this retrograde period.

November

Best Days Overall: 3rd, 4th, 11th, 12th, 21st, 22nd, 30th

Most Stressful Days Overall: 5th, 6th, 19th, 20th, 26th, 27th

Best Days for Love: 1st, 2nd, 3rd, 4th, 9th, 10th, 11th, 12th, 21st, 22nd, 26th, 27th, 30th

Best Days for Money: 3rd, 4th, 5th, 6th, 11th, 12th, 14th, 15th, 21st, 22nd, 24th, 25th, 30th

Your natural psychic ability – greatly enhanced this month – enables you to sidestep the emotional pitfalls of the coming month. The unusual line-up of planets in Scorpio is making people overly sensitive, extremist and uncompromising. They take passionate positions on the religious and political issues of the day. You can see this coming a mile away and thus can avoid getting involved in conflicts. Like a fish in water you sense the current and swim away.

Though this is a tumultuous month the upheavals in the world and in those around you create opportunities for you to exercise your genius – giving balm to the afflicted and the unfortunate. The universe likes to have you around, Pisces, for precisely such purposes.

Your deep connection with the invisible world is even deeper at this time. The edginess and restlessness you feel are coming from the environment around you, not from within yourself. Your health is excellent most of the month.

If you invest in stocks, the eclipses of this month bring short-term upheavals in your investments. But these losses are only paper ones and you will make them back if you hang on. There is a conflict this month between your spiritual/religious interests and your financial life. It would seem to be an ethical conflict of some kind over a financial deal, or perhaps your boss wants you to do things that you are not comfortable with ethically. But there is a way out. Focus on what you are comfortable with and do that.

Your feelings of self-esteem and self-worth are strong this

month but earnings come with difficulty. Glory and prestige come easily, but not wealth. After the 23rd you get the whole package – increased professional status and increased earnings. Work in the meantime towards acquiring knowledge and the education you need to advance your career.

Love is passionate, intense and altruistic, but conflicts over finances need to be resolved. Your lover has quite big financial ideas this month and you feel somewhat inadequate. After the 23rd you will feel more successful. Romance is expensive now – but fun. Singles may find love in a foreign country.

December

> Best Days Overall: 1st, 8th, 9th, 10th, 19th, 20th, 28th
>
> Most Stressful Days Overall: 2nd, 3rd, 16th, 17th, 23rd, 24th, 30th
>
> Best Days for Love: 1st, 2nd, 3rd, 8th, 9th, 10th, 11th, 12th, 19th, 20th, 23rd, 24th, 28th, 29th
>
> Best Days for Money: 1st, 2nd, 3rd, 11th, 12th, 13th, 14th, 21st, 22nd, 23rd, 24th, 30th

After a year of stretching your mind through travel, education and philosophical studies you are getting ready to shift over to the practical application of all this knowledge – most notably to your career and life's work. If you have expanded your 'higher mind' it is inevitable that your public esteem will increase. You become more valuable to society at large. And this is what you desire right now. You want your ideas to affect the wider sphere. You want to exert your influence with the public at large – either directly or through your business deals. You want – and will get – greater policy-making power.

Those of you who have found your true life's work will experience great expansion and promotion within it. Those of you who have not yet found it will be led to it this month and in the coming year. Enjoy this, for it is one of the great revelations in life.

All your ambition is taxing to your vitality, so rest and relax more until the 22nd. Emotional calm and a pure diet are important factors in maintaining good health right now. After the 22nd your health improves dramatically and you will see your fondest dreams beginning to come true. You won't get the total package at this time – that will come in a year or so – but you will see the initial blooms.

Your social life is active all month. With Mars in your 7th House of Love and Marriage you are too charming to resist. You go after what you want with great courage and fearlessness. You don't take no for an answer and surprise even yourself with your social forcefulness. But this social activity is not merely in pursuit of passion. 'Networking' with friends brings you extra earnings. Your contacts and connections are an important form of wealth. They make you more valuable to your employer or business associates.

Earnings are quite strong, especially after the 22nd. Before then you are overspending – probably on gifts and the like. But after the 22nd you get more rational about gift-giving, providing others in correct measure. Though a pay rise is in the making – and perhaps you've even been promised one – you probably won't receive it until next year.

Also available . . .

YOUR CHINESE HOROSCOPE FOR 1994

Neil Somerville

Chinese astrology is an ancient and increasingly popular subject, a system of character analysis and prediction which has inspired renewed interest in the West.

In this best-selling annual guide, Neil Somerville introduces the 12 signs of the Chinese zodiac, and outlines the main qualities and weaknesses of each. In addition, he reveals how the Five Elements influence the signs, and provides prospects for 1994, the Year of the Dog.

All you need to know is the year you were born; then you can discover a wealth of information about the hidden depths of your character.

Whatever your sign, you'll find plenty to interest you in this informative and amusing guide. Not only can you learn what lies ahead for you in 1994, but also how you relate to other signs, what your ascendant is and which famous people share your sign. Find out what the Year of the Dog holds in store for you!

STAR
QUALITY

Marjorie Orr

Who are the Aries actors, Sagittarius singers and Pisces politicians? Do you share your star sign with your favourite film star, or a member of the Royal Family?

If so, you will share many of their strengths, the weaknesses and their talents.

In *Star Quality*, leading psychological astrologer Marjorie Orr tells you what these strengths and weaknesses might be. For example, wouldn't you like to know

- how each star sign rates as a wife, husband or lover
- whether Taurus bosses are better than Libra, or which signs make the best slaves
- how your Gemini child is likely to behave?

Each chapter concentrates on one of the twelve sun signs, and answers all these questions, as well as giving your horoscope up to the year 2000. The birth charts of three celebrities are analysed in depth for every sign.

Star Profiles include:
Madonna, Michael Jackson, Joan Collins,
Arnold Schwarzenegger, Cher,
Sean Connery, Princess Diana and Pavarotti.

SUN
SIGNS

Sasha Fenton

Much has been written about astrology and, in particular, Sun signs. However, in this unique book Sasha Fenton turns her inimitable astrological skills to the subject, revealing once and for all exactly what you want to know about your Sun sign.

Sign by sign, the book fully explains the significance of each sign, including such details as the Elements and the Qualities of each sign. It dispels any confusions regarding cusps or Summertime, and compares well-known celebrities with yourself. It will leave you with vital knowledge about health, hobbies, shopping habits, possessions, work, sex and, most important of all, not what it is like to *be* a particular sign, but what it is like to *live* with one.

Together with the other books in this trilogy, Sasha Fenton's *Moon Signs* and *Rising Signs, Sun Signs* will enhance your understanding of astrology, of yourself, and of those around you.

YOUR CHINESE HOROSCOPE FOR 1994	1 85538 290 3	£4.99	☐
STAR QUALITY	1 85538 179 6	£4.99	☐
SUN SIGNS	1 85538 021 8	£4.99	☐
RISING SIGNS	0 85030 751 1	£4.99	☐
MOON SIGNS	0 85030 552 7	£5.99	☐
UNDERSTANDING ASTROLOGY	1 85538 065 X	£4.99	☐
POWER ASTROLOGY	1 85538 160 5	£4.99	☐
SUN SIGN SECRETS	1 85538 076 5	£4.99	☐

All these books are available from your local bookseller or can be ordered direct from the publishers.

To order direct just tick the titles you want and fill in the form below:

Name: _____

Address:_____

_____

_____ Postcode: _____

Send to: Thorsons Mail Order, Dept 3, HarperCollins*Publishers*, Westerhill Road, Bishopbriggs, Glasgow G64 2QT.

Please enclose a cheque or postal order or your authority to debit your Visa/Access account —

Credit card no: _____

Expiry date: _____

Signature:_____

— up to the value of the cover price plus:

UK & BFPO: Add £1.00 for the first book and 25p for each additional book ordered.

Overseas orders including Eire: Please add £2.95 service charge. Books will be sent by surface mail but quotes for airmail despatches will be given on request.

24 HOUR TELEPHONE ORDERING SERVICE FOR ACCESS/ VISA CARDHOLDERS — TEL: **041 772 2281.**